Responding to Loss

John D. Caputo, *series editor*

PERSPECTIVES IN
CONTINENTAL
PHILOSOPHY

ROBERT MUGERAUER

Responding to Loss
Heideggerian Reflections on
Literature, Architecture, and Film

FORDHAM UNIVERSITY PRESS
New York ■ 2015

Library of Congress Cataloging-in-Publication Data is available from the publisher.

Printed in the United States of America

17 16 15   5 4 3 2 1

First edition

for Monika
    more is more . . .

Contents

Illustrations

Preface

How can we deal with what befalls us in life? Jean-Luc Marion's phenomenology of givenness describes how what comes to us appears contingently, "falling upon us" so as to make an "unpredictable landing" in our lives. Phenomena arrive "discontinuously, unexpectedly, and by surprise."[1] Once landed and factical, phenomena appear as *fait accompli* over me; they cannot be denied—as we ordinarily say, "what is done is done."[2] Marion's phenomenology thus develops how it is that phenomena arrive, crashing over my consciousness that receives them. Not surprisingly, where "phenomena must fall on and arrive to consciousness in order to come to themselves," they are given in different degrees of intensity of intuition in relation to intention.[3] Even though ever eventful, producing themselves in giving themselves to us, phenomena can become "dulled, attenuated, and disappear" when lowered into mere objectivity or into everydayness,"[4] where insofar as they appear according to well-worn categories they occur in the mode of what can be known beforehand: "fixed so we don't really have to see them . . . objects appear to us transparently."[5] Or, in other cases, what comes is poor in intuition, just as formal mathematical abstractions are empty, that is, without content of individuation.[6]

More interesting for our purposes than either common or intuition-poor phenomena is a third type: the most intuition-rich phenomena, that is, the most powerful or primal phenomenalities.[7] These phenomena prove to be saturated with intuition, even to the point of overwhelming intention. That is, what is given is "so saturated with given intuitions that significations and corresponding noeses are lacking"; correspondingly, our task as those to whom the gift is given "is to transmute, up to a certain point, the excess of givenness into a monstration, to an equal extent, that is to say, unmeasured."[8] In the aesthetic mode, even an earthquake or avalanche witnessed at a safe distance may be experienced as sublime. In the realm of human making, painting exercises considerable positive power since in its giving an excess of intuition comes to us in saturated phenomena. As Marion vividly explains, when a burst of light and an image come from the pigment on canvas and flood over us, visibility and seeing themselves come forward into visibility, as happens in works such as Claude's, Turner's, or Rothko's.[9] Instead of the common gaze passing from one visible to another where nothing holds it, where the look comes up against the painted semblance it no longer traverses the latter but is swallowed up and engulfed there.[10]

Negatively, the overwhelming force of a hurricane, flood, or tsunami is terrifying; many cruelties humans visit upon one another are so great that we may not be able to bear their impact. Battered by them physically or psychologically, we commonly find ourselves blankly uncomprehending, puzzled or frozen into inaction, or perhaps fainting. Crashing over us in a negative manner, these events are powerful enough to fracture our preexisting worlds and disrupt our sense of self, thus forcing upon us the most serious stresses and unavoidable problems. It is with these overwhelmingly destructive happenings that I am concerned in these chapters.

Of course, from Plato to Kierkegaard and Heidegger, philosophy has long advised us that the breakage of what we take for granted may, rather than finally harming or numbing us, open us to deeper reflection and understanding of ourselves and the world. As Claude Romano says in working out this tradition (most specifically the implications of what Marion has called to our attention), "Thus, it is only on the occasion of an event—a bereavement, an encounter, an accident, an illness—in the shipwreck of the possibilities that gave shape to the world, that the evential meaning of the world can be revealed to me."[11]

But, again, what are we to do when we find ourselves in such circumstances? Though we might, it seems, "instinctively" withdraw from the world—most obviously and immediately trying to eliminate the perturbance or, if that is not possible, at least to remove ourselves from the source of the distress—with a corresponding "turning inward upon ourselves." As an armadillo curling itself up, protective shell outward, soft parts inward. We may faint as an immediate response or hide. At the same time we also know that except for dealing with that which is too short lived or too weak to threaten our resilience, trying to ignore what presses itself upon us does not work. It likely will overwhelm us. If it turns out that we have managed to suppress the event or to have no memory of it, that does not indicate that it has passed away from us. Rather, it means we have not faced it. It will surface, later if not sooner. Additionally, because at all times we have only finite capacities there always is a delay in our response to saturated experiences. There is a lag between our taking in and being able to respond to such positively rich or negatively overwhelming events.

Thus, for example, beyond any psychology or anthropology, the phenomenon of despair bears witness to a fundamental anonymity of the human adventure, which lets us bring to light, negatively, the evential meaning of selfhood. The latter is always a deferred response to events, such that I respond to what happens to me without ever being its origin. Rather, it is events, as origin, that alone allow me to respond, by *taking up and making possible* the possibilities they open and thus appropriating them as such. This response is itself constituted entirely by the disparity between possibility, as primary and fundamental openness to events, and the capacity to *hold myself open*, to insist in this openness: *availability* to events.[12]

Insofar as I cannot respond adequately to what is given immediately, even if I don't experience it as such, the gap puts me at a distance from the moment and force of initial impact, enough so that while I do or do not explicitly deal with it I am (respectively) an either alert or suppressed witness to what has happened to me or/and what continues to happen to me.

In the pressing task of engaging what overwhelms us, we often do so, or at least try to do so, over time and with the help of others, with whom we can talk about the events. We usually work out a number and variety of accounts of what happened and what it means. We shape it into at least a semi-intelligible narrative, so that a story emerges that enables us to hold together what we remember happening or of which we only now start to become aware. In the course of struggling with what has been given it normally also is important to listen to what others have to say: to their viewpoints concerning what occurred and to the way the multiple dimensions seem to hang together, to their accounts of their own experiences when something parallel occurred, to their advice as to how to go forward.

Because of this gap between what happens to us and our response, between what we can do alone and what can more fruitfully result from dialogue with others, and because I am neither qualified nor in a position to counsel anyone as to what to do with what overwhelms him, the reflections in these chapters operate at the remove of witnessing what has occurred and what further unfolds in alternative modes of response. Hence also my focus on what we ordinarily call works of art. For it is not just dialogue with friends, neighbors, colleagues, others who shared the very same event of givenness or occurrences somewhat the same (living through the same wartime experiences together as comrades or through the same flood as community members), or professional therapists that helps. As Heidegger helped us think through, what we consider to be significant poems, paintings, and buildings are those that set-into-work some dimension of our life world, or, better put, that are the catalysts whereby the dimensions that constitute a coherent gathering of what belongs together are evoked and joined together in a continuing dynamic—the latter itself an event that brings forth for the first time or holds onto (enactively maintains) a world.

We can learn, then, from artworks that witness what also has happened to other people in other times and places and that, whether actual or imaginary, open a realm for us to reflect not only on what is given in testimony but on how what is unconcealed bears on our own lives. As we will see, we are called to receive and respond to what others and artworks lay before us. To deploy something of this complex play of setting out and taking up loss in unfolding conversations, the chapters here cover Cormac McCarthy's intense novel *The Crossing* as set in discussion with Heidegger, who is in dialogue with Anaximander; Daniel Libeskind's Jewish Museum Berlin in intersection with the writings of Hannah Arendt and Emmanuel Levinas; and Wim Wenders' film *Wings of Desire* and Martin Heidegger's late homey talks and writings, seen in interaction with each other and with Jean-Luc Marion's ideas. The novel, architecture, film, and community addresses considered in these three chapters all focus on the particularity of situated events and, at the same time, on the inherently social dimension of our experiences, their interpretation, and subsequent actions. To be human is to be-with (*mitsein*), Heidegger tells us.

The common thread or focus of the works explicated here is loss—a phenomena that does indeed crash over us, sometimes as dramatic trauma, sometimes as chronic, but in all cases unquestionably given to each of us individually, as unsubstitutably mine or yours, to bear. Yet at the same time, what is given just as surely is something that we share and that binds us together, as "survivor" and sympathizer, as co-survivors, as survivor and witness, survivor and perpetrator, and the multiple combinations thereof. At core, each alone, sundered in fact from the "others" in our worlds—the persons, or places, or bio-physical-cultural subconstituents from which our body, our embodied consciousness, emerges—and then various of us in specific secondary historical, contextual combinations need to deal with the event and aftermath that unfolds from the unavoidable loss of ourselves as who we had been, of our world as we lived it. Of course, no matter how strong the force overtaking those of us reflecting at a remove and attempting a dialogue concerning what is given, a singular priority attends he who has undergone what came overwhelmingly in, he to whom the substantial events occurred, the one who, because he is capable of experience, of unsubstitutably undergoing an event in which he himself is altered with no way back, has the possibility of understanding *himself* in his selfhood starting from the possibilities articulated in a world that the event has pushed forth, and consequently, to advene himself precisely as the one to whom what happens happens.[13]

The saturated, potentially crushing losses commended to us in the works reflected upon in these chapters have not directly happened to those of us thinking about them today. For which we need be thankful. But the violence, exclusion, displacement, and injustice that befell many who have come before us or who are fictively burdened with their impact indeed has been set before us to take to heart, as Heidegger puts it, by what we commonly call novels, films, museums and their exhibitions. These works lay out something of the specific phenomena of loss and call for a response to what is given and taken away in the world, to individuals in their relationships to others, to places, and thus to their own possibilities, including finally ourselves. Further, we may learn from and respond to two of the major structures of experience itself: that what is given can come to visibility only insofar as it is received, so that it is shown insofar as we are witnesses, and that, in receiving the given, we are called, called to receive and respond, so that we ourselves come to be, to be shown, as we are. In this double reception and recognition the world unfolds for us as our life world, and we become human, responding to the call of the givenness that still is given and still gives. We would respond appropriately by receiving what comes in a manner adequate to help render it visible, both witnessing that givenness is not gone but instead continues to come and also by actively passing along what is given by McCarthy, Libeskind, Wenders, and Heidegger and in our own life worlds today, that is, by finally passing on the call itself.

A few words on the submotif of witnessing. As just explained, the primary subject matter of these essays is loss—loss that occurs suddenly and violently or gradually but no less surely (perhaps as a stressful injustice to be borne over a long time)—and our troubled responses to it, not witnessing. Witnessing, though important, is but one dimension of the unfolding of the experience of loss. My approach to the phenomena intends to understand the ways in which literature, architecture, and film are fundamental hermeneutic enactions that proceed by setting-into-work and thus bringing forth ways in which we try to make sense of loss.

Though these essays were not written in response to Kelly Oliver's fine book *Witnessing: Beyond Recognition*, it is important enough to help in an initial orientation.[14] She undertakes the major task of developing a theory of subjectivity by challenging the thus-far dominating notions of Hegel, Butler, and Kristeva, aiming to develop a "new model" by "starting from othered subjectivity" with an adequate ethical and political "normative force."[15] Though in light of the hermeneutic fact that all reading and seeing, indeed all experience, is always already interpretation, I cannot claim with Newton that "*no fingo*" (I feign no hypothesis). My project is much more modest. It is congruent, though, with Oliver's more ambitious project of arguing against the notion of what we can call the "received" notion of vision and space, that is, the metaphysical-representational view (in the course of which she attends to the scientific and philosophical investigations of our integrated visual and motor systems).[16]

As Oliver shows in her ninth chapter, "Toward a New Vision," the evidence and argument provided by Gibson, Merleau-Ponty, Irigaray, Levinas, and others establishes that we are "fundamentally connected to our environment and other people through the circulation of energies that sustain us" and as "the result of our *responsiveness* to the energy in our environment."[17] That engagement as address and response critically opens us to her specific characterization of witnessing's dual character: "seeing for yourself" is tensed with "bearing witness to what can't be seen."[18] My chapters here attend to the way literature, architecture, and film operate at precisely this juncture. As both Heidegger and the artists themselves tell us, they set into work what they see that we too may see; moreover, in their variable modes of enacting visibility, the art works bring forth for us the invisible. My goal simply is (variously) to read, hear, look at, imaginatively and physically move through, and then reflect on what McCarthy's novel, Libeskind's museum, Wenders' film, and Heidegger's "homilies" give to us concerning the relationships among human-natural environments (*Umwelts*) and loss.

This project aligns with Oliver's contention that "insofar as we are by virtue of other people, we have ethical *requirements* rooted in the very possibility of subjectivity itself. We are obligated to respond to our environment and other people in ways that open up rather than close off the possibility of response."[19] Though it would be far too much to claim as accomplished by my chapters, I do demonstrate that the works considered here in fact do successfully trace out the trajectory of eros as Oliver exhorts: "If we conceive of subjectivity as a process of witnessing that requires response-ability and address-ability in relation to other people . . . then we will also realize an ethical and social responsibility . . . to open personal and social space in which otherness and difference can be articulated."[20] Perhaps the reader will even find that these artists and works, by critically yet compassionately delineating somber environments of loss, help us (to use her enobling phrase) "see others with loving eyes that invite loving response."[21]

Finally, in regard to the project of this book, we need to ask about the role the arts play in our current situation wherein we need to understand and attempt to deal with destruction, loss, trauma, and the need to go on. Given the chapters' tactic of meditation or reflection, which is neither art nor philosophy but moves in the "between," there is the question of the relation of the arts to philosophy, such that what the chapters attempt, including engaging them with the originary thinking of Martin Heidegger, makes sense. Further, why these three modes of art (literature, architecture, film)? Why specifically Cormac McCarthy's *The Crossing*, Daniel Libeskind's Jewish Museum Berlin, and Wim Wenders' *Wings Over Berlin*?

How or why is it legitimate to spend time and energy engaging with the arts in a way that involves neither their making or production, nor traditional philosophy in the strictest sense, that is, conceptualization of aesthetic objects or experiences? The answer seems to lie in the active movement back and forth between art and philosophy. The art works themselves do not "tell" us something in a simple, direct manner as do statements and most "extra-aesthetic" discourse such as technical manuals or scientific publications that claim, demonstrate, or "prove" something. Art, rather, shows us something, laying it before us that we might, as I noted above, take it to heart. If we follow Heidegger's ontological position, art even has the high task, and sometimes accomplishes, a gathering of primal dimensions into world. Philosophy, in the traditional sense, aims to make clear and explicit the categories and themes of a given field, as well as the differences from other spheres. Thus, we have philosophies of language, beauty, the sublime, and aesthetic distance.

But, if particular art works do not themselves "speak directly" to us, though we need to make sense of and learn from them, and if philosophy treats univocal or universal concepts, it is necessary to explicate the former without losing their specificity by shifting to the overly abstract. Such unfolding of the art works would be a thinking and saying that gives them voice. This middle way would need to respect the autonomy of the art, not pretending itself to accomplish the gathering and showing that art does; at the same time, it would need to respect the autonomy of philosophy as the development of the specialized content of metaphysics, epistemology, aesthetics, ethics, and related fields.

The question of the relation of the arts and philosophy, then, leads to the need for and legitimation of the reflections presented here. Of course, more philosophy proper could be done: claims could be developed concerning what language or art are (as is part of what is occurring right here, as I write this section). But that is not the task at hand: what is needed and taken up is attention to the singularity of individual works. In speaking to his hometown neighbors Heidegger says: "Meditative thinking need by no means be 'high-flown.' It is enough if we dwell on what lies close and meditate on what is closest; upon that which concerns us, each one of us, here and now; here, on this patch of home ground; now, in the present hour of history."[22] What is closest in regard to the essays treated here? The three art works themselves and what those works lay before us (pain, death, apparently senseless violence, mortality, the enigmatic realm of the divine).

Our time certainly is an age of disaster, not only of natural disasters evidently exacerbated by climate change but within the seemingly constant state of war and displacement around the world. Hundreds of thousands of people have been disabled or turned into refugees, countless communities and ways of life destroyed. The acute traumas suffered in such events not only change lives immediately but often generate chronic stress (as with PTSD), lowering the long-term ability to cope with what comes next. All this in addition to the inevitability of our own deaths, which each of us face. Here and now, we find ourselves in the midst of terrible events that are not "past" but that as effective history still bear on our individual and social lives, that is, on whether and how we might realize our potentials and limitations, our shared ethical and political possibilities and obligations. Here and now, how can we deal with loss and our mortality? How to do so in regard to the divine (which for many appears to be absent though at the same time is believed in by millions, while still others seek some kind of spiritual, though not necessarily religious, meaning and value)?

Art works are one important means to engage these issues, both because they set into work the saturated phenomena of violence and loss and because the works themselves are given to us as saturated phenomena. Thus, our immediate task is to take up the specific works by reflecting upon them in a way that lets their particularity and what they bring forth befall us (avoiding reduction to abstractions). This explicating can be thought in terms of the way one "tours" a painting, which proceeds by explicitly calling attention to this and that feature, to what appears in a given spot and how it might be seen and interpreted. Aspects can be attended to without separating them: one can see how the pigment is applied, how a tree is rendered, how a shadow is cast, so that the relationships of these internal elements and the interplay of parts and whole can come to the fore; additionally, the materials, forms, techniques, and subject matter also can be connected "externally" to such elements in other paintings, to the artist and social movements, to political implications, and so on. By avoiding the use of representational concepts in unfolding what is specifically brought forth in the work, the tour stays clear of philosophy, in fact moving in the between—between the arts and philosophy. Because we can see everything but unavoidably miss much, because the relationships to the external world (which itself changes) multiply meanings, the possible responses are never foreclosed. In a very positive sense "nothing" is "resolved." Insofar as successful, the reflections in the between help us stay open to the works and allow the works to perform as the openings that they are.

If these essays stay clear of the univocal philosophical concept of "art," instead taking up three specific works, each of a different mode (literature, architecture, and film), it is fair to ask, as one reviewer of the manuscript put it, "What is it about art that, as Jean-Luc Nancy (in *The Muses*) indicates, always means that art cannot be thought simply as art, but always be thought as the arts (in the being singular plural)?" There would be several approaches to answering this question. From the viewpoint of cognition studies, it is clear that we not only have multiple senses with which we take in what is given but that there are many ways in which people respond to the world and learn. To cite but one example, the famous Jungian Myers-Briggs typology of differing psychological preferences and emphases explores the various combinations of the four factors at play in the ways people utilize their perceptual (sensing and intuition) and judging (thinking and feeling) functions. Then, too, there are material and technological developments that bear on our bodily consciousness and spiritual condition, as seen in the shifts of our psychological understanding of cognition and perception (such as the appreciation of retinal persistence and afterimages), in our responses to experiences of increasing speed in the nineteenth century with its attendant disjointed perceptions (such as occur when looking out a train window while crossing a bridge with heavy girders), and with appreciation of afterimages— all paralleled by the creation of moving pictures. In these ways of thinking, we would hold that the world is a rich and changing realm, such that many arts are needed better to approximate an adequate response to that which shows itself and, congruently, that each of the arts is able to disclose the world in a distinctive and valuable mode.

Or, considered archetypally, there have been multiple modes of art that emerged simultaneously with our human beginnings and that still perdure, with more being created along the way. We could follow the clue provided by Northrop Frye, who asserts that, no matter what the content, the forms of the arts do not exist outside of them: "poetry can only be made out of other poems; novels out of other novels."[23] Thus, painting and sculpture move from and within the site opened by our earliest cave painting and figural carving, literature from our first uses of language and storytelling, architecture from the primal stacking of stones to make altars and later dwellings. (As Kant pointed out, an arch imitates nothing in nature; its form has its ground only within the representation of architecture itself.) New perceptual-technological hybrids such as film have resulted from the synthesis of painting, photography, drama, the static circular panoramas before which viewers moved to follow a story or take in a large-scale landscape, dioramas that moved about immobile spectators, the phenakistiscope and zootrope, the kaleidoscope and stereoscope, and processes of editing visual material by cutting and rearranging as is done with montage.[24]

No matter what approach we take, recognizing the particularity of each work, then going on to group them according to type is about as far as we should go without generating unjustified univocal concepts. There are myriad art works. It is reasonable and practical to say that they are arts of this or that sort, but it would be unjustified for philosophy (at whose conceptual edge I am here moving, while wanting to pull away as soon as I may) to attempt to abstract to "art." Better for us to proceed individual work by individual work, artist by artist, connecting them as we go, sometimes moving backward to earlier works and "outward" to the extra-artistic. The three art works, then, provide modes of access to the richness of what can be given to us, but they do not constitute a hermetically sealed realm. Rather, they permeate our historical worlds and our lives therein—or, as Heidegger contends, in their deepest accomplishments, actually gather together the primal dimensions of and opening those worlds.

As ancient as our humanity itself, language enables us to live ecstatically, simultaneously here and imaginatively elsewhere. Stories in general, including novels, involve distinctive settings, of course, but still allow unrestricted saying and free reflection, so that through the characters, dialogue, and events presented the work allows readers to join in. Cormac McCarthy's novel *The Crossing* takes up the issues of loss, questioning of the character of the cosmos and our possible reactions through a complex set of conversations and reflections. More than that, though situated in ruins within historically Christian Mexico, its consideration of fate and freedom, of human and divine mysteries, operates at such an almost mythic level that it invites further dialogue, via Heidegger, with Anaximander, who thought at the time when the early Greek world was struggling with the juncture of sacred beliefs and profane philosophy.

Taking up Daniel Libeskind's Jewish Museum Berlin shifts us from language to the built environment and things (as Heidegger does in treating the temple, house, and bridge) and from the destroyed church of McCarthy's tale to devastated Berlin after World War II (a half-century later). The city and museum are sites we physically enter, thus emphasizing the bodily dimension of our human condition as *embodied* consciousness (though, of course, our encounters with buildings, their urban surround, and the things exhibited within a museum also involve memory and imagination). This museum is exceptional in that it not only commemorates the radical exclusion and deaths of the Jews in and from Berlin but provides a site for action since the qualitatively charged spaces and things within evoke a direct experience that disturbs us out of the everyday and calls for a responsible ethical and political trajectory.

Film is a third mode between literature's powerful imaginative realm, which stimulates the readers' capacity to visualize what is virtual, and architecture's qualitatively distinct spaces (and artifacts in exhibition) that involve physical experience. Film effects virtual realms as does literature, but the former does so with specific and detailed visualization of places, events, and dialogue not otherwise achievable; it projects us into, invites us into, an astonishingly convincing experience of spaces that architecture cannot make available physically. Wenders' movie, *Wings Over Berlin*, continues the focus of the Jewish Museum on the historical sites and events following the city's destruction as well as on the questions facing the survivors and we who come after or from elsewhere. So situated, the characters and audience again move through the dissembling and gathering of the fourfold (to use Heidegger's figure): heavens and earth, mortals and divinities (in the mode of immortal angels). The characters witness and question the pain surrounding, really permeating, the city but remain open to the possibility of affirmative responses. They do not deny, hide from, or flee the destruction but face the loss that has been, is now, and is yet to come. This again connects with what Heidegger experiences and has to say. After the war, he too meditates on the loss and possibilities that remain or occur anew. In his own mode, he responds from a rural situation, not because that is a conceptual opposite to the urban or because he is hopelessly nostalgic but because that is where his life actually unfolds.[25] He asks what can be done in this time, what he and the rural might contribute. He says the same as Wenders' characters: stand and act honestly as you yourself can yet remain open to others and to the reassemblage of multiple places and social spheres.

The film, then, moves on from the novel and museum building, but in continuing to lay out before us the grim and simultaneously positive, even joyful, dimensions of our mortality within the senseless, historically repeated human violence—and perhaps cosmic forces—beyond our control, it returns to what we encountered in the works of literature and architecture considered. The interpretations, perhaps, will help readers agree that these three works are themselves saturated phenomena well worth further thought, even as they let emerge a portion of the saturated phenomena of violence, loss, trauma, and the mystery of our lives within them. Overall, my hope is that this book's explications of *The Crossing*, Jewish Museum Berlin, and *Wings over Berlin* not only unfold what emerges from the works' dialogues, actions, and settings, and from what Heidegger can bring forth, but engages readers to participate by continuing the reflections.

Acknowledgments

I want to thank Joshua Polansky, Director, Visual Resources Collection, College of Built Environments, University of Washington, for his capture of stills from *Wings of Desire* and for exceptional effort in tracking down a usable image of the Kaiser-Wilhelm-Gedächtnis Kirche (Memorial Church) in Berlin.

A special debt is owed to the late Helen Tartar, Editorial Director at Fordham University Press. She not only was graciously supportive of this project but consistently went above and beyond the call of duty in her interest in and support for continental approaches to interpreting the built and natural environments, for example attending the meetings of the International Association for Environmental Philosophy and sponsoring new series.

I am grateful to the Press's reviewers for their positive critique and suggestions, which certainly led to an improved final version. It was a pleasure working with Fordham University Press—Assistant Editor Thomas Lay, Managing Editor Eric Newman, and Assistant Marketing Manager Katie Sweeney were all that could be hoped for by an author.

Responding to Loss

The Hermit's and the Priest's Injustices
Reading Cormac McCarthy's The Crossing *with Heidegger and Anaximander*

Homer was wrong in saying "Would that strife might perish from among gods and humans." For if that were to occur, all things would cease to exist.[1]

Toward an Introduction

I want to inquire into the mysterious relationships among the greatest realities—nature, humans, and the gods—and to approach the core enigma of whether we live in a chaos or in the well ordered, that is, within a cosmos. How should we live within what appears to be radical flux, where our all too transitory lives seem to count for little within the overall ebb and flow? Perhaps with the hope of the orthodox Jew, Christian, or Muslim? Or, in the manner of the stoic, whether personally world weary or responsible for vast realms of public life, as was Marcus Aurelius? Yet again, in the manner of Buddhists, either in a purer Eastern way or as appropriated by Westerners such as Schopenhauer? Or, congruent with more typically individualistic assumptions, should we should fight and resist to the end, as Dylan Thomas says, refusing to go gently into the night? How to face death and respond to violence?[2]

Indirectly. Since I am no seer and have neither the call nor the courage to be blinded by the ultimate forces to become one, any approach to the subject will have to be through others who have seen and said more than I am able but whose stories I can recall and relay to you. So I begin by considering Cormac McCarthy's philosophy and Martin Heidegger's fictions. Even this, I fear, is extremely difficult. Specifically, I find McCarthy's novel *The Crossing*, as all his other work, imaginatively mesmerizing but emotionally draining. Similarly, Heidegger's writings are dauntingly dense since they so completely consist in taking apart and reconstructing 2,500 years of thinking.

It might be that to prevent us from becoming smug (a danger inherent in the varieties of orthodox religious faith that apparently indicate to some that they have salvation at hand, or the correlate of a profane belief that science and technology provide all we need and all that is possible in a purely material universe, or the result of everyday thoughtlessness), we may need to have our faces pushed into death and violence. Hence the importance of engaging the darker realities witnessed by McCarthy and Heidegger. Just as there are the "hard sayings" of the New Testament (such as that it is harder for a camel to pass through the eye of a needle than for a rich man to enter heaven), so there are the dark tests or contests of Job and Satan, witnessed—even condoned!—by Yahweh.

McCarthy as Witness

I turn, then, to the unflinching witness of violent destruction, Cormac McCarthy. I also deliberately take only one section of his noble *The Crossing*—specifically the story of the ex-priest and the hermit[3]—and that out of context, knowingly violating a fundamental tenet of literary theory and criticism, namely that the unity of a literary work is such that its form and content are indissoluble. This violence of reading (to which I shall return in the end) at least allows us to consider a philosophy of the whole, since in the novel there are sections that speak of the cosmos as a harsh intertwining of nature, humans, and God.

To refocus our questions: in this section of *The Crossing*, what do McCarthy, his characters, and we readers witness about humans, nature, and God? What do we come to understand about the chaos or cosmos within which we live? Do we find any implications for action?

In our era of positive science and technological accomplishments, many generally believe that life is understandable, that it is stable and predictable, and that it can be brought under control.[4] We well might believe that the whole of McCarthy's corpus shows us the opposite vision: that where the violent bear everything away we have not cosmos but chaos, that is, a flux of ever-eruptive destruction that is unintelligible, transitory, and unpredictable and that defeats all our deepest human hopes and dreams. Without repeating the incidents that flow through his novels so unrelievedly as to numb both the characters and readers—for I have neither the space nor the heart to do so—it is enough to note that in these novels, and specifically in *The Crossing*, all one cares for, and even what no one cares for, is taken away: all family and place, as well as animals wild and domestic, law and civility, youth and innocence, old age and the prospect for peacefulness. Not only does all pass away; it is stripped away seemingly without human or divine pity of any sort.

McCarthy does more than narrate this flow of merciless events; he presses the issue with an interior tale in which the young protagonist encounters a former priest who has become the heretical caretaker of "a huge adobe church whose roofbeams lay in the rubble." This story within the story is cast in philosophical language and thoughts that are strikingly like those of the ancient Greek thinker Heraclitus. Recall that Heraclitus was nicknamed "The Obscure" because of the enigmatic manner in which he spoke of the cosmos, using images that emphasize the interaction of apparent opposites: flux, violence, the sun, the bow, and human misunderstanding.

> Fragment 6: The sun is new each day.
>
> Fragment 8: That which is opposition is in concert, and from things that differ comes the most beautiful harmony.
>
> Fragment 10: Joints: whole and not whole, connected-separate, consonant-dissonant.
>
> Fragment 12: Those who step into the same river have different waters flowing ever upon them.
>
> Fragment 19: Men who do not know how to listen or how to speak.
>
> Fragment 46: The bow is called life [*bios*], but its work is death.
>
> Fragment 49a: In the same river, we both step and do not step; we are and we are not.
>
> Fragment 51: They do not understand how that which differs with itself is in agreement: harmony consists of opposing tension, like that of the bow and the lyre.
>
> Fragment 53: War is both king of all and father of all, and it has revealed some as gods, others as men; some it has made slaves, others free.
>
> Fragment 60: The way up and the way down is one and the same.
>
> Fragment 102: To God, all things are beautiful, good and just; but men have assumed some things to be unjust, others just.[5]

McCarthy tells of the boy's crossing into the ruined town in terms that, deliberately or not, echo Heraclitus's emphasis on things that operate by joining oppositions. The protagonist fords a stream, stopping to loosen and let go his handmade bow: "Legacy of some drowned archer, musician, maker of fire" (137). Next, still using Heraclitus's language at most every step, McCarthy presents the tale that the ex-priest-turned-custodian tells the boy about the life of a man born in nearby Caborca, who then lived for a time with his wife and child in this town of Huisiachepic.

The ex-priest tells of a heretic hermit who philosophized as a good empiricist and, in his legal exactitude, as a worthy heir to Job. Also now become heretical himself, the caretaker contends that the hard lesson of the world—the one story only that we have—is that everything is necessary, every last and every terrible thing. All the violence, all the destruction. Some of the events that befell the man who became a hermit form part of the tale of nature, for the earthquake that also destroyed the church in neighboring Bavispe and killed his young son was a natural phenomenon. Obviously, nature often is cruel and indifferent to us. Other aspects of the violence are human. The hermit was himself an orphan and first set upon his road to the city where his little son died because his own "parents were killed by a cannonshot in the church at Caborca where they had gone with others to defend themselves against the outlaw American invaders" (144). Thus, we hear the tales of the human evil and natural disasters that ripple across our lives, expanding into more and more violence. It appears that this condition simply is the case.

But the empirical, legalistic hermit will know how this is so. It would be bad enough to live in a hostile chaos but even worse to be in some sort of perverse cosmos, where the violence and evil somehow are not only permitted, as in the Book of Job, but necessary and not to be despised. The heretic anchorite seeks the answer in the creator of nature and humans. He tells us he had come to the ruined town and its church because

> I was seeking evidence for the hand of God in the world. I had come to believe that hand a wrathful one and I thought that men had not inquired sufficiently into miracles of destruction. Into disasters of a certain magnitude. (142)

After the loss of his son to the earthquake, neither his wife, nor nature itself, nor its God holds for him: "All that he loves is now become a torment to him. The pin has been pulled from the axis of the universe" (146). And the murder of his parents as well as his later experiences of political executions left him with the belief that humans are unable to plot effectively their own courses of action. Yet his losses, his disbelief in human or natural ease, even his heretical stance bound him closer to God, in a dance of challenge. In his persistent wrestling with God, making his case against Him, which was madness, he "began to see in god a terrible tragedy" (154).

The hermit came to believe that since nothing lay outside God, not even chaos, God could have no witness, that is, no other or nothing by which he could define himself and have his identity. But the old man died in ignorance and error, the caretaker tells us, for "God had outwitted him." We are told that the caretaker himself (the former priest who had argued with the hermit for years) came to see "what the anchorite could not. That God needs no witness. Neither to himself nor against" (158). At the same time, we are told that the former priest, locked in his struggle with the hermit, also was mistaken about God and was blind to His terrible countenance. As the narrator tells us,

> And the priest? A man of broad principles. Of liberal sentiments. Even a generous man. Something of a philosopher. . . . He heard the voice of the Deity in the murmur of the wind in the trees. Even the stones were sacred. He was a reasonable man and he believed that there was love in his heart.
>
> There was not. Nor does God whisper through the trees. His voice is not to be mistaken. When men hear it they fall to their knees and their souls are riven and they cry out to Him and there is no fear in them but only that wildness of heart that springs from such longing and they cry out to stay his presence for they know at once that while godless men may live well enough in their exile those to whom He has spoken can contemplate no life without Him but only darkness and despair. Trees and stones are no part of it. (152)

At this point in *The Crossing*, we find a devastated boy (the protagonist) who, in addition to his own horrific experiences with natural beings and people, is told by a heretic once a priest about the man who challenged him and shattered his faith, where the latter is bereft of any comfort, much less understanding of or control over humans, nature, or an apparently indifferent God. What do the characters, McCarthy, and the reader hear in these tales that form chains of witnesses? Seemingly the same dark vision spoken by Heraclitus: all is flux, violence, and—undifferentiated—neither good nor bad to God.

So it may be in the world articulated in *The Crossing*. Yet in the novel there surprisingly are things stubbornly stable, things that refuse to pass. These things, to use Heidegger's way of speaking, linger awhile. Even more than that, they linger more than their expected or allocated while.

In the caretaker's story of the hermit, McCarthy includes a partial counter-site to the church at Huisiachepic that was ruined by the same earthquake that killed the hermit's son. The "parallel" church is the one in Caborca (where the hermit's family was killed and to which he returned to rail against God and where, in turn, the priest contended against him). This church at Caborca is both beautiful and, unexpectedly, one of those few things in the novel that remain still standing.

> By the flooding of the river through the years much has been destroyed. The sanctuary and two bell towers. The rear of the nave and most of the south transept. What remains of it stands on three legs so to speak. The dome hangs in the sky like an apparition and so it has hung for many years. Most improbably. No mason could devise such a structure. (149–150)

An odd thing, this church. It never could not be built this way, nor could it be—has it been—destroyed. It not only endured as a major building might (or should be expected to), but even when without a "foundation," that is against and despite human neglect, natural disaster, and what appears to be the default of God.

Perhaps this is another aspect of McCarthy's Heraclitean vision. The opposites of passing away and lingering may need to be brought together. But why would only part of one church be in such a condition if this were a "law" or "logic" of the cosmos? In any case, we have heard multiple testimonials that neither humans nor nature have aught but violent fluctuation, as usually perishing sooner rather than later in the destruction presided over by a God most awe-ful.

> It was never that [the hermit] ceased to believe in God. No. It was rather that he came to believe terrible things of Him. (148)

As we already have seen, the narrator confirms, as against the priest's earlier broad views and formlessness by which "he sought to make God manageable," that God indeed maltreats those to whom he speaks. This God of *The Crossing* is somewhat like Yahweh in His worse moments and somewhat like the primal force witnessed in Heraclitus's thought. Whether or not intended by McCarthy, the Greek convention whereby the gods, such as Zeus, play out the universe in a to-and-fro movement of scattering and gathering appears in these passages of *The Crossing*. Heraclitus's Fragment 52 says:

> Time is a child playing dice. . . .

The mad hermit testifies about God:

> The man could see Him bent at his work. . . . Weaving the world. In his hands it flowed out of nothing and in his hands it vanished into nothing once again. Endlessly. Endlessly. . . . Not chaos itself lay outside that matrix. And somewhere in that tapestry that was the world in its making and in its unmaking was a thread that was he. . . . (149)

Given what McCarthy's novel and Heraclitus both say, it would seem that the world, though violent and cruel beyond bearing to tender humans with our vested emotions and interests, appears as one dynamic of indifferent gathering and scattering if seen from the vantage point of God or the gods (that is, from the vantage of the whole cosmos itself). God appears to gather and scatter animals and people across the natural world, indifferent to their own beliefs, desires, and plans, their military and religious boundaries and territories. He flung the hermit from Him, drew him in, flung him away again, and finally drew him back, done in by death; He drew in the priest, scattered him through the hermit's truthful condemnations, then gathered him in by the lesson he saw in the hermit's self-oblivion. In this divine or cosmic dynamic that moves to and fro, we are expendable; from it we should expect nothing but pain and the grief or resignation of living amid all the passing away and to which the illusion of individuation is an added source of misery. A dark philosophy, indeed, to which *The Crossing* bears witness.

Heidegger Testifies About What the Greeks Saw

What of Heidegger's fictions? I insist that his work is a kind of poetizing because I take him at his word. Not because he writes bad verse, though he does, but because he speaks the saga of the round dance of the primal fourfold of heavens and earth, mortals and divinities. Even more so because he weaves his saga from the earliest thoughts of the West and from poets such as Hölderlin. As Northrop Frye says, in their anagogic or cosmic phase, all literary symbols are drawn from and return to the whole literary universe.[6] In speaking of the thinking of the earliest Greek thinkers (whom we characterize as the first philosophers of nature) and his own thinking that recollects and weaves thoughts together, Heidegger says

> thinking is poetizing, and indeed more than one kind of poetizing, more than poetry and song. Thinking of Being is the original way of poetizing. . . . thinking is primordial poetry, prior to all poesy, but

also prior to the poetics of art, since art shapes its work within the realm of language. All poetizing, in this broader sense, and also in the narrower sense of the poetic, is in its ground a thinking. . . . Because it poetizes as it thinks, the translation which wishes to let the oldest fragment of [Greek] thinking itself speak necessarily appears violent.[7]

According to Heidegger, then, the thinker's poetizing language, which moves back and forth from earlier texts, gathering them together, also is essentially violent, not only because we have to move from one language and thought to another, yoking them together by force, but because "we are bound to what is said in the saying . . . as though what is to be heard and said here necessarily suffers violence" (EGT, 19).

When Heidegger translates the early Greek thinkers, making from his dialogue with them yet another saga about the characteristics and relationships of humans, nature, and gods, it is not surprising that he is as exempt from nostalgia for pastoral bliss as is McCarthy. Explicating the famous chorus from Sophocles' *Antigone*, Heidegger notes how humans violently contest against nature not only in sailing against the stormy winter seas but also in agriculture, ripping up the oldest god, mother earth, with sharp plows to obtain crops. From the first, *techne* (technology) is a *poesis* (making) that violates nature and gods to satisfy human needs.[8]

Neither natural elements nor gods proceed gently. As Heidegger notes, Heraclitus says in Fragment 64: "Lightning steers the universe." Human steering, of course, "is an intervening, transfiguring movement that compels the ship along a specific course. It has the character of violence."[9] Yet, even when Zeus effortlessly rules, all animal and human life feels his blows. Heraclitus's Fragment 11 tells us: "Everything that crawls is tended and driven to pasture by the blow. The whip blow drives the herd forward and tends it while it is on the pasture" (HS, 31). Thus, whether by cosmic lightning and its voice, thunder, or by Zeus's prodding bolts, or yet by human custom and law, we not only are driven forward and guided but given our allotment, dispensed whatever we shall have (HS, 32). "The coerciveness of what befalls is connected with the tranquility of grazing" (HS, 32). Heraclitus here gathers many things together:

greedy, pursuing, and steering of the blow and being driven. To the latter there also belongs a tending and being steered. Allotment also belongs to the tranquil sense of grazing. Grazing as allotment is protection as well as getting steered in the sense of being forced. (HS, 32)[10]

"The kindness of the gods unites in itself the grace and the coercion which we must listen for . . ." according to Fragment 11. The swing between night and day and the cycle of seasons (HS, 35) also drive us forward, apportioning and measuring our lives and activities, our allotment of time here on earth beneath the heavens.

Heraclitus's experience of the world, put in terms of the contention among fire and earth, water and air in Fragment 76, is a tale in which "the annihilation of what precedes is the birth and arising of what follows. What follows comes forth in that it lives the death of what proceeds" (HS, 89). Animals and humans live their brief lives in the midst of a great dynamic of dark and light, death and life, annihilation and generation, war and peace, hunger and satisfaction (HS, 92). Here, insofar as we are like to the gods at all, we would witness and partially understand this dynamic. The gods, the everlasting immortal ones who do not die, are the great witnesses of death and thus strangely related to it, "from which they are free" (HS, 91). While "the fall of living things into death is irrevocable and final" the gods live on, "spectators and witnesses who accept the death of humans as offerings" (HS, 92, 94).

As noted, for Heraclitus, from the vantage point of the gods, tensed with that of mortals, things are not oppositional but the same, not valued positively and negatively but as the same. (Recall Fragment 102.) For the gods witnessing our rise and fall, "Living and dying are one and the same; waking and sleeping are the same; young and old are the same" (HS, 94–95). What this sameness means and the place of such sameness are questions to which we will return later. At the least, we hear that in the saga running from Heraclitus to Heidegger, the human experience and measure of what belongs together and apart, of the relationships among what is experienced in a harsh life, are quite different than what obtains in the sphere of the gods—where the genuine measure appears to be provided (cf. HS, 111ff.)

How humans can glimpse and catch a hint of understanding what the gods see and say has long been thought to depend on intermediary figures who pass, back and forth, between us: the seers. Heidegger reminds us that "The seer . . . is . . . the madman. . . . A madman is beside himself, outside himself: he is away. We ask: away? Where to and where from?" (EGT, 35).

The seer speaks from the . . . measure [*Wahr*] of what is present. He is the sooth sayer [*Wahr-Sager*]. As protector of Being, preservation belongs to the herdsman, who has so little to do with the bucolic idylls and nature mysticism that he can be the herdsman of Being only if he continues to hold the place of nothingness. Both are the same. (EGT, 36)

Of course, "The seer is the one who has already seen . . ." (EGT, 36). He stands in knowledge, having been struck and blinded by the lightning bolts of Zeus, by the lighting of Helios and Being. And because of this originary seeing, his subsequent saying is a remembering common to the genuine thinker and poet alike. "That is why, Heidegger notes, "*Mnemosyne* is the mother of the muses" (EGT, 36–37).

In fact, Heidegger unfolds this characteristic of the seer with Homer's *Iliad* in mind, specifically the scene at the beginning when the Greeks were ravaged by the plague sent by Apollo and "at an assembly of the warriors Achilles commands Kalchas the seer to interpret the wrath of the god" (EGT, 36). McCarthy writes about the hermit in the same terms. Recalling the torment of the hermit's life, the violent deaths of his parents and little boy, as well as his struggle with God, it is not surprising that he not only is "like a dreamer who wakes from a dream of grief to a greater sorrow yet," but after abandoning his wife in the ruins of his life, he becomes in the capital city "a bearer of messages," the content of which he does not himself know nor care about (147).

> He was simply a messenger. He had no faith in the power of men to act wisely in their own behalf. It was his view rather that every act soon eluded the grasps of the propagator to be swept away in a clamorous tide of unforeseen consequence. He believed that in the world was another agenda, another order, and with this power lay whatever brief he may have had. (147)

Thus, he was turned—truly called or not, who could know?—toward God. The man dreamt of God and returned to Caborca to dwell beneath the impossibly still-standing dome of the ruined church, as considered above. McCarthy tells us,

> The people of the town came and stood about. At a certain distance. They were interested to see what God would do with such a man. Perhaps he was a crazy person. Perhaps a saint. (180)

After the heretical hermit drives off the priest by hitting him with verbal blows that correctly assert that the priest knows nothing, the novel says that, contrary to the priest who left the scene and remained outside the ruined church, "and [who] by this choice sacrificed his words of their power to witness,"

> the old man [the hermit] by whatever instinct, stood [inside the church] on ground at once blessed and fraughtful. . . . On that perilous ground he had made of himself the only witness there can ever

be and if some see in his eyes the rapture of madness what else could one look for in one who had enjoined the God of the universe on ground of that God's own choosing. For that is always the nature of such ground, perilous and transitory. And it is indeed so that you must make your case there or nowhere. (152)

McCarthy's narrator goes on two pages later,

Now we may speak of madness. Now it is safe to do so. Perhaps one could say that only a madman could pace and rend his clothes over the accountability of God. What then to make of this man with claims that God had preserved him not once but twice out of the ruins of the earth solely in order to raise up a witness against Himself? (154)

It goes without saying that it is not our place to evaluate this mad witness, any more than it was that of the Greeks before the walls of Troy to evaluate Kalchas. But it is appropriate, even necessary, for us to ponder what the hermit saw and what is related in his tale. This is our task as readers, thinkers, and translators of testimony into our lives.

What the mad hermit saw included the things that passed so violently, so painfully out of his life and that which remained unavoidably—even colossally—present, thought just as violently and powerfully: that is, God. Hence, the odd status of the hanging dome of the ruined church in Caborca in which he came to dwell. Though the hermit and his distress passed away, the dome that sheltered him itself "floated on in the pure air" (150) and, though already a ruin, or perhaps as and because it was a ruin, seemingly was exempt from the cosmos's rule on the transitory character of all earthly things.

What to make of this? If we read McCarthy through Heidegger, we find that the hermit seer shows us a tale of injustice, the injustice of things against one another and against the order of the cosmos itself. To come to this, we first need to hear how Heidegger retells the tale of the oldest text, "of Western thinking," the Anaximander fragment from the end of the seventh century BC (EGT, 13). In Nietzsche's translation, it reads:

Whence things have their origin, thence they must also pass away according to necessity, for they must pay penalty and be judged for their injustice, according to the ordinance of time. (13)

Heidegger recalls and translates the text into his own words insofar as he speaks of the world as what is present to us as such and in terms of things that linger awhile. The thinkers and poets and seers all would witness not only the transitory nature of animals and humans but also of

> everything present, everything that presences by lingering awhile: gods and men, temples and cities, sea and land, eagle and snake, wind and light, stone and sand, day and night. (EGT, 40)

For Anaximander and Heidegger, the basic trait of things is that they are present. But, thinking more deeply, Anaximander says that this presencing is an injustice. What does this mean? Remember that Heidegger recounts how Heraclitus says that from the oblivion of one thing there arises the appearance of another, next thing. Similarly, according to Heidegger, Anaximander holds that all is not right with things, with what is present. He says that "something is out of joint." The character of things as lingering in presence, in the present, indicates that the jointure is one of "time." Between the absence of what withdraws into the past and the absence of what approaches from the future but is not yet here, what is present lingers in the present. According to Heidegger's reading of Anaximander, the result is a kind of hubris. Heidegger says,

> What has arrived may even insist upon its while solely to remain more present, in the sense of perduring. That which lingers perseveres in its presencing. In this way it extricates itself from its transitory while. It strikes the willful pose of persistence, no longer concerning itself with whatever else is present. It stiffens—as if this were the way to linger—and aims solely for continuance and subsistence. (EGT, 42)

Thus, in insistently lingering, even if the insistence is necessary to their being things, to presencing at all, things are disjoined. They throw things out of joint. They generate injustice. He continues,

> Lingering as presencing . . . is an insurrection on behalf of sheer endurance . . . In this rebellious whiling whatever lingers awhile insists upon sheer continuance. . . . In the jointure whatever lingers awhile keeps to its while. . . . The jointure is order. (43)

Whereas order [dike] involves the proper transitory flow of what comes to be and what passes away, disorder [adikia] occurs insofar as things insist on their own lingering, as opposed to their letting come about the lingering of other things, and as opposed to their own passing on and away in a timely manner.

Recalling and retelling this saga, Heidegger's treatment of Anaximander arrives at a resting point where what he says seems to be the same as McCarthy:

> According the fragment . . . those beings that linger awhile in presence, stand in disorder. As they linger awhile, they tarry. . . . They hang on; they cling to themselves. When what lingers awhile delays, it stubbornly follows the inclination to persist in hanging on, and indeed to insist on persisting; it aims at everlasting continuance and no longer bothers about *dike*, the order of the while.
>
> But in this way everything that lingers awhile strikes a haughty pose toward every other thing of its kind. None heeds the lingering presence of the others. Whatever lingers awhile is inconsiderate toward others, each dominated by what is implied in its lingering presence, namely, the craving to persist. . . . Inconsiderateness impels them toward persistence, so that they may still present themselves as what is present. (45–46)

Beyond Humanism

Does not what Heidegger says name the dynamics of *The Crossing*? How better to interpret its violent destruction than in terms of the inconsiderateness of things toward one another, an inconsiderateness that compels things to cling to their own persisting at the expense of other things, at the cost of disordering, that is, with cosmic injustice.

Even a quick tally of events in the novel seems to confirm the coincidence of McCarthy's story with Heidegger's, Heraclitus's, and Anaximander's about the "urge to continue lingering," futile though it is for each thing and as destructive as it is for all the rest of the world. The boy's family is murdered in bed by someone who wants something from them; the wolf, caught while seeking her own kind and for killing cattle as is her way of living, is trapped, degraded, and destroyed; on the roadways and in the villages of *The Crossing* we encounter incident after incident in which property, virginity, life itself is violently wrenched away by others who want to assert only themselves. The cosmic gathering and scattering appears to be a matter of things (people, but animals too) gathered in by others who take what they want or need in order that the latter may cling to enduring, in a process that scatters the debris of the consumed and destroyed all about us, which scatters to destruction and death all that does not manage to be the thing that does unto others that it may endure instead of them.

Overall, McCarthy's tale is one in which most everything falls, in unpredictable and ungovernable turn, as part of the violently transitory character of the universe. Hence, those things that manage to perdure, to insist on lingering beyond what might be their customary or regularly allotted time, are especially noteworthy. As we have already seen, this is the case with the church dome at Caborca, in contrast to the church at Huisiachepic, which was destroyed, and to the town of Caborca, which is gathered up and scattered in regard to the earth and time as "the ruins of a town slumping back into the mud out of which it had been raised" (137).

And of course, the God to whom the church was raised and who witnessed its destruction, this Judeo-Christian God endures. Everlastingly. Outside of time, we understand. The protagonist, scarred and numbed, persists by at least lingering to the end of the story, though he exists, in terms of his noncomprehension and nonparticipation in many events, at a level of humanity that arguably is far lower than was Job at his lowest.

Perhaps the most strikingly insistent and thus most unjust character is the hermit who dwells under the hanging, persisting dome. He lived on, extending his while, after his parents died, after his son died. He was spared, or prevented from, the peace of death insofar, the narrator says, "he'd been called forth twice out of the ashes, out of the dust and rubble" (146). With the loss of his parents and child, we are told, "In his sparing he found himself severed from both antecedents and posterity alike. He was but some brevity of a being" (147).

In the language of Anaximander and Heidegger, he remained present while the others had departed and in a manner in which nothing more from him and his wife would emerge. He persisted for over seventy years, still there, caught between the passing away of others and the never to come of those who forever would remain absent. He lingered so long that he never came out of the rubble of the town or church; he was not called forth from the ashes a third time but left there by God. God outlasted him, of course. God left him dead.

The hermit railed against God for the "injustice of his past life. The ten thousand insults. The catalogue of woes" (155) but was oblivious to his own proud insistence on lingering, on persisting in the face of God and over against all the other things that came to be and passed away while he endured. To his own disorder, his own injustice, the mad seer was woefully blind.

So, what do we witness, we who witness the testimony of McCarthy, Heidegger, Heraclitus, and Anaximander? The thinking and poetic saying of all these authors, of their characters and interior narrators, appear to indicate that the usual human understanding of nature and God are pitifully inadequate. We essentially attempt to know and manipulate the world for our own benefit—most deeply for our very being or presencing, which consists in a persistent lingering in the flux of the transitory, even if this means persisting at the expense of all other things, by destroying animals and people and by wrestling with God himself. What else can we do? How else can we be things?

McCarthy and Heidegger bespeak a nonhumanistic alternative, akin to the stance taken toward the cosmos 2,500 years ago by Anaximander and Heraclitus. In the works of all four of these we hear one tale, the tale wherein to become fully human means to learn to understand that our human vantage is in deep shadows compared to the sun's lighting or the lightning of the gods. Whereas we are certain that justice and injustice are to be measured in terms of our mortal desires (in the modern world, that means in terms of our individuation), for the gods all is the same. Heraclitus says in Fragment 102:

> Everything is beautiful, good, and just for god. Only humans make a distinction between the just and unjust.

In McCarthy's version, the priest-become-heretic says,

> The events of the world can have no separate life from the world. And yet the world itself can have no temporal view of things. It can have no cause to favor certain enterprises over others. The passing of armies and the passing of sands in the desert are one. There is no favoring, you see. How could there be? At whose behest? (148)

Here we find something like the final testimony of McCarthy, Heidegger, Anaximander, and Heraclitus. In these words we have a kind of summation of what the narrator and characters witness. We witness the same, in a sequential telling of the tale, from one incident to the next. As the readers, however, we are at the end of the chain and are left with a question. How shall we respond to what we have received?

The testimony from Heidegger, Anaximander, and Heraclitus that the very lingering of things generates injustice is harder to fathom than the fact that we and McCarthy, his characters and narrator, all witness the transitory nature of things in the world and the reality that many of them insist on maintaining or extending their while at the expense of others, even if it comes to murder. Of course, if we testify honestly, we implicate ourselves too: we kill daily for our food, in our delegation of force and desire not just to the butcher and the soldier but to many others, as the voices on behalf of environmental and social justice point out.

Yet there is more to be told, to be called into question. Commonsensically, we know that we could not exist—could not be at all, not here and now or anywhere, ever—if we did not persist, presencing for our while. And, if we did not presence, lingering, how would we ever make room for others? Do our children not emerge as the result of our lingering in love or lust with one another, as the result of lingering with each other "making love" for a while, which then leads to the while of gestation and birth, and then to the lifetime of a next generation? Anaximander thinks so, whether for these ordinary reasons or not. Remember that in his surviving fragment he acknowledges "necessity": "Whereas things have their origin, there they also pass away according to necessity. . . ." Animals, mortals, all things presence a while and pass away—necessarily, or they would not come to be; they never would be things at all.

If it is in some way necessary that for things to come into being and to linger and thus also insist on having some while, it not only is because it is unavoidable but because that is proper for what is something rather than nothing. The injustice too would be necessary as would be the final penalty to be paid. Is this to arrive at a position where we bear no responsibility, since we simply exist by lingering, which unavoidably means holding off and destroying the contending current and future coming of other things?

No. Neither ontologically nor existentially. Heidegger contends that for Anaximander no such passive dimension or consequence follows for mortals from the fact that by our lingering we contend with others that also could come to stay awhile or, if already here, might stay a while longer. Two-thirds of the way through his essay, Heidegger unexpectedly shifts our attention to a complicating dynamic by retranslating another portion of Anaximander's fragment and arguing that "what is present . . . does not simply disintegrate into inconsiderate individualities; it does not dissipate itself in discontinuity. Rather, Anaximander's saying [goes on to say] 'beings which linger awhile let belong, one to the other: consideration with regard to one another'" (EGT, 46). Apparently, for Anaximander, we not only expel others from presence (generating injustice) but, at the same time and in tension, somehow also let other things belong together (letting justice occur) (EGT, 47).

Just as things turn against one another, bringing destruction and ultimately disorder into the world, they simultaneously have the possibility of "turning-themselves-toward" one another, in what Heidegger translates as "solicitude or care" (EGT, 46). Indeed, the allowance of one thing by another would not be a kind of option or choice that things or humans make but itself a necessity. Transforming the commonsense observation made above into tighter language: no thing could come about, as or within lingering, except insofar as other things admit it into their while and presence, that is, turn toward it. How can anything come about and remain, for its while, present? Heidegger says, "each one giving [care] to the other, is the sole manner in which what lingers a while in presence lingers at all, i.e., granting order" (EGT, 47).

If we think of what this means at an existential level, we recall that even in McCarthy's dark novels, there is care among the devastated, along with the callous violence. In the hermit's tale, the story itself continues only after the near-starving boy is fed by the now heretical ex-priest and as one of the cats delicately enjoys the remains of the meal. Just as for the Greeks in the *Odyssey*, hospitality to the stranger is observed before the tale is told. First, eggs, something as coffee, and the offer of the makings for a cigarette; only then unfolds the dark saga upon which we have focused.

Indeed, scattered amid the horrors, and no doubt overlooked because of the latter (if other readers respond as I do), McCarthy places lovely and moving instances of the simple ways things are positively oriented to one another. To consider only the section of the hermit's tale, we find, in addition to the generous portion given to the boy an almost still-life where "the cat rose and looked at itself in the white porcelain of the plate and stepped away and sat and yawned and set about cleaning itself" (141). Before his son was killed, the man who became the hermit had shared beautiful moments:

> He is youthful. Perhaps not thirty years of age. He rides a mule. The boy rides in the bow of the saddle before him. It is the springtime and the wildflowers are blooming in the meadows along the river. He has promised to return with a gift for his young wife. He sees her standing there. She waves goodbye to him as he sets out. He has no likeness of her other than that which he carries in his heart. Think of that. Perhaps she is crying. Standing there watching him out of sight. (144)

A touching scene. So much given all at once. So much to treasure and remember in this ordinary splendor. It is to be savored, as the heretical priest acknowledges: "This is a journey I have thought of many times" (144).

Yes, McCarthy's story is all the crueler, we well may believe, in relating such realities, for they make subsequent life more heartbreaking still. Just as I note that I can barely bring myself to read McCarthy because of this trait, something compels me. The wolf is dragged through the story, treated with an odd combination of controlling violence and respect (largely for its character as a savage killer?) by the boy and also because he, and the reader, are mysteriously drawn to it or its power. One might suspect that we merely are being manipulated by McCarthy, though his utter lack of sentimentality would suggest only a cynicism or nihilism—unless, as we are now examining, there might be another dimension of meaning. At any rate, the sweet scene of parting and the promise of a gift on the return are turned so bitter that the man not only loses his son to death but abandons his wife, further impoverishing his life and hers too, eventually fleeing his country and moving to Guatemala, Trinidad, and the capital. Even the little he has is taken away:

> What thoughts must have been his? Who cannot feel his anguish? He returns to Huisiachepic bearing across the mule's haunches the corpse of the child with which God had blessed his house. Waiting for him in Huisiachepic is the mother of the child and this is the gift he brings her. (146)

Of course, we too are overwhelmed by the destruction and pain. Yet the simple beauty is there too. Quiet and small. The ruined church in Caborca is breathtakingly beautiful still, and oddly so because of its surreal ruination: "The church is very beautiful. . . . The dome hangs in the sky like an apparition and so it has hung for many years" (149). Indeed, in the narration, the beauty and destruction mix together through the sentences on pages 148–149, just as seamlessly as happens in Anaximander's saying.

In the midst of the natural and human destruction, where things indeed do contend with and discipline one another, they also cooperate, making room for one another side by side (as happens with the ex-priest and the boy, the to-be-hermit and his young son in the saddle, the gathering of hermit, priest, and townspeople). They are generous to one another, yielding to one another's needs and prospects from their meager allotments in life. Typically, amid the description of the hermit's dying days, when he and the priest argued to the end, McCarthy notes that the townsfolk had been feeding the madman all these years: "The food, the pitcher of milk—which the people of Caborca had become accustomed to leave for him at the edge of the shadowline . . ." (156).

Even as a ruined thing, the hanging dome and vaults of the church, to use the language of the later Heidegger, sheltered the priest so that he might dwell there in his odd manner, gathered with the earth and heavens and his God.[11] And, in this place, here too the priest and hermit and townspeople were gathered in a strange manner, but as community nonetheless. All these things turned toward one another, made openings to and for the others. Each welcomed and helped sustain the others' lingering their while—longer than they would have otherwise. The giving of the means for whiling and the accepting of the opening given happen together, at the same time: food is offered by the hermit and gladly accepted by the boy and cats. Yes, we may contend that this little "good" is almost completely overwhelmed by the "bad." But the "good" is there, no matter how small the portion, and perhaps with the destruction looming so large, the wonder is that there is any simple beauty and solicitude among things at all.

What do these parts of the story tell us? One possibility, in Heidegger's words:

> If what is present grants order, it happens in this manner: as beings linger awhile, they give [care] to one another. The surmounting of disorder properly occurs though the letting-belong-of [care]. (47)

If so, as lingering in their while, sometimes some things rudely insist on themselves at the expense of other things; yet, sometimes some things open to each other, sheltering and caring for each other.

In McCarthy's novel, this doubled dynamic happens in several ways. Some people care for others; the splendor of fields and animals is given to mortals. Even after all the events he has witnessed and that he relates to the boy, even after he has been driven from his faith by the penetrating words of the anchorite, the ex-priest names himself with the word "care": "I am the custodian. The caretaker" (140). Though he abandoned the church and its parishioners, he remains as caretaker of the tale, to give testimony and thus care for the hermit and the fallen church and God. Is this what enables him also to care for the boy? And, ultimately, for the reader, who becomes heir to what is witnessed? Supposedly this tale and its puzzling meaning are meaningful to the reader. ¿Verdad?

In what ways do things open to one another? By providing for physical sustenance, of course. That is why the gracious sharing of a portion of the characters' meager apportionment of life's necessities is all the more worthy of respect. And, as noted, beauty is beheld as things manifest themselves. More important, the mutuality of the openness that things give to one another is shown in how many of such events of gathering are actually communal in character. Companionship and company are given. The ex-priest welcomes the forlorn protagonist, and the boy repays the hospitality with his polite and attentive company; the cats, boy, and caretaker temporarily make a content community. As the boy and the heretic priest talked,

> A large gray cat came up the table and stood looking at him. It had one ear missing almost entirely and its teeth hung down outside. The man pushed back slightly from the table and the cat stepped down into his lap and curled up and subsided and turned its head and gravely regarded the boy across the table in the manner of a consultant. A cat of counsel. The man placed one hand upon it as if to secure it there. He looked at the boy. (154–155)

The heretic's gestures are quite the right ones. Though we know things cannot hold and that this moment all too quickly will pass, it is just what we do—and long to do. Hold the moment. The battle-scarred cat, the deeply wounded boy, and the host stripped of all he had desired and sought as a priest are able to gather together and comfort one another. With all their internal and external scarring from the damaging scattering that they wreak unto one another, things also can gather together in caring belonging. Only the slightest gesture is needed: a nod of empathy, a hospitable push of corn husk and tobacco, the making room on a lap. Mc-Carthy's tale, then, tells us fully the double dynamic of which Heidegger and Anaximander speak: that

> whatever is present, as that which lingers awhile, is released into reckless [careless] disorder; . . . [also, such] present beings surmount disorder by letting order and care [reck] belong to one another. This letting-belong is the manner in which what lingers awhile lingers and so comes to presence as what is present. (EGT, 48)

More precisely, what is the manner in which things may so mutually open to one another and gather together? We find a first answer in what we are doing: reading what McCarthy, Heidegger, Anaximander, and Heraclitus think and say in writing. The manner of opening and giving to one another, for mortals, is that of language. With the novel, in a story inside it, the protagonist and ex-priest talk to one another; within that tale we hear of the priest and hermit arguing for a long time, of the latter becoming a messenger in Mexico City and then of his praying and arguing with God and muttering into his Bible. When the preacher ceased speaking on behalf of God, the hermit-barrister worked out his case against Him.

Through language, the company of people extends to their gathering with animals. Animals and people provide one another company; people do their part largely by talking, not only to themselves ("It occurred to the boy that he hadn't been speaking to him," 139), but regularly by addressing animals. Horse, dog, and wolf. So it is with the caretaker and his cats. The boy considers the ex-priest talking:

> He looked at the man and he looked at the cats. They seemed to be sleeping to a cat and it occurred to him that the man's voice was no novelty and that he must talk to himself in the absence of any god-sent ear from the outer world. Or talk to the cats. (143)

Remember that one of the cats, gathered into the man's lap and engaging the boy with its look, as it listened to the two of them in conversation, was called "a cat of counsel" (155).

More importantly, so we do not overlook what the narrator just said in a whisper, the boy was a "godsent ear." The novel names the core of the manner of the gathering-together of animals and people when they open to one another and let order reign by their compassion and conversation: a language-borne care of each to the other, of one letting, even helping, the other to be. The care is a gift. The caring is the giving of the opening to each other. How does the care come? As a gift born by the animal that comes and attentively stays. By the horse and the dog. Or by mortals who make a place through the slight, efficacious gestures that provide a portion of what is physically or spiritually needed, or as "any god sent" thing or event.

In the manner of the nourishing-gathering given by the generous act and attentive language, we have only to press one more step in order to think what may matter most in the mutuality of the gift giving that lets order happen. What is the gift that is given by the giving of company and conversation? Is it just the food and understanding that comes? One could object that in the bleak landscape, these gifts should be more than enough. Perhaps I am greedy. Perhaps I am just as all the other things that want more, that are not satisfied with their little while.

Lest my readers think it is just me who is greedy here, note that McCarthy does not scruple to be generous on this point. With his usual economy, McCarthy—surprisingly?—tells us what the ultimate outcome of all this giving has been for the heretic priest. The expanse of what is given to him by all the things, events, and discussion of his life is covered in a scant nine printed lines (as the text originally was set), which sweep from his origin to his final, current state.

> I am a Mormon. Or I was. I was a Mormon born.
> . . .

They came here many years ago. Eighteen and ninety-six. From Utah. . . . I was a Mormon. Then I converted to the church. Then I became I don't know what.

Then I became me.

What do you do here?

I am the custodian. I am the caretaker. (140)

Because this self-identification is related at the beginning of the priest's and hermit's tale, at that point we cannot yet appreciate what it means for him to be or become himself or to be named "caretaker." And even with the hints we have just discovered above about how things open to one another in care, what anyone genuinely is remains a mystery and so will remain long after they pass away. Still, the gifts given by things, animals, mortals, and God appear to play a part in the priest coming into his own. The priest himself tells us this.

Once again, McCarthy and Heidegger say the same, as we see in the latter's gloss on what care or solicitude [*reck, rouche*] mean:

> The Middle High German Word *rouche* means solicitude or care. Care tends to something so that it may remain in its essence. This turning-itself-toward, when thought of what lingers awhile in relation to presencing, is *reck*. Our [German] word *geruhen* [to deign or respect] is related to *reck* . . . : to esteem something, to let or allow something to be itself. (EGT, 46)

The gift that things give to one another—that the other is let into its own—also means that things let one another into the deepest mode of their being present things. The other is not merely let have some physical space, mappable onto a coordinate system, for some time period, measurable by a clock. Instead, what is bid and allowed to become itself comes to its proper while—to the time apportioned or given to it—and to its individual and historically concrete essential nature. Somehow what is given in the mutual opening of things results in order rather than disorder, justice rather than injustice, being joined in the gathering together of what solicitously belongs together rather than being disjointed in a scattering by contentious destruction. In Heidegger's terms, what is given

> enjoins matters in such a way that whatever is present lets order and [care] belong. The [order] lets such enjoining prevail among present beings and so grants them the manner of their arrival—as the while of whatever lingers awhile. (EGT, 49)

This claim seems comforting. We appear to have arrived at a positive position in which we see that things help one another to while as present and have the possibility of coming into their own. But we cannot forget the dual character of things as they also come—first and foremost in McCarthy's novels—compulsively and violently so as to "expel one another from what is presently present" (47), from their own sphere of lingering.

I noted above that neither McCarthy nor Heidegger is romantically nostalgic for a lost age of harmony and bliss. Both resolutely admonish us to bear in mind the necessity of the tensed dynamic between pushing away and opening toward other things, between order and disorder, justice and injustice. McCarthy and Heidegger dedicate much of their thinking and writing to telling us not only *that* such destruction and care play out across the cosmos but (as best they are able) *how* these dimensions play as the cosmos. Here, too, we need to remember and again face up to the darker side that accompanies the light of the caring belonging. Otherwise we also will fail to comprehend the mystery of the gift of the possibility of coming to one's own characteristics and to the whiling that things can give to one another in opening by way of care (because both dimensions are given at once). To adopt a few of Heidegger's sentences to the point:

> What mortal can fathom the abyss [of insurrection of things on behalf of their own sheer endurance at the expense of the others]? [We] may try to shut [our] eyes before this abyss. [We] may entertain one delusion after another. The abyss does not vanish. (EGT, 43, 51)

A Hint at the Cosmos's Unified and Diverse Dynamic

Are order and disorder, gods and mortals, wanton destruction and solicitous care, justice and injustice, earth and sky all partners in one cosmic dynamic? McCarthy's novel and Heidegger's works are full of things and "forces" or "dimensions" of the cosmos that usually are themselves opposites but, as we have just found, that mutually shape and respond to one another. As we already have heard: Heidegger says that what is so tensed belongs together in their differences, as the same. Heraclitus says: "Living and dying are one and the same . . . ; the sameness of what seems to be different" (HS, 94–95). McCarthy has written: "So everything is necessary. Every last thing. This is the hard lesson. Nothing can be dispensed with. Nothing despised. Because the seams are hid from us, you see. The joinery" (143).

How can that be? How can we begin to understand it? In *The Crossing*, things that are generated out of themselves (animals, mortals, all of living nature, or what the Greeks name *phusis*) and those that we generate by human *techne* or *poesis* (the cities and the churches or the stories, respectively) encounter one another. Obviously. But the point is what happens in the novel. It is what is reported to us by the characters and narrator. We are told about the encounters and are left to ponder what it might mean for us. What are we to make of the testimony about the overwhelming disorder and, to a lesser extent, it seems, of order in the cosmos?

In the encounters, as noted repeatedly, things seldom cooperate. Instead, they go counter to one another. They appear to move so as to realize a world of opposition or collision rather than conjunction. Yet, as also noted, the novel's tale of the relations among humans does not seem to be its major story, its news. Surely, the bulk of the novel is concerned with such encounters. But the most thought-provoking parts of the hermit's and priest's tales focus on the relationships humans have with other humans, animals, and God. The protagonist and the wolf, or he and his horse and dog, present a deeply problematic set of affairs, specifically the nonintegration of the moments that approach a caring attitude or responsiveness on the boy's behalf toward these animals and the moments when he is callously indifferent to anything but, or even to, his own varying drives and drift. Or, as we have considered in some detail, the hermit and priest contend with God—a genuine encounter since each goes counter to the other.

To consider one example, since I have been arguing that the ex-priest is a Job-like legalistic detective, here is how he begins to explain to the boy why he came to be where he is:

> I thought there might be evidence that had been overlooked. I thought He would not trouble himself to wipe away every handprint. My desire to know was very strong. I thought it might amuse Him to leave some clue. . . .
>
> Something. Something unforeseen. Something out of place. Something untrue or out of round. A track in the dirt. A fallen bauble. (142)

Could it be that what appear as opposites, scattered, or even scattering themselves apart are in their differences able to encounter each other and in that tensed countering to each other somehow belong together? Could this somehow be necessary to what they each are and to what the cosmos as a whole might be?

Heidegger and Fink read Heraclitus to say that we come to understand who we are as mortals by seeing ourselves in reference to the gods. As immortal, the gods provide our measure as morals. But in this encounter the counter is just as true: the immortals understand themselves by witnessing "humans who constantly disappear in time" (HS, 98). Whereas in treating McCarthy we hear from human witnesses about their railing against God and that God outlasts and has outwitted humans, with Heraclitus we hear that gods and mortals come to live in their own differences and relationships with each other via the distinction that emerges for each of them out of their encounter with death (HS, 98, 100, 105).

Heraclitus thus holds that when mortals reach the abyss—of death, that is, of not remaining in presencing—we need our counter, the gods, for the sake of knowledge. It is by realizing our great deficiency with respect to the gods that we can begin to understand our mortality and our relationship to the rest of the cosmos. Both our own deaths and the immortal gods are necessary for us to understand and become who we are as mortals (HS, 105). And, in reverse, immortals have need of mortals for the same reason (HS, 112). In this way mortals and gods do not stubbornly hold out against each other or contend against each other for their own whiling at the expense of the other—that is not intelligible, save through fruitless and hubristic intentions of humans to be immortal. Instead, mortals and gods open themselves to the other and thus open themselves to themselves too. In measuring each other, "against" each other, mortals and gods "hold themselves close to each other" (HS, 109).

Insofar as this is so, Heidegger points out, Heraclitus does nothing less than attempt a major shift in Greek mythology. Whereas the Greeks had thought the autonomy of gods and mortals from each other, Heraclitus would be expressing them in "a mutual constitution," as "standing open to an intertwining of understanding their relationship" (HS, 111). To say that the gods and mortals need each other ultimately is an ontological claim: each can be what they are only in mutual measuring and response. Cosmologically: together in such measuring of difference by way of passing away into death or not, the humans and immortals respectively allow each other to linger their appropriate while. They allow justice rather than injustice to occur. Their encounter as proper counters, rightly joined, articulates order rather than disorder; that is, it carries out the jointure of cosmos.

A parallel debate about whether God needs humans occurs in *The Crossing*, where witnessing and measuring also play a prominent role. We have heard how the mad hermit is said to be mad because he came to believe that God had twice saved him "only in order to raise up a witness against Himself" (154). This view appears to be based on the same position as Heraclitus's. The deranged hermit, we are told, hardened in his resolve to be a witness to God because he thought

> That the existence of the Deity lay imperiled for want of this simple thing. That for God there could be no witness. Nothing against which He terminated. Nothing by way of which his being could be announced to Him. Nothing to stand apart from and to say I am this and that is other. Where that is I am not. He could create everything save that which would say him no. (155)

What to make of this? According to what Heidegger has said about Heraclitus, the latter tells us that the old anchorite is on the right track. He and God would need each other to provide measure and self-understanding. Thus, in witnessing God, even if inadequately, failingly, or falsely, he would be in the service of God. At the same time, insofar as he "hardened" his resolve to be a witness to God and to render God accountable, as would seem the point of a witness's testimony, his hardening risks the danger of which Heidegger has warned us: "strik[ing] the willful pose of persistence. . . . It stiffens . . . and aims solely for continuance and subsistence" (EGT, 42). Would the hermit, then, by his belief that he is and needs to be the witness against God, open himself to God and God to himself? Or would he be insisting on his while in such a way as to interfere with the whiling of God and thus risk putting the cosmos out of order, rashly initiating an injustice against the Most Just?

At this point in the novel, the narrator tells us that God had "turned even the old man's heretical usurpation to his own service" (156). "How could there," we are asked, "have been another possibility" (156)? The priest, however, comes to another conclusion, not that the railing hermit was serving God by insisting on testifying against Him but that God is not in the least in need of a witness (158).

The priest's position corresponds to another facet of the Greek thought we have been considering, Heraclitus's idea that we learn from our own counter, now applied not directly between God and humans but between what is said directly and what is to be learned through indirect reflection upon what the witnesses say. Subtly, the narrator points out that one does not, cannot, know the meaning of what one says or pronounces. Think of the Greek tradition of oracles, who articulate an enigma but do not univocally interpret it. That task falls to those to whom the pronouncement is directed, that is, to those whom it concerns. Similarly, in *The Crossing*, the hermit, earlier in life, already had been characterized as a "bearer of messages" who "had no way to know what the messages said" (147). In a densely worded page, the narrator tells us,

> In the end what the priest came to believe was that the truth may often be carried about by those who themselves remain all unaware of it. . . . They go about ignorant of the true nature of their condition, such are the whiles of truth and such its stratagems.[12]
>
> What the priest saw at last was that the lesson of a life can never be its own. Only the witness has the power to take its measure. It is lived for the other only. The priest therefore saw what the anchorite could not. That God needs no witness. Neither to Himself nor against. The truth is rather that if there were no God then there could be no witness for there could be no identity to the world but only each man's opinion of it. The priest saw that there is no man who is elect because there is no man who is not. To God every man is a heretic. (158)

These paragraphs seem to say the same as Heraclitus: to God or the gods, all human endeavor is the same, and the priest comes to understand what God does through his human counterpart (the hermit) and thereby also comes to see what would be necessary to have a counterposition about God and about God's relationship to humans. We may be swayed to the likeliness of the priest's position because it also seems to apply in the case of the protagonist. How better to say what he comes to in the end, what the lesson of his life is for us? Do we not find that the events narrated have, together, so numbed him, and have been so beyond his capacity to think about or articulate his feelings about them, or been so concealed in some other way that he stays in oblivion about their meanings and his own possibilities? Do not the priest's words, reflexively, tell us, in regard to the protagonist, that "the lesson of a life can never be its own" (158)? As the priest might learn from the anchorite, so might we learn about or from the protagonist. Or, perhaps the same thing from them all.

For the narrator to say that the priest comes to see that the lesson of a life "is lucid for the other only" (158) seems to echo Heraclitus's position that we understand only by measuring ourselves against our counter. If Heraclitus's sayings about gods and men learning through their encounters as counters is true, and if Heidegger's view—taken, he says, from the Greeks—that truth as unconcealment always and necessarily is twinned with concealment, then it would seem plausible, perhaps even inescapable, for two so intertwined opponents as the priest and hermit that the priest "therefore saw what the anchorite could not" (158).

The narrator presses on, identifying what the priest saw: that God needs no witness. This is the opposite of what the hermit saw. We suppose, because the priest's insight comes second—last—that it now is the final word. The truth. The hermit was wrong; the priest learns from him and so is correct. Why would we believe this? Perhaps because of the way we learn to read and to do bookkeeping—guided or governed by discursive logic. These activities have answers that are worked out and pronounced as the final statement. Q.E.D. The bottom line. The answer, we are taught, is given at the end. This, of course, is complexly connected to the historical development and use of our concepts, unified by the secular myth of progress, whether in Darwinian evolution or Hegelian dialectics.

But, we know better. A poem or novel is not a sum or argument with a tidy conclusion. Here we do not need to summon the mighty ideas of Heraclitus on the everlasting and necessary tension of supposed opposites. We only need to note the unity of the literary work and how in figural thinking such as Heraclitus's and Heidegger's each thing that is said stands in relation to all that is said in the whole. Applied to these passages at hand, what the priest and anchorite say stand in opposition. Period. They are counter. We encounter both, in a given order, since the text is linear. But it is not discursive, running on to a conclusion (*discursis*) as does propositional language. Instead the novel is a saying that says—lets-lie-present-before-us (to put it in Heidegger's language): priest-hermit; God needs human witnesses–God needs no witness; concealment-unconcealment. We have heard all there is to hear. We are not told any answer. We have only the testimony. Testimony on both sides of the case. Perhaps. Perhaps not.

In any event, these fictive characters cannot tell us what they or the novel mean. The task of interpretation is ours alone and unavoidably. Is that not how and why we read a novel? Here I only note that the two possible insights stand, persist for a while, in a manner in which they both open to each other, both allow the other to come forth into its own. Indeed, each is necessary that the other have its meaning. They genuinely are counter because they let us measure each other and become aware of our assumptions about meaning and judgment, about mortals and gods or God. As together necessary, they too, in their way, let order occur while they linger. But they also yield when their while is over and so do not cause disorder or injustice. As counters and deferential to each other and their respective whiles, they are exemplary.

Developed to this point, the story within the story includes the two countersagas in relation to the rest of the protagonist's experiences and to those of all the other characters natural, human, and divine, as well as to those the narrator conveys, and to the hermeneutics that are divided on what this means about God's intention and relation to his world. I claim that these inner tales do not trespass against one another or move in insurrection against their while. As evidence, I note that at this point the story within the story comes to an end and passes away. Its while is gone. The next page is headed with three centered asterisks. The boy and the ex-priest exchange a brief goodbye, and the boy moves toward the river. The next paragraph either agrees or disagrees with Heraclitus's saying that one cannot step into the same river twice:

> The boy would cross and recross the river countless times in the days following. (159)

Beyond Both Gods and Mortals

A major difference between McCarthy's tale and the sayings of Heraclitus and Anaximander has been ignored in what has been remarked upon thus far. Orthodox Christians would not take God to be the same as the Greeks' gods. Supposedly, the Greeks would agree that the difference is great. For the Greeks, the gods are not an ultimate reality. Hence, just as from the vantage of the gods the things of nature and of human affairs are all the same and are driven by the blows of lightning, so too from a "higher" vantage point gods and mortals alike are set into—driven to—their relational opposition and belonging by a cosmic force whose name returns us to our starting point of violent destruction, of transitory passing away into death and oblivion: War. Heraclitus's Fragment 53 says, "War [*polemos*] is the father and king of all things" (EGT, 23). Whereas before we heard how gods and mortals could come to understand themselves and allow each other to come into their appropriate nature because they could measure themselves against each other through the study of death, which one undergoes and the other only witnesses, now we hear that both come to be what they are insofar as Strife establishes some as gods and some as humans. Evidently, all that crawls, human and animal, is delivered by the blows of the gods' whip, yet the highest force, directing gods as well as mortals, is War.

According to Heraclitus, naming War does not dissolve the tension between scattering and gathering in favor of the former. War is not wanton destruction nor disorder—chaos—as is clear because Heraclitus uses the name for the unifying ontological principle of the cosmos. Further, in Greek thought about the parallel existential aspect, War has its norms and provides pathways to virtue and excellence. War in this sense is not ultimately the scene of the reckless (careless) but the place where the value of those who know and act well (the *aristoi*) show themselves genuine against their counter (the *polloi*). It is in war that we find the heroes who properly seek honor and teach us how to live and die nobly.

In this context, for Heraclitus to say that "living and dying are one and the same" would be more than an observation concerning human experience and duration, whether from a pessimistic, resigned, or cynical point of view. Nor would it be from the vantage point of the immortal gods, witnessing our deaths (though, as we have observed, this does occur as one of their tasks). Rather, it would speak from or about that which is other than both gods and humans: to translate the fragment from the larger, more discerning and unifying dimension, the ever-living things—the gods—and those things that always are dying—mortals—are one and the same. Though dramatically different in respect to the measure of death (by which, as we have heard, they measure against each other and thus have the possibility of coming to understand and fulfill their natures), according to Heraclitus, in some other respect they are one and the same. In what respect? In relation to what cosmic dimension?

Within the tradition that Heraclitus and Parmenides begin and that Heidegger freshens, both gods and mortals, as distinct beings, yet remain among the many things of the universe, which the earliest Greek thinking came for the first time to think as One. We understand this reflection about the relation and state of the many and the One as the beginning of philosophy. At a more ontic or existential level, the relation of the many and the One was thought to be played out as the many of natural things (mountains, trees, birds, and fish) belonged together in or as *phusis*, the name for the natural world that emerges out of itself and as the many that humans make through *techne* and *poesis* that also are gathered together: "seafaring, temple building, conversation at social gatherings" belong among human activity, all of which belong among beings (EGT, 80).

Heraclitus's Fragment 53, we might remember, tells us that things are flung into the universe, scattered by the occurrence of "the setting-apart-from each other," which happens as the lighting "manifests some of those present as gods, others as humans, and brings some forward into appearance as slaves, and others as free" (HS, 119). Nor yet is it the case that natural elements are left out of the account, as might be surmised from the way McCarthy, Heidegger, Heraclitus, and Anaximander emphasize the disappearance of animals and natural features in the face of the violence and selfish concerns of humans and before the scattering of the gods and cosmic Fate. Heidegger notes the difference between becoming quiet about something and becoming oblivious to it.[13] He contends that in searching for the Unifying One in Fragment 53 (cited above) Heraclitus

> seeks to know what tacitly collects and embraces also those present beings which are not to be counted as among the regions of gods and men, but which are nonetheless human and divine in another sense—present beings such as plants and animals, mountains, seas, and stars. (EGT, 119)

Zeus and Helios, Dionysos and Hades all belong together and are the same in that they are gods manifesting the divine (EGT, 71). At the same time, mortals and immortals are the same insofar as they are beings. Thus, they are gathered together as many into or by a One. At this ontic level, the Greeks experienced and thought both mortals and gods as subject to higher cosmic dimensions. Unlike the Judeo-Christian-Islamic tradition, in which God comes to be thought as the Absolutely Other and the Source of his creation and thus is identified as the "ultimate reality," for the Greeks, this is not the case. Heraclitus puts the position succinctly in Fragment 30:

> This ordered universe [the cosmos], which is the same for all, was not created by any one of the gods or of mankind, but it was ever and is and shall be ever-living Fire, kindled in measure and quenched in measure.

The Greeks' gods too—in a manner proper to them—were subject to the ultimate forces. The philosophers came to think this final, unifying dimension of the cosmos as: The One, as the One unifying the all. Others, more existentially, said that the gods were subject to what they sometimes called Fate of Destiny.

This earliest Greek thinking points our reflection about McCarthy's novel beyond the human and indeed beyond the divine. In terms of what Heidegger says of Anaximander, it is "not we who are the place of the sameness of the great opposition of life and death"; "rather, the place of sameness must be sought after in [the One, *hen*], to which humans comport themselves and . . . resemble in a certain sense" (EGT, 95). Clearly, we are in the midst of some other-than-humanistic vision, as noted at the beginning of this essay. Heidegger affirms this shift, along with Heraclitus and Parmenides. Perhaps McCarthy does also.

If gods and mortals could come to understand themselves and their mode of belonging together more profoundly in light of each other as counters, would not this insight be an instance of coming to understand identity and difference at one and the same time? That is, would it not be an understanding of the most fundamental relation: that of the One and the many (HS, 97)? Just as we heard that, as cattle to pasture, humans are driven by the whip blows of the gods' lightning bolts and thunder, so ultimately, according to Heraclitus, gods and humans both are struck by the lighting of the cosmic unifying force, in which they belong together in its gathering happening (HS, 117). We could summarize this by further amending the translation Heidegger and Fink are making of Fragment 88 to say that "The ever-living gods and the ever-dying mortals are one and the same—they are scattered and gathered by the One Unifying All, by Fate itself" (HS, 94–95).

Some cosmic dimension or force dispenses the span of whiling for things and the place for whatever lingers. Both mortals who linger but a short while and gods who linger immortally must yield to this Necessity [*chreon*] that delivers them into the cosmos and keeps them in their different ways. According to Heidegger, Anaximander tells us:

> [Necessity] delivers what is . . . to its lingering. [Necessity] dispenses to what is present the portion of its while. The while apportioned in each case to what lingers rests in the transition between the twofold absence (arrival and departure) [of time]. The jointure of the while bonds and confines what is present as such. That which lingers awhile in presence . . . comes to presence within bounds. (EGT, 53)

In Parmenides' parallel terms, "*Moira*, the apportionment, . . . allots by bestowing" what endures with its while, so that it may come to be present in the mode of its lingering. Its "dispensing" or governance" metes out the presencing of what is present (EGT, 97–98).

What the early Greeks thought and we translate as the One, the One Unifying All, *Logos*, Necessity, or Fate-*Moira*, according to Heidegger's reading, all name the same ultimate cosmic "enjoining and presencing gathering of what is present in the presencing which lingers awhile according to each particular case" (EGT, 57). Under the name *Moira*, the early Greeks experienced the dispensation of portions to the gods and mortals in terms that we would translate as Fate or the Fateful. The Unique One "lets lie together before us" all the many natural, human, and godly things that "are usually separated from, and opposed to, one another, such as day and night, winter and summer, peace and war, waking and sleeping . . ." (EGT, 71).

In a deeper way than we heard before, just as gods and mortals exercised their natures by coming to understand themselves via each other as counters, now we hear that they can come to their own possibilities insofar as these are dispersed from, and they respond to, "the unique One Unifying All [which] is alone the fateful":

> The fateful, . . . [the] destining proper, . . . is the assembly of that which sends everything to its own. The Laying that gathers assembles in itself all destiny by bringing things and letting them lie before us, keeping each absent and present being in its place and on its way and by its assembling it secures everything in the [whole]. Thus each being can be joined and sent into its own. (EGT, 72)

The One Unifying All appears in another mode in *The Crossing* in the tale of the priest and hermit. In his dying words, the hermit

> told the priest what he had learned. . . . He held the priest's hand in his own and he bade the priest to look at their joined hands and he said see the likeness. This flesh is but a memento, yet it tells the true. Ultimately every man's path is every other's. There are no separate journeys for there are no separate men to make them. All men are one and there is no other tale to tell. (156–157)

In McCarthy's properly literary mode of speaking of the Unifying One, the novel fuses thoughts about animals, humans, and gods in the tales told by or about the characters and through the narrator. The motif is amplified as the ex-priest speaks to the boy, when "outside the abandoned village, the profoundest silence pertained" (143). Though not yet so identified at this point in the narrative, the ex-priest also ponders the unity of men, their journeys, and their stories:

> I came here because of a certain man. I came to retrace his steps. Perhaps to see if there were not some alternative course. What was here to be found was not a thing. Things separate from their stories have no meaning . . . . When their meaning has become lost to us they no longer have even a name.[14] The story on the other hand can never be lost from its place in the world for it is that place. And that is what is to be found here. The *corrido*. The tale. And like all *corridos* it ultimately told one story only, for there is only one to tell. (142–143)

He continues, weaving the many into a unifying one, by beginning the story within the story about the hermit who was born and died in Caborca and who lived once in the town where they now are speaking, in Huisiachepic,

What does Caborca know of Huisiachepic, Huisiachepic of Caborca? They are different worlds you must agree. Yet even so there is but one world and everything that is imaginable is necessary to it. For this world which also seems to us a thing of stone and flower and blood is not a thing at all but is a tale.[15] And all in it is a tale and each tale the sum of all lesser tales and yet these also are the selfsame tale and contain as well all else within them. . . . And those seams ["the joinery," the way in which the world is made] that are hid from us are of course in the tale itself and the tale has no abode or place of being except in the telling only and there it lives and makes its home and therefore we can never be done with the telling. Of the telling there is no end. And whether in Caborca or in Huisiachepic or in whatever other place by whatsoever other name or by no name at all I say again that all tales are one. Rightly heard all tales are one. (142–143)

This passage seems to say the same as Heidegger, who asserts that all the early Greek thinkers think the same by whatever other names. The ex-priest's words also apparently articulate that upon which he and the hermit are in accord. Despite that the ex-priest listens to the hermit's confidences about what he learned only mistakenly to "take [the hermit's] telling for confession," and despite the fact that the two of them hold contrary positions about whether God needs a witness, they agree on one point, that there is but one tale to tell. Moreover, their opposite insights, and perhaps for us as readers their opposite lessons, are held in tension—unresolved—in the novel. Neither finally overcomes the other: both stand in encounter, as lingering counters to the end. The two tales held together as a "twinned vision" exemplify what there is to say.

Whether or not there would be only one story and whether or not all men are the same, if "things separate from their stories have no meaning," clearly there is great need for storytelling. I began this chapter (intended to consider the character and relations of animals, humans, and gods) by acknowledging the need for and the usefulness of poets and thinkers, specifically of McCarthy and Heidegger and their colleagues. The ex-priest agrees. His role in *The Crossing* appears to be one of recollection, of passing his testimony to the boy.

If, as we earlier found Heidegger contend, thinking is a kind of primal poetry, and if McCarthy philosophizes a good deal in his novel, a case can be made, in Heidegger's words, that thinking and poetizing are the same. Still, I have omitted—or deferred—the most critical point. One more important than that poetizing and thinking are the same, or even than that there is but one tale about all men who are the same. Overlooked thus far is McCarthy's whispered variation of the One and many: "Rightly *heard* all tales are one" (my emphasis, 143). These words, occurring in the ex-priest's opening comments to the boy, direct us from our preoccupation with telling the story toward what usually remains unsaid: our task is a matter of hearing, of taking in and responding properly. The ex-priest has heard the hermit's story and whether he has heard correctly, well, only the reader could judge. The novel lets stand, apparently opposite, the two interpretations of the hermit's story (those of the hermit himself and of the priest). The boy hears the testimony of the priest about all of this. At times, the narrator adds another voice. The choir of witnesses finally includes us, the readers. We are challenged rightly to hear the stories, the novel as a whole. And it seems we are called to hear that, and perhaps to judge whether, all tales indeed are one and whether all things in the world are the same. Apparently, we are called on to be very thoughtful.

The narrator of *The Crossing* tells us that, through his experience with the hermit, the priest "came to believe that the truth may often be carried about by those who themselves remain all unaware of it,"

> Then one day in that casual gesture, that subtle movement of divestiture, they wreak all unknown upon some ancillary soul a havoc such that that soul is forever changed, forever wrenched about in the road it was intended upon and set instead upon a road heretofore unknown to it. (158)

It could be that the story within the story not only contains the hermit's unintended message to the priest, but if "such are the whiles of truth and such its stratagems" (158) the novel's witnesses might have the possibility of delivering to us, the readers, such a sudden blow with unpredictable impact.

We are implicated, of course, not just generally as human readers of the novel but in a special way because the chain of testimonials that runs from Anaximander, Parmenides, and Heraclitus to Heidegger and McCarthy ends with evidence about our current scientific-technological world. The setting of *The Crossing* in the American-Mexican West and its timeframe has specific connotations. The placement, thought in terms of Heideggerian topology, indicates the scene of the drama of the essential unfolding of Being in which the West (the Occident) is the evening-land (*das Abendland*)— the land of death.[16] It is the place where the sun "dies" each day, as it moves to oblivion, swallowed in the sea or plunged into the concealing earth. Since we currently live on a planet dominated by the paradigm of scientific method and knowledge and its mate, technology, we live in the twilight between day and night. Not only at the twilight of the gods, as Nietzsche said, but at the twilight of entire species and perhaps of nature itself, as environmentalists tell us. McCarthy's novel, in fact, spans the history of the modern, Western era, portraying parts of Mexico as still in the heritage of European military and hacienda boundaries and ruled by cruel force, and in the same sweep, the military destruction and atomic age of World War II, where our technological appropriation of the sun dawns in the protagonist's New Mexico. In this west, both old and new, the story ends as the boy unsuccessfully tries to enlist and is rejected and hurt in yet further ways.

When explaining that gods and mortals alike are subject to the ultimate dispensing of their allotment, Heidegger contrasts our derivative and basely utilitarian senses of "necessity" and "use" with the still-powerful, primal meanings he would resuscitate from the early Greeks. Originally, he says, the Greek word usually translated as necessity (*chreon*) meant something more closely connected to "the hand."[17] Thus, he proposes retranslating it keeping, in mind "the hand," "to place in one's hand, and thus to deliver" (EGT, 50–51). We see here that the word "means: I get involved with something, I reach for it, extend my hand to it. At the same time [it] means to place in someone's hand or hand over. Thus to deliver, to let something belong to someone" (51–52).

Delivery also has many meanings. In *The Crossing*, almost everything and everyone is delivered over to its enemy or what would destroy it. In the Old Testament, Job was delivered over by God to Satan.[18] In the New Testament, Jesus teaches us to pray to our Father with precisely this meaning in mind: "Deliver us from all evil." In addition to desiring to be spared or preserved from what will harm us, we seek and pray for what we would have delivered unto us: "Give us this day our daily bread."

Whereas Heraclitus and Parmenides may have thought of the Ultimate Unitary One and *Moira* ontologically, as the Presencing that delivers the handing over of lingering in presence to what is present (EGT, 52), the modern sense of "usage" matches the world portrayed in *The Crossing*. Heidegger tells us that our derivative and reduced sense of the word means to consume, to gobble up. We think and act as crude utilitarians. Here we need to remember the overall thrust of the novel, whether or not interpreted in terms of the rebellious refusal of present things to yield to each other, where, in order to remain insistently a while longer, they destroy the other things that would come along. McCarthy gives us the modern, postcolonial world ravaged still by marauders both settled and nomadic. Here the playing out of the violent destruction continues to ripple across the West, where the red sun dies in the sea.[19]

The Crossing is written and comes to us at a time when the ideas that *Moira* or God dispenses our characteristics and allotted durations upon the earth have fallen into oblivion. Indeed, sophisticated as we supposedly now are, we deny such ancient ideas as mere delusions. With our technology and power we are reshaping nature and society according to our preferred human measure, and with medicine and genetic engineering we are challenging even death itself.

> Man has already begun to overwhelm the entire earth and its atmosphere, to arrogate to himself in forms of energy the concealed powers of nature, and to submit future history to the planning and ordering of a world government. (EGT, 57)

Our actions against one another and nature, according to Heidegger, are intimately connected with our reductive way of thinking, which with its representational concepts "exhausts itself in securing," that is, violently manipulating and consuming all that is present (EGT, 121). Our perceptual and conceptual engagement with things proceeds "like an appetite which seeks out the particular being and attacks it, in order to grasp it and wholly subsume it . . ." (EGT, 82).

Heidegger is warning us here of a staggering oblivion that is beginning. Our usual modes of thought and action fall within the realm Anaximander describes as the disorderly and unjust. "Mortals accept whatever is immediately, abruptly, and first of all offered to them. They keep . . . only to that aspect which immediately makes a claim upon mortals; that is, they keep to what is present without considering presencing" (EGT, 99). In our conceptual and pragmatic seizure of everything that stands over against us, Heidegger warns, mortals "turn from the lighting, and turn only toward what is present, which is what immediately concerns them in their everyday commerce with each other" (EGT, 122). Hence his life's work to retrieve and hear and say anew what is becoming forgotten. In our defiance, we are becoming unable to hear or say how things are in the cosmos. We are becoming blind to their simplicity and nearness.[20] We no longer think of, or think that there is, a cosmic ultimate. We do not attend to any interest or task other than making and taking what we want to consume.

Heidegger understands his entire effort to be moving back and forth in the realm between the early Greek insights and our own current oblivion, in order to hear and pass on to us the originary meaning of the cosmos, which still calls to us. He would be a witness to the possibility of mortals belonging with and responding to things, to heavens and earth, to divinities.

Is there any rescue? Rescue comes when and only when danger is. Danger is when Being itself advances to its farthest extreme, and when the oblivion that issues from Being itself undergoes reversal.

But what if Being in its essence needs to use [*braucht*] the essence of man? If the essence of man consists in thinking the truth of Being?

Then thinking must poetize on the riddle of Being. It brings the dawn of thought into the neighborhood of what is for thinking. (EGT, 58)

That our technology, military power, and consumptive way of living plan and execute everything according to the measure of our base, arbitrary desires is by now a common cultural theme. Not that its ubiquity leads to self-reflection, understanding, or a change in our actions in regard to the environment or one another. It also is a commonplace that we question or even discard the gods and God. The hermit in *The Crossing* makes this issue the focus of his later years. He taunts God in the ruins of His own house. McCarthy's narrator tells us,

It seemed that what he wished, this man, was to strike some *colindancia* with his Maker. Assess boundaries and metes. See that lines were drawn and respected. (151)[21]

Later, after the hermit dies, the narrator comments further on his fate.

The old man was buried in the churchyard at Caborca among those of his own blood. Such was the working out of God's arrangement with this man. Such was his *colindancia* and such perhaps is every man's. At his dying he told the priest that he'd been wrong in his every reckoning of God and yet had come at last to an understanding of him anyway. He said that his demands upon God resided intact and unspoken also in even the simplest heart. . . . For the path of the world also is one and not many and there is no alter course in any least part of it for that course is fixed by God and contains all consequence in the way of its going and outside that going there is neither path nor consequence or anything at all. There never was. (157–158)

Again it seems that we have a convergence of stories that say the same, though with difference in practical response. Anaximander tells of the necessary insurgence of things that linger in the present, the disorder and injustice they wreak. The Greeks understood much about hubris—at the least that it was part of the character of things, human and otherwise, to revolt at times against their fated allotment or what was appropriate to their own excellence or potential. But yield they did, whether by insight and choice or when finally driven by the overwhelming blows of the gods or Fate itself. Orthodox Jews, Christians, and Muslims, for all their comfortable talking to God, well know that one lesson of the Book of Job, which I have cited repeatedly, is that Job too railed in his legalistic, righteous manner. He may have been innocent at the beginning of his story, but he fell into pride in his self-defense. He finally yielded, beaten down by the flash of God's majesty and power. But these lightning bolts from Zeus and Yahweh's speaking from the storm fail to impress us today. We regard them as projections of fears of the father or as indigestion. We do not take them seriously in the least. They are faded into oblivion. Now we have only the light we make ourselves. We are in the dark.

Hence the archaic ring to Heidegger's and McCarthy's language. Critics are quick to note the pompous, "pseudo-oracular" tone of their work. Heidegger apparently thinks he is an early Greek sage, and McCarthy would speak as the Old Testament (at least we might be relieved that *The Crossing* is toned down compared to the manic *Blood Meridian*). The narrator in *The Crossing* is just as insistent as is Heidegger that we recognize our oblivion to the true measure and acknowledge and act according to our proper place in the cosmic scheme of things. After telling us what the priest took to be the lesson of the hermit's life and death, the narrator goes on to affirm the contention (introduced above) that all men are the same in God's eyes and that we all are guilty of pride and contention against one another and Him:

> To God every man is a heretic. The heretic's first act is to name his brother. So that he may step free of him. Every word we speak is a vanity. Every breath that does not bless is an affront. . . . For nothing is real save his grace. (158)

These words conclude the hermit's and priest's stories before the boy mounts up and rides out. These words also return us to Anaximander's sayings about the ways present things resist the coming forward of other things—we insist on our own whiling at the expense of the others who would also come and linger to develop their own possibilities. We betray or even strike down our brother that we may have more, that we may have more life—a longer lingering, even if it is beyond the portion allotted by *Moira* or God the Creator. Heidegger notes,

> Mortals, whose essence remains appropriated in [One as the Same] are fateful when they measure the [Logos] as the [One Unifying All]

and submit themselves to its measurement. Therefore Heraclitus says, in Fragment B43: Measureless pride needs to be extinguished sooner than a raging fire. (EGT, 75)

Since Heidegger does not hold a humanistic view of the world, he often remarks that the oblivion of That which is ultimate (which, though always occurring in different ways throughout history, is especially dangerous in our own reductive, scientific-technological epoch) is not merely a human phenomenon. Where the fullest meaning of things and of the cosmic dimensions are not anything given solely by humans, though we play a critical role in the dynamic, the shift toward oblivion largely results from their own withdrawal and self-concealment. Heidegger speaks of a doubled dynamic in which, as we heard above, in turning toward what discloses itself in the present and as the present, we turn away from what dispenses the presencing. Simultaneously, That which grants all things their apportioned while, precisely by lighting them in the present, as things in our shared world, withdraws itself into self-concealment. "The destining of the disclosure of the duality yields to what is present to the everyday perceptions of mortals . . . [a] fateful yielding. But then . . . self-concealing reign[s] at the heart of disclosure" (EGT, 100). Though these ideas are too complex to develop here, the ontological position appears to be confirmed by recent human experience: God is silent; Zeus no longer hurls thunderbolts; the One Unifying All, *Moira*, or *Logos* would appear either vanished or inefficacious.

Toward a Conclusion

At this point, we might ask about our texts, as Heidegger does of Parmenides' verses, "How do these bring" nature, humans, and God "to light? They seem rather to obscure" them, since they themselves lead us to darkness and "leave us without counsel" (EGT, 80). That is true, especially since thinkers and novelists do not proffer, as do scientists and politicians, unambiguous statements about how the natural or social worlds necessarily are nor how they must become.

Still, many of us like a moral as the fruit of our attentive reading and listening to authors whom we respect and seek out because they are more insightful than are we. At least many of us seek a lesson or two about ourselves or our relationships to the world. Though now not fashionable in literary theory or criticism, I warned the reader of this bent at the beginning of the chapter. But, if as it appears, McCarthy and Heidegger "leave us without counsel," are we to be denied?

We shall not, will not, be denied. We are not the type of beings who voluntarily will turn away hungry or lacking in any way. Ever, if we can help it. We will get what we want from McCarthy's novel, and from this chapter too, for that matter. Such fierce taking is a necessary part of human character. The immediate problem, however, is ours, not our authors', for according to McCarthy and Heidegger, the burden finally rests not with them, nor even with the witnesses whose testimony they unearth or invent, turn over and sort as they shuffle toward a new brief. Recall that the ex-priest told the boy that unity is not the product of the telling but of the hearing: "rightly *heard* all tales are one." Heidegger too speaks of the critical importance of hearing, even of hearing what is unsaid. The burden of insight or judgment is not borne by the witnesses but by the jury. Those who hear must put the various, fragmentary, even apparently contradictory versions together. As readers, we must interpret the testimony and thus unify the many into one. Further, we may need to act on what we come to understand only partially or incorrectly, given our situation and the unavoidably piecemeal condition of individual stories, forgetfulness and misunderstanding at every junction, and our own all too finite character. We must judge and act accordingly, if not upon someone on trial in a court before us, then in our own lives, which are called into question by all genuine questioning, testimony, and hearing.[22] Heidegger's and McCarthy's writings contain language that says we are responsible for recognizing our monumental human pride and for our refusal to accept and bend before what is given to us—which lead to rebellion against ceding that our lingering shall stay in the bounds of what fate appropriates to us. What Heidegger and McCarthy say seems to be in accord. What they agree upon would be a good lesson.

Of course, the point is not that we should attend to two idiosyncratic personalities. Quite the contrary. Heidegger and McCarthy weave the Old and New Testaments, Heraclitus, Parmenides, and Anaximander into what they relate to us (and I have added Stevens and Shakespeare) because the basic strands of the Western tradition all say that human hubris needs to be given up, that pride must yield to what ultimately reigns in the cosmos, which though largely intelligible to us, nonetheless does indeed reign. Only by properly responding to what is given and to the other-than-human cosmic measure can we participate in the orderly flow of events. Only then will there be justice.

Since, in our Western tradition, we have been given such directives by the Greek as well as the Judeo-Christian traditions, one might think we would get the point. Evidently not. Twenty-five centuries and countless wars and disasters have not informed us much nor changed our ways. As to those of us here and now inhabiting the twenty-first century, two world wars and many others just as savage have not been enough to deter us from our busyness seizing, controlling, and destroying nature and one another.

I write this chapter self-consciously, of course, as a comfortable member of major research communities in two of the most self-satisfied, self-promoting, self-styled "world-class" cities and states in the new globalized capitalistic system, that is, in the techno-communication-information age. Central Texas and Puget Sound, as much of California, see themselves as heirs to the tradition of the West because in these places knowledge comes into power over nature and society. Living in the world we have made, secured, and exploited, there is little discernable impulse to set aside our pride of authorship and control, as might seem to occur as a result of living in the world. Most of us are oblivious to what is most deeply real because we are too busy with our projects and too greedy in the pursuit of fulfillment of our crassly utilitarian and selfish goals. Many of us are, indeed, the perpetrators of violence and destruction lavished on so much of the rest of the world. To prolong our stay and satisfy ourselves with a disproportionate share of the world's goods, we go counter to others, to our counterparts whom we manipulate or eliminate. Just as Anaximander says. Evidently, according to our authors, it thus has ever been with mortals. In any case, it now is so with us.

Precisely because we are oblivious to our pride and to our refusal to grant what is needed to other things we need the gods, and their helpers, the poets and thinkers. Because we are, as Søren Kierkegaard might say, even oblivious to our oblivion, we are driven from what is immediately before us toward where we next should be—for our own good, as well as for the balance of the whole environment—only by the blows administered by the gods or their herders and shepherds. Driving us away from what is comfortable and familiar, from what immediately occupies our attention and desire, is among their chief tasks. Whether or not any god or God sends us blows or directives via *The Crossing*, I could not say. But I have been making the case that through the accumulated testimony they have gathered and presented, McCarthy, Heidegger, Anaximander, and Heraclitus have done their jobs. These authors have tried to drive us toward a genuine alternative to the modern-contemporary, self-absorbed oblivion that reigns within our scientifically-technologically constructed world of consumption. Heidegger is hopeful that he, or his forebears at least, have given us ways to think the cosmos by strategically using the resources of our tradition:

The word of thinking rests in the sobering quality of what it says. Just the same, thinking [and writing] changes the world. It changes it in the even darker depths of a riddle, depths which as they grow darker offer promise of a greater brightness. (EGT, 78)

Such might be our motto. Few would disagree that what our authors say is complex to the point of being perplexing and perhaps, rather than being a riddle, is deliberately, stubbornly, obscure. Certainly McCarthy's novel gives us "darker depths"—the problem of dealing with this staggeringly dark destruction motivated this chapter in the first place. So, how to respond to the dark testimony? For their part, McCarthy and Heidegger already have responded to it by attending to what they have heard in the Western tradition and history, by thinking it over carefully, and by saying what they have. They have written down the testimony for us. We have read these texts and now need to decide what to make of them. How to interpret these stories, literary and philosophical, as we label them? How subsequently to act?

Again we have to ask: what have McCarthy and Heidegger said? In fact, though we may claim we want to be told something definitively, the evidence indicates that in the name of pride or independence or freedom we do not want to be told what to think, much less what to do. Just as well, for Heidegger asserts and McCarthy stresses that no guidance in the form of an answer is forthcoming. In *The Crossing*, as befits a novel, we hear much, but nothing is stated. All is in the mode of a hypothetical verbal structure, as Northrop Frye observes.[23] That is why the differing insights and testimony of priest and hermit are left standing in opposition, as counters. Precisely in their differences, which must remain, they belong together and present, in miniature, the dynamic at play throughout our world. They are slivers of the many that must be unified. Together, the tales, in their tension, are and yield but one tale. This story within the story finally must, along with the rest of the novel, be read into a whole. Again, as Frye points out, here following Blake, unless we proceed on the basis of such an assumption, how could we begin to make sense of any literary work?[24] Why would we try? There is no "bottom line" or "conclusion" that acts as a directive to what to do next. To yet again note the priest's words:

So everything is necessary. Every last thing. This is the hard lesson. Nothing can be dispensed with. Nothing despised. (143)

What Heidegger says of Heraclitus certainly applies reflexively to himself and McCarthy:[25]

Heraclitus does not teach this or any doctrine. As a thinker he only gives us to think. With regard to our question . . . he certainly gives us difficult matters to think about. (EGT, 72)

In *The Crossing* and in Heidegger's works we encounter a gathering together into belonging of that which maintains its differences. The dynamic counterpoints of the human and the other-than-human play their parts in the establishment and unfolding of the cosmos. So does our mortal resistance and our yielding to an ultimate measure. A complex sentence at the end of Heidegger's interpretation of Heraclitus's use of *aletheia* [unconcealment, truth], because of its complexity and because of the amount of material we have been reading, could slip by unnoticed:

The invisible shining of the lighting streams from wholesome self-keeping in the self-preservation of destiny. (EGT, 123)

To begin to unpack this, the sentence simultaneously presents us with the currently dominant humanistic and crude utilitarian viewpoint as well as the other-than-humanistic one developed by Heraclitus, Anaximander, and Heidegger. The counterpositions may be better seen if written diagrammatically (drawn from EGT, 122). The two alternatives read across—horizontally—as usual, but the four subsections can be compared vertically.

wholesome	in self-keeping in self-restraining	preservation	of destiny
versus	versus	versus	versus
unhealthy	self-insistent self-imposing	destruction	of ourselves

On the one hand, our Western culture is the scene that has developed as we have learned how to violate and destroy, as we choose, any other we encounter in our path while underway in our self-insistent, self-imposing projects concerning what immediately promises to satisfy our desires or to help us prolong our stay in life and power. As Anaximander puts it, the result is injustice or disorder, and if some care to call this unhealthy [*unheil*], so be it. In contrast, if we take to heart that there is a measure beyond the human and the possibility that there is and that we might partially know a setting or giving of bounds within which we have our proper place and our appropriate relationships to other people, to natural things, and even to the gods or God, then we could act in a self-restrained manner.

By such attunement, which would be a coming into accord with our other, our counter, we would care for and preserve our apportioned place and while and thus let order, justice, and destiny reign in the cosmos. This would be self-keeping and wholesome, both for us and for all that flows into and out of the world. The former way is what Anaximander spoke of as self-insistence against others; the latter is the mode of turning ourselves toward the other in solicitude and care, so that in heeding one another, things let others belong together. Here each can persist, lingering in a manner such that, in their differences, each can come into their own. By so opening to one another and by letting order come and care belong to one another in the cosmos, things would surmount disorder. We remember that the Anaximander fragment with which we began says in part (in two contending translations, first Nietzsche's then Heidegger's):

> . . . According to necessity; for they pay one another recompense and penalty for injustice. (EGT, 20)

and

> . . . along the lines of usage for they let order and thereby also [care] belong to one another (in the surmounting) of disorder. (EGT, 57)

In this nonresolution of alternative translations, as both linger, standing together, they become open to each other. They remain in encounter. They call us, inviting us in. Beyond question, we cannot comfortably or conveniently, much less smugly, suppose that we understand much of what has been said by our authors. Not only is the greater portion of the testimony painfully dark, but even the lighter parts fall somewhere between the very difficult and the entirely opaque. To remind ourselves of these difficulties so as not to backslide after all this work, we recall the witnesses one last time to reconfirm their testimony. McCarthy still says, a third and final time, that "Everything is necessary. Every least thing. This is the hard lesson." Heidegger also reaffirms that the words set down by our witnesses "lead us into darkness and leave us without counsel."

So, though we have heard much, we finally are not relieved of our charge, of our necessity, if we would care about what we have read and would avoid falling into forgetfulness and injustice in our lives in the world. Even while attending to the possibility of wholesome opening to other mortals, natural things, and gods or God, we still need to face and reflect on death and destruction in the world, for everything but the gods and perhaps the ultimate dimensions pass away, and even the latter suffer if disorder, injustice, comes to prevail. I end, then, with fateful Fate itself that apportions our while, whether we accept the short spans of our lingering gracefully in openness to others or contemptuously resist it by attempting to prolong our while at the cost of the others, at the cost of disorder and injustice. One last testimony by Heidegger. He ends his essay on *Moira* with these words:

> But anyone who only expects thinking to give assurances, and awaits the day when we can go beyond it as unnecessary, is demanding that thought annihilate itself. That demand appears in a strange light if we consider that the essence of mortals calls upon them to heed a call which beckons them toward death. As the outermost possibility of mortal [being-in-the-world], death is not the end of the possible but the highest keeping (the gathering sheltering) of the mystery of calling disclosure. (EGT, 101)

2

Art, Architecture, Violence
Daniel Libeskind's Jewish Museum Berlin

Art and Architecture Witnessing Violence

Art and Technology

Architecture is distinct from but belongs together with poetry and the other arts, especially when thought originarily, as Heidegger has taught us to try to do. Art works can be sites of disclosure: as things they gather together the dimensions of historically unfolding worlds. Because they are particular, to approach them thoughtfully and to respond to them adequately we need to inquire into specific works and worlds. In regard to violence and loss we could begin by asking what it would mean to use a Heideggerian kind of thinking to interpret Daniel Libeskind's Jewish Museum Berlin (originally titled the Extension to the Berlin Museum with the Jewish Department), both in light of Heidegger's positive accomplishments with nonmetaphysical, nonrepresentational thinking and of his negative association with National Socialism. Despite the former achievement, given the scandal and terribleness of the latter, the project could in itself seem incredibly inappropriate—something we need to face. With both the subject matter and the approach we are in the heart of the political.

How to begin? Heidegger's account of how art works (including architecture) disclose the violence and loss inherent in human lifeworlds demonstrates at the least that they also hold the phenomena for nonconceptual, recollective thinking (*Andenken*, related to *Gedächnis*—memory).[1] Hannah

Arendt and Emmanuel Levinas (as many thinkers of the twentieth century) have learned and utilized much from Heidegger but go on to develop their own positions—which will turn out to be more important for us here, both in general and specifically in regard to the Holocaust. Levinas explores how, beyond our violence toward things and the killing of animals, the distinctly human capacity to murder necessarily affirms rather than obliterates the personhood of the victim—as well as, uncannily, that of the murderer. Arendt stresses our continuing obligation to try to comprehend and marshal political action against the repressive violence that destroys a person's spontaneity and political participation—a position correlate with Levinas's contention that our face-to-face encounters unavoidably call us to and testify to our primal responsibility to the other.

We have, then, questions of political life, of acting and giving witness. What are we to do and not do? What is sound testimony? What do these matters have to do with architecture and design? It might be scandalous to apply Heidegger's thinking directly to an encounter with the Jewish Museum Berlin and to reflect on the violence of the Holocaust using what he has said. Maybe his words ring hollow, or worse. All Heidegger scholars would say we need face up to that. But what would we say about the phenomenon, what would we say about violence, about witness, about museums as testimonies to the past? These issues need to be thought in some way. We also need to hear and consider Heidegger's words, whether they are proper or not, since they are a dimension of the historical events. What kind of witness is Heidegger to what art is? To what violence is? What kind of testimony does Heidegger give as to what design amounts to, whether in poetry or buildings? To hear Heidegger, to have him as a witness, one option is to force him to contrive answers, as bad lawyers do, by asking him questions such as "Where were you in the 1930s? When did you stop denouncing progress?" But forcing his words to fit into our concepts is not a proper path to follow. We have to try to hear his words, hear what he actually says when giving testimony, which after all is our task when reading or listening to all authors. We need to hear them in their own words. In Heidegger's own words, what would we learn about art and architecture, museums and design, violence and loss, if we tried to listen to what is said about all of them at the same time?

One of the interesting complications is that Heidegger has many voices.[2] That there are many Heideggers is one of the things to which we need pay attention. While we are concerned with the credibility of what we hear, we need to appreciate that the relevant parts of the Heideggerian corpus that this chapter can cover do not develop in a straight line. What is possible and useful here is not a report but more of a meditation or a weaving together of telling motifs.

To begin considering art and architecture it is not necessary to distinguish between landscapes, buildings, and smaller artifacts. All of these are some kind of building, something that we make, related to poetry, tools, and to political actions (remembering that Arendt insists that political and ethical acts are not to be subsumed under the categories of production). When we think about human action, about the political, we also are thinking about technology, how we make things, how we make factories, how we make cities. But the technology in fact also involves our relationship to the earth, so while we can distinguish them, we cannot actually separate technology, environmental ethics and action, architecture, and urban design. All of these phenomena make possible the ways in which we live on the earth.

Of course, we know from artists working in the twentieth century that we live in a time when a received holistic view cannot be taken for granted. To appreciate that modern art struggles to delineate a "broken" world is not to exaggerate our situation as exclusively negative. Even during the period of the two world wars and specifically during the Weimar Republic in Germany the arts began to disclose fascinating aspects of our emerging contemporary experience: multiple perspectives, simultaneity, structures underlying objects (for example, following Cezanne), the fluidity of time, and traces of dynamic processes all freed or opened up deeper senses of time and space. Still, of course, fractures and isolation had—and still have—to be faced, as we see from the gaunt figures of Alberto Giacometti and the alienated figures of Duane Hanson, through the theater of the absurd, the haunted scenes painted by Giorgio de Chirico and Max Ernst, to the novels of Cormac McCarthy, J. G. Ballard, and G. W. Sebald. Ansell Kiefer transcribes the scene of twentieth-century technology, of the post-Holocaust, where intellectuals and artists are as much implicated in our problems as they are anything resembling prophets or guides to a solution. The artists and their works show that we and our production have become incredibly problematic—which is the way it should be because we are in fact dangerously close to, at times even far past, being "out of control." Again, today, we need to become more adequately conscious of our situation and responsible for what we do.

In the *Introduction to Metaphysics* Heidegger talks about how not only action in general but specifically violent action appears to be basic to human beings. If we look at what the past shows about what humans beings do—as with the famous Cretan bull jumping, which celebrated the human capacity to leap, literally, over the animal powers—we find that indeed we are people of action (e.g., depicted in the *Toreador Fresco* from the

Palace of Minos, Knossos, Crete). In these ceremonies of life and death, of power and domination, we somersaulted off the bulls' backs; we were in awe of them but also were conscious that we have great capabilities. Of course, we are connected to the animals, but "look at what we can do!" In short, a primal part of what we accomplish in our action is triumph over animals, over the life force of the world. Other early works, kept for us in the museums of our establishing cultures, such as the Vaphio cups, inlaid dagger blades (from the royal tombs at Mycenae), Near Eastern bas reliefs, and Egyptian tomb paintings show our hunting prowess. The history of culture in many ways is a documentation of our inventiveness and *techne*: of how with the cunning of words Odysseus bent events in the direction he wanted, of how with our woven nets we capture and control things as archetypal and powerful as the great bull. Thus technology, as it has developed from the Greeks to us, is mainly a matter of control. We need to be careful here not to overlook the violence. We didn't need to wait until the modern mechanical universe or nuclear technology: technology has been violent, or a means to violence, from the start. That is part of what it means to be a human being. In some measure to be human is to exert violence and control over the world. Indeed, Arendt insists that one of the distinguishing features of violence, differentiating it from power, is that the former is instrumental.[3]

When we look at these great hunting scenes today we see much more than the acquisition of meat: we witness the killing of the great animals and the way we triumphantly lift ourselves up. Of course, there have been many and still are a few cultures where animal spirits are respected, but the dominant technological realm is one of power as domination. Nor does Heidegger find this history to be a weird aberration (though it is "strange" in a different sense). We are violent all the time. In the *Introduction to Metaphysics* he cites as testimony to this phenomena the famous passage of the chorus in Sophocles' *Antigone*:

> There is much that is strange, but nothing
> that surpasses man in strangeness.
> He sets sail on the frothing waters
> amid the south winds of winter
> tacking through the mountains
> and furious chasms of the waves.
> He wearies even the noblest
> of the gods, the Earth,
> indestructible and untiring,
> overturning her from year to year,
> driving the plows this way and that
> with horses.

And man, pondering and plotting,
snares the light-gliding birds
and hunts the beasts of the wilderness
and the native creatures of the sea.
With guile he overpowers the beast
that roams the mountains by night as by day,
he yokes the hirsute neck of the stallion
and the undaunted bull.
And he has found his way
to the wind-swift all-understanding
and to the courage of rule over cities.
He has considered also how to flee
from exposure to the arrows
of unpropitious weather and frost.[4]

Just as we control the natural world by capturing and killing the animals, we do similar violence to the earth so we can have beautiful crops. To have wheat, corn, and flowers, we tear the earth open with plows; we cut into it. If with van Gogh we might appreciate the sheer beauty and sensuousness of wheat fields or sunflowers it is because it is possible to focus on that dimension, which certainly are phenomena worth attention, but in doing so we let slip into oblivion the violence of plowing the earth with steel plows (or the exhausting labor of the peasants shown in others of the artist's works).

To counter this forgetfulness, Heidegger wakes our memory to a complex that needs to be rethought: *Riß* means tear, cleft, fissure, gap; *Aufriß* means sketch, design. Thus, to cut the fields with plows: that is a design.[5]

> The "sign" in design [Latin *signum*] is related to *secare*, to cut—as in saw, sector, segment. To design is to cut a trace. Most of us know the word "sign" only in its debased meaning—lines on a surface. But we make a design also when we cut a furrow into the soil to open it to seed and growth. The design is the whole of the traits of that drawing which structures and prevails throughout the open, unlocked freedom of language.

The fact is, then, that the design is in the cutting. On the earth, the draft, the drawing of the plow (which is why a draft horse is so named) is a violent drawing. But we don't think about it, neither in immediate practices nor, as Lefebvre demonstrates in *The Production of Space*, in the conceptual representations of space that are later put into practice. When the highway engineer draws a dotted line on a map, it cuts through somebody's neighborhood; this act is an initiating cutting with the political authority and economic power such that the subsequent construction makes it physically so.

We have, then, this drawing, this drafting that we do as farmers, engineers, intellectuals, artists, and poets—a dimension of which cuts into the world in a violent way. But in itself, to witness is not to be judgmental (though sound judgment would first call up and attend carefully to what is witnessed). The art works, in any case, are not simplistically judgmental. Sophocles' play does not say, "this is terrible, we shouldn't do it." Even living as a vegetarian requires that someone takes a sharp stick to poke holes in the ground in order to pierce mother earth and grow something; then one takes what has grown, either while still developing or when deemed ripe, and eats it (rather than letting it return to the earth as seed). Unavoidably, some violence is part of what we do, how we live, who we are. That is why the whole tradition of human life and the question of what it is to be human still has to be encountered. It is not a passing matter or local problem to be solved; nor can we turn away.

Other forms of life depend on and manifest this same kind of violence. We design landscapes, our cultural habitation in dwellings and cities, factories and highway systems. Here we see the reach of technology that increasingly has its own power in the realm of subjects and objects. We design factories, which are objects that control subjects who are going to produce objects, perhaps by further steps of designing and building machines that produce even more objects or better shape the behavior of subjects. There is an interesting connection between the technology we have, our control of nature, and the aesthetic tradition of the sublime. The sublime is that which is so overwhelming as to surpass understanding or exceed any idea or conceptualization, though the imagination might witness them in painting, literature, or even architecture (a category very interesting to Kant, Burke, and the poststructuralists since in the sublime we encounter something for which a concept is inadequate, thus displaying a limit condition for reason proper).

Nature, either in particular volcanic eruptions, avalanches, or violent storms or as the infinite cosmos provides phenomena that apparently do surpass our conceptual understanding. In paintings by Salvator Rosa, Joseph Wright of Derby, Joseph M. W. Turner, Caspar David Friedrich, and many others tiny human figures are humbled before the natural world. Of course, part of the feeling for the splendor of the natural world derived from beliefs that divinity was behind it.[6] The natural sublime had as the crucial element the religious belief in a creator God: when one saw the splendor of the mountains and heard an avalanche, that was a sign of God and God's power. This tradition comes fairly straightforwardly from Genesis, where God is revealed as the origin of everything, and from Job, where God's terrible power surpasses understanding. The natural sublime or natural divinity occurs as a first stage in which we understand ourselves as humbled before nature or the divine. Schopenhauer and Buddhism, in their different ways, both counsel how we might deal with these fundamental relationships.

The early experiences of travelers on the Grand Tour of Italy who were overwhelmed by nature and then appreciated the divinity behind it provided the cultural horizon of the American experience of wilderness, of Niagara Falls, or of the Rocky Mountains as painted by Thomas Cole, Frederic E. Church, Albert Bierstadt, Thomas Moran, and their colleagues—a tradition continued today by many wilderness enthusiasts. Not surprisingly, however, a historical transition from the natural sublime to the technological sublime occurred when the dominant Western attitude shifted so that what really astonishes us is not nature but our own technology. Our machines amaze us and are commonly seen as surpassing understanding in their complexity and reach. In its positive version we have the hydrological systems proceeding from awesome dams or the rockets blasting off from Florida toward the moon. The negative technological sublime appears in the form of the technology that threatens us, as when machines consume the workers (*Metropolis*), robots take over (the renegade computer Hal in *2001* or the cyborgs in films like *Blade Runner* and *Terminator*, which are the heirs to *Frankenstein*), or nuclear destruction is at hand. Part of the aesthetic and experience of the negative technological sublime is the voyeuristic psychological thrill of threatened harm or death experienced from a safe distance. For many, the thrill of being frightened while apparently but not actually in danger is much enjoyed, which is why we pay good money to be scared on increasingly "awesome" roller coasters.

Our machines are what truly impress us. Our technology overwhelms us to the point where we find the sublime not in God, not in the natural world, but within ourselves—or in what we produce. Thus, the movies starring cyborgs and space ships have to do with our preoccupation with ourselves, a humanistic fascination with our own power that has come to us in a straight line from the Greeks. Thus, what Heidegger finds in Sophocles that we inherit, and the latest way this power is implemented by our creations, still is found in our technological systems. In an everyday situation this may not directly be the giant power systems, the highest skyscrapers, or the most polluting industrial complexes but appears in the seemingly benign form of familiar modular products. Much of what architecture does, as Heidegger points out in "Building Dwelling Thinking," is design modest living units that are often cost efficient, well lit, and clean.[7] We are happy to have them, especially given the alternative of being in a refugee camp or in a terrible place after a war. Architecture does design and see to the building of these kinds of things, but the process is such that we forget both the violence we are doing to the environment and the loss that is incurred when we become modular people with modular heart implants living in a modular, homogeneous world.[8]

The combination of human character, violence and the drive to control, and technology that has come to dominate our ways of life politically and economically have yielded a world whose character is well named in the wonderful book title *The Machine as the Measure of Man*.[9] Clearly, technology is not apolitical but rather the instrument that in modernity defines those with power. There is a most sobering record of how in speaking of indigenous peoples; of the colonized in Africa, Asia, and South America; or generally of the "Third World" and "developing nations" the main reason Westerners have seen themselves as superior is that we have had superior machines. We have had superior technology. For the most part oblivious to the outrageous character of our attitudes, though lacking comparably deep spiritual practices we in the United States and Europe have not felt inferior to Africa or to the subcontinent of Asia. Such a thought does not occur to us. We have the technological knowhow, the muscle, the latest stuff, which provide the basis of almost all of our positive actions. When we feel compassion for the hungry of the world and decide that we need to help feed people who are starving to death, we initiate huge programs to green the earth and grow crops with tractors and fertilizers. That is positive action. But it also is violent, creating environmental disasters, dependencies on industrial-chemical products, and irreparably destroying traditional ways of life. Accordingly, not only art works but also our practices in the world witness our heritage of technology. Along with Heidegger I contend that there is no simple way to talk about innocence and guilt in regard to our complex historical technological and political attitudes toward nature and humankind.

Architecture, Design, and Pain

If we return to the themes of violence and the hunt (for example, by recalling the hunting scenes painted on cave walls from the time of the first humans or depicted by Assyrian narrative art (such as the relief from the Palace at Nimrud depicting *King Ashurnasirpal II Killing Lions*), we can reflect on the ways technology has to do with death, with violence, in a manner that does not cover up the phenomena. We need not always be oblivious to what is fundamental. Our earliest art works deal with these facts: that we live by killing and eating other living beings. In the cave or hide paintings there is an encounter held for us to consider; there is an honesty. Such images and the correlate myths and stories manifest the mystery and power of life, the mystery and power of animals, the mystery and power of earth or *phusis* (that which comes forth of its own accord, without human making). Today we are witnesses both to the testimonials given (left behind) by earlier witnesses—that is, to the works we consider primal art—and possibly through those works to the realities they disclose. It would appear that such sources testify that animal or life power, the upsurgence of what comes forth of its own accord in its own way, is not to be taken lightly. The adequacy and appropriateness of our usual taken-for-granted responses in brought into question. We hear the same thing in the stories of indigenous healers today and, in another way, find it in the planet's environmental changes and in biological mutations (as with viruses). For the most part, of course, we do not pay attention to such testimony or the challenge it issues us; we do not find it credible or relevant to our lifeworld of biomedical technology and chemical pharmaceuticals. We are out of touch with such earthly and animal power.

From the ancient Egyptians we learn that we not only need to deal with the hunt and the death of birds, fish, and animals but with human death. Here is the beginning of architecture, that is, in the substantial form of what was intended to endure, to enact an "eternal present" in the words of Sigfried Giedion.[10] Beyond the very earliest transitory woven structures (which could be considered the first architecture),[11] there is what counts in official architectural history and theory (whether deemed a second architecture or the first): Near Eastern and Egyptian monumental architecture. Here is the origin of what needs to be said in our context about museums and monuments. These buildings, their exterior cosmic alignments, and their interior spaces all have to do with the afterlife of the *ka* (soul). In these built environments the weighing of the soul and the decision concerning the conscience of the dead person takes place. The architecture is an abode, a holding place where the *ka* (the vital force of life) may rest before connection with its singular source: the eternal, infinite, and transcendent sun god, Ra.[12] In Heidegger's terms, here we encounter the metaphysics of presence. At the same time, something primal has been lost as soon as this position comes to prominence.

As the standard interpretation goes, after the Egyptian phase architecture next developed in Greece. In "The Origin of the Work of Art," while fully respecting the historical particularity of the Greek temple, Heidegger gives his powerful interpretation of the event of disclosure that occurs there: the temple is the gathering of earth and heavens, of mortals and immortals, all of which belong together and, when gathered for their allotted while, bring forth a world. Architecture, then, as other genuine art works, has the capacity both to accomplish and witness the discontinuous epochs within which mortals live. For example in Judaism, in Christianity, and in Islam religion gives us valued accounts about our relation to the eternal creator-God. The latter two belief systems go further with their visions of eternal life so that the just believe that though they will die, beyond death they will be safe.

The Judaic tradition is more complex: the ancient view of the dead lingering as shadows in *sheol* (an underground) was later combined with apocalyptic views on the soul existing separately from the body after death so that in the context of the continued doctrine of resurrection in Rabbinic Judaism and in the neo-Platonic Aristotelianism of Moses Maimonides it was held that the dead will be raised and judged, with the righteous going onward to eternal life in the world to come.[13] (I am not at all competent to follow the variations that obtained across Europe in the practices of German Orthodox Judaism in the early twentieth century, details of which are far more specialized than my point here.)

In the gestures of believers orienting themselves upward (from Egyptian papyrus images of worship of the *Rising Sun in the Form of Re-Harakhty* (c. 1150 BCE); to the catacomb frescos of Orans figures, which depict Christians raising arms heavenward in prayer (fourth century CE); to manuscripts showing Jews pointing upward to an envisioned Jerusalem (such as *Bird's Head Haggadah*, southern Germany, c. 1300), we find evidence that the believers were able to be less anxious about this earthly life and death than they might have been otherwise because they were confident about being immortal in some way. Part of Heidegger's reason for naming us mortals in his later works is to continue the project begun in *Being and Time* to criticize our thoughtless average, everyday attitude. If we remain inattentive to the meaning and responsibilities of our lives and deaths and to what we need do in decisive moments to live worthily, we may believe we are carefree but in fact we are lost in oblivion. Or, as Thoreau more sarcastically notes, if you don't have any problems you must be in such wonderful shape that he has nothing to say to you.

In the varieties of religious buildings we can read what is in effect at a given time and place concerning death and what might lie beyond it. Within the hermeneutics of architecture we can see that, as in the great mosque of Harum, the building is designed so as to give us a chance to pray, to put us in touch with a power greater than ourselves (a case of the architectural sublime, complementary to the tradition of natural divinity rather than to the technological).[14] The mode of entry and orientation, the lofty dome and substantial pillars, the prayer rugs on the floors, the dark and quiet atmosphere inside are not part of a tentative or lonely activity; the building opens for confident, social activity. It enables the gathering together of a community of believers and their God. Of course, there are violences in these spheres too, violences between Christians and Muslims (certainly nothing to be very proud of, though a religious basis has been found by many believers on both sides). Or, the ruins—now memorials— of churches and abbeys in England resulting from what that King Henry did testifies that there was violence then too, in the further fractures of religious differences. Obviously, the worldly and material dimensions of these religions is not exempt from regularly operative human behaviors.

No matter what a culture holds about the possibility of a city of God in the afterlife, there is no avoiding dealing with death, loss, and violence in the city of humans. In our shared, overlapping lifespans, mortals gather together in settlements and political relationships, aspects of which are facilitated by what is designed and built. Before there can be political life in a proper sense and its communal reflection, as Arendt explains, a site needs to be established. Not only does the settlement boundary need to be demarked ritually from the chaotic outside, but pragmatically the architect, engineer, and lawgiver need to precede political life. The first stage in the formation of a public realm is the building of a place. Such a founding event—a making, technically, according to Arendt—requires the double leadership of the architect and lawmaker. For the Greeks,

> The lawmaker was like the builder of a city wall, someone who had to do and finish his work before political activity could begin. He therefore was treated like any other craftsman or architect and could be called from abroad and commissioned without having to be a citizen, whereas the right to *politeuesthai*, to engage in the numerous activities which eventually went on in the polis, was entirely restricted to citizens. To them, the laws, like the wall around the city, were not the results of action but products of making. Before man began to act, a definite space had to be secured and a structure built where all subsequent actions could take place, the space being the public realm of the polis and its structure of law; legislator and architect belonged in the same category.[15]

Within the settlement once bounded and already comprising one's life world, a doubled second sphere was delineated: the agora, for public political debate and decision making proper, and the theater, with stage and seating, where the community members gathered together and engaged their specific, historically founding and confounding mythos. Alberto Perez-

Gomez reminds us that research has established that the "communitarian character of the Athenian scene, [was] tangibly displayed in the spatial relationship between a factitious community . . . and the arena of dramatic action—a relationship which reproduces that between a real community and a forum of political action."[16] The countertensions among the factions of a community had to be recognized existentially and worked through. Even more potent than the agora with its public political debate, the Greek theater provided the site where the community engaged the operative mysteries. The audience all knew the story, the mythos. The real project was to recall, reaffirm, and reconsider yet again, and together, what to make of the apparent facts, for example, that a measure was given—thought by way of *dike*, fate—that was greater than even the gods themselves and that human life with its allotted span breaks across laws impossible to follow, impossible not to follow. Thus the continued vitality of the polis depended on the ways in which the architecture brought citizens together with one another and with their mythos—the stories that held the true accounts of the nature of the cosmos and human existence—so that the forces in charge of human life as well as our relationships with and responses to them could be considered.

Architecture also plays an irreplaceable role in allowing the community a place to protest, to air grievances, in the flesh. Open spaces have long been a bulwark against tyranny, under which public gatherings are often forbidden. For example in the Plaza Major in Buenos Aires we still find witnesses to the violence of the military regime from 1976 to 1983 in which people were "disappeared." What kind of testimony is there to those killed and vanished? What stands witness to this violence? Here, not a monument, not a thing, however artfully potent such may be. Rather in Argentina the mothers themselves have been brave enough to come and stand witness, to give embodied testimony to the fact that their loved ones, their family members, are disappeared. But the disappeared, the violently murdered, those thrown out of airplanes or buried—they are absent.[17]

Witness and testimony, violence and architecture, are much more bound together than we normally acknowledge because, as is often observed, it appears that as Americans we prefer to be cheerfully optimistic while considering critique to be negative and thus to be avoided, even though critique is essential in trying to find any genuinely promising positive course of action. As an example concerning violence and testimony drawn from political life and space, the American courthouse, where it stands in the public square as it does in much of the U.S. South, Midwest, and West, is considered the place where a community can gather to vote in order to elect our government officials and decide contested issues, come together to commemorate and celebrate socially important events, such as our independence on the Fourth of July. As to the interior spaces, the courtroom appears as the site where one accused of a crime has the right to face her accuser and as the place where a jury hears testimony. This certainly is correct. Yet it is also on courthouse grounds that legally mandated hangings were carried out and lynchings flaunted acceptable bounds of law and justice. In regard to this location more questions are forced upon us: when you have to give witness, when you are called to come before a judge and jury in the course of a trial, what kind of testimony do you give? What kind of justice is there? Arendt and Levinas seem to be entirely trustworthy in what they say (even if we disagree with them, it is not likely that we would consider that they fail to speak the truth as best they can). Again, though, we also need to ask whether and how we might use Heidegger to talk about these issues, especially when a case in point involves the Holocaust. These are major problems.

Levinas is famous for the injunction that we are responsible for the other, not in an abstract way to be considered conceptually and through a system of rules but concretely. He contends that we are not free but that from the beginning, before any rationalizing, we already are placed under "a responsibility ordered to the first one on the scene, a responsibility for the neighbor, inspired by the other"; "A being (*l'etant*) is a human being and it is as a neighbor that a human being is accessible—as a face."[18] In his familiar phrase, we are responsible for "the stranger, the widow, the orphan".[19] Heidegger might probe our disposition as a lawyer might inquire of a prospective juror in a case involving harm stemming from the trauma of loss and exclusion, "What experiences do you have dealing with strangers?" or "What views do you have about our responsibility to them?"[20]

In fact, Heidegger himself brings forth an "expert witness," Trakl, cross-examining the testimony preserved in his poem "Winter Evening." Heidegger unfolds what the poem says by moving back and forth among the lifeworld evoked, the implications for neighborliness, and the potent, multiply meaning words of the poet. The poem sets before us a scene in which household members are in their house, happy and warm on a winter night when a stranger (ominous, and perhaps dangerous because a stranger?) treads the path outside and looks in—"the Stranger who disturbs the being with oneself" (*le chez soi*).[21] What is to be done? Normally the inhabitants keep the door barred. That has been the point of walled cities for centuries and remains so for gated communities and guarded enclaves today. Because it is a basic architectural and social element that connects inside and outside, even connects what is concealed with what is unconcealed, Heidegger focuses on the threshold.

Heidegger begins by pointing out that Trakl uses the word *Riß*, which as we saw above in relation to Sophocles says tear, cleft, fissure, gap. To cross a threshold, of course, is to go across a divide, a gap that occurs or is deliberately established, between one side and another, between one thing and another. The threshold, then, establishes and holds the different apart, but it also bridges them, bringing and keeping them together in their difference. Insofar as we don't want to share with the stranger—the stranger on the outside hungrily looking in, the stranger on the outside who might want to do violence to us—our resistance is raised up. We fear the pain that we might have to endure, perhaps even more than death (Levinas contends that in the context of the prospect of death we have a fear not of nothingness but of violence, of which more below).[22] The dread of violence and possible pain that we might suffer, which in fact separates those inside and outside, simultaneously binds us together. It binds us together as potential friend or potential enemy, as us and/versus them. Alternatively, our compassion or self-assurance might allow us to respond positively to the stranger. We might invite the other person in. If we do, will the outcome be a friendly hospitality offered and accepted or what we find in Flannery O'Connor (where "the violent bear it away") and in Cormac McCarthy (that we are blown away)?

But, it turns out, such dilemmas are not the issue. The stranger is not another person outside our family circle but a dimension and trajectory of all of us: "Trakl's work sings the song of the soul, 'something strange on the earth,' which is only just about to gain the earth by its wandering."[23] The stranger is ominous because in encountering wandering personified we come face to face with "a wandering into the whiling of life and toward death," with the necessity of learning to bear ourselves toward death, as capable of dying.[24]

Thus, in exposing us to ourselves in "A Winter Evening" Trakl goes on to write

Wanderer quietly steps within;
Pain has turned the threshold to stone.[25]

As Heidegger interprets these lines, they name something that persists and that has already persisted. It is only in turning to stone that the threshold presences at all. The threshold is the ground-beam that bears the doorway as a whole. It sustains the middle in which the two, the outside and the inside, penetrate each other. The threshold bears the between. What goes out and goes in, in the between, is joined in the between's dependability. The dependability of the middle must never yield either way. The settling of the between needs something that can endure and is in this sense hard. The threshold, as the settlement of the between, is hard because pain has petrified it.[26] And pain has turned the threshold to stone because in contrast to an anthropological understanding where pain would be an internal sensation, a matter for medicine and therapy, originarily, Heidegger explains, pain names the separating of what belongs together, a pulling apart and gathering together. An odd thing to say, but Heidegger's originary thinking listens to the poet's words, in this case learning from Trakl what "pain" more deeply names and says to us.

> But what is pain? Pain rends. It is the rift. But it does not tear apart into dispersive fragments. Pain indeed tears asunder, it separates, yet so that it draws everything to itself, gathers it to itself. Its rendering, as a separating that gathers, is at the same time that drawing which, like the pen drawing of a plan or sketch, draws and joins together what is held apart in separation. Pain is the joining . . . in the rendering that divides and gathers. Pain is the joining of the rift. The joining is the threshold. It settles the between, the middle of the two that are separated in it. Pain joins the rift of the difference. Pain is the dif-ference itself.[27]

In a direction surprising to English speakers, Heidegger already is developing the ideas about pain not only with those of threshold and stone but with design. In German, however, there is play among the terms, especially for the poet and originary thinker who recall what words themselves say. Whereas *Riß* means tear, cleft, fissure, and gap while *Aufriß* means sketch, design, draft, or elevation as a building perspective, in another modality, as we learn from Trakl and Sophocles, we also sketch and design in language when we compose the words of a poem, draft an essay, or outline a building project.[28] We can think here in terms of architectural design (say, of a house, of a museum). These designs also evoke a pulling along since the related term *zeigen* means both to design and to draw (as in the directive to pull the door toward you rather than push it away)—according to Trakl all of these dimensions would be connected to pain.

Why explicitly connect the ideas of design, pain, and threshold? Heidegger is reflecting on how within art and architecture as design (*Aufriß*) we find hidden a *Riß* (tear, cleft, fissure, gap). Here the play of the hidden and disclosed words and phenomena (*Riß* concealed within *Aufriß*) is like Heidegger's more famous explication of truth as disclosure, in which he unfolds what happened world-historically and what needs to be recovered from the event in which *letheia* (forgetfulness, concealment) was concealed within *aletheia* (disclosure, unconcealment). The tearing is hidden in many ways. For example, we focus on the completed design and building, not on the process that brought it forward. But of course the design is carried out through the tracing of ink across paper, the cutting of the woodblock, the engraving of the plate, or when clearing the ground for building by using the plow or bulldozer. This tearing and cutting is as pain: both separate.

But they also gather. Of pain Heidegger says "it draws everything to itself." In the case of the design-pain-threshold, that which joins and separates also draws us. Here we find that other sense of drawing: just as when the draft horse pulls the plow that cuts the earth, architecturally there also occurs a kind of drawing. In the cutting, tearing pain within the phenomena of violence, testimony, and architecture now given to us there is something that pulls at us, that tugs at us.

From the perspective of Trakl's testimony about the design, threshold, and pain that sunders but also brings together it is rather trivial to stress that the interiorized modern subject and the excluded, external other(s) need to be joined. More significantly, here we find that our proper comportment to one another as mortals shows itself to be a more fundamental issue:

> Only a being that lives soulfully can fulfill the sending of its nature. By virtue of this power it is fit to join in that harmony of mutual bearing by which all living things belong together. In keeping with this relation of fitness, everything that lives is of it, that is to say, good. But the good is good painfully.[29]

At the same time, since attention also needs to be given to the more subtle differences that obtain within our shared finitude we are returned to Levinas and Arendt. We need to reflect further on the problem of our social-political responsibility, especially our failure to bear witness and to resist violence actively, to do what we can to constitute and hold open a genuinely public realm. In the architectural figures of dwelling and threshold—and the historical existential case of the Berlin Wall, running between and separating East and West Germany—we encounter our finitude and are called to open beyond our everyday comfort that we may cross over to and even embrace our disquieting mortality.

Daniel Libeskind's Jewish Museum Berlin

The Subject Matter

Because the only proper way to engage the substance of architecture's relation to violence and loss is by attending to and responding to particular concrete things, I shift now to focusing on a specific type of building— the museum—as a site of witnessing and testimony. One reason to talk about the museum, of course, is that (as noted at the beginning of the essay) Heidegger points out the linkage between originary thinking as *Andenken* (recollective, memorializing thinking) and *Gedänknis* (monuments, memorials). In part, the things that gather together the dimensions of world can also hold meaning and memory because they themselves endure.[30] Like a series of Russian dolls, each one holding another doll inside itself (with human culture on the outside), museums are large things that hold smaller things that hold meaning. The museums and artifacts last; they hold. Specifically, there is one museum that stands out as an exceptional manifestation of architectural accomplishment in regard to our subject matter: Daniel Libeskind's Jewish Museum Berlin (as renamed during the process that began as the project for the Extension to the Berlin Museum with the Jewish Department).

Our task here is to try to see and think this museum, which is a challenge because of its design's complexity and the seriousness of the memories it holds and sets before us that we may take them to heart (as Heidegger, in *What Is Called Thinking?*, characterizes what it means to say and think).[31] Just as great is a barrier we face before we can even begin the task: the fickleness of architectural academics and practicing professionals. The building was heralded when first designed not only because of its inherent importance but—and perhaps even more so—because it was a spectacular instance of deconstruction. It was one of the first major appearances in designed and built form of Derrida's insights.[32] Those designs no longer interest architects, who are notoriously oriented toward "ideas of the moment" and who have since moved on to folds (from Deleuze), blobs (including the hype about projects in Bilbao and beyond), globalization (Dubai), and environmental sustainability. Indeed, the embarrassing thoughtlessness already began before the building was even constructed! A session of the Association of Collegiate Schools of Architecture Conference held in Dallas rejected a paper on Libeskind's project in 1998 on the grounds that "we already have heard too much about this museum." Shame on us. The Jewish Museum deserves our thoughtful attention. As Heidegger says, we would no more expect to understand fully a painting by Klee after standing briefly before it than we would to understand Heisenberg's theory of subatomic physics after a first encounter.[33] So too with an architectural design. Now, from a perspective outside of designers chasing after the "idea of the month" with a fuller grasp of the story of the design, and having had the chance to experience the building reflectively and what it brings forth, we may do fuller justice to the Jewish Museum and what it evokes.

The design not only temporally precedes any experience of the completed building, its spaces, and the materials held there but raises questions concerning the relation of concepts and practices, both generally and in this specific case. Overall, using the work done by Heidegger, Lefebvre, and poststructuralism, architectural and spatial theory have developed the critique of representation and of the dominance of conceptual processes over lifeworld practices. Heidegger, of course, has demonstrated how in the historical unfolding of metaphysics the primal originary thinking that brings forth the disclosures of the lifeworld has been displaced by what are in fact the secondary abstractions of calculative "scientific" conceptualization. Lefebvre, often echoing Heidegger, distinguishes three dimensions of the production of space and argues vehemently that we need to restore the primacy of the lifeworld's spatial practices. He traces the history of spatial production and its theorization, showing that the basic shaping of places is accomplished by our work (for example, building the streets and piers of cities, planting and cultivating the fields of the countryside, burying our dead in cemeteries adjacent to our churches that are oriented to the east and west in alignment with the realms of life and death). From our emplaced practices and experiences we have abstracted the idea of space, eventually developing the concept of space as absolute, homogeneous, infinite, and isotrophic, which held until the accomplishment of the tradition of Newton and his forebears yielded to the articulation of relativity by Einstein and his colleagues.

Our contemporary problems in theory and praxis occur because these scientific "representations of space" have displaced and now exert control over practical activity: we conceive of how we want a parcel of land to be developed and then, often from afar, send directions and delegate the power to make it so. Lefebvre describes how in a healthy dynamic interplay (1) the lived spatial practices come first, (2) conceptions of space are developed from them, then (3) both are symbolically reworked, especially by the arts and religion that elaborate the first two so as to provide the historical, social lifeworlds within which we practice and conceptualize.[34] I mention how what would be an appropriately continuing dynamic has come to a broken state perverting our lifeworlds because the critique of conceptual representation calls for reinstating originary thinking while the critique of the dominance of abstract space calls for reestablishing practices responsive to particular places, actual materials, and embodied persons in specific historical lifeworlds. Good design and architecture are essential if we are to accomplish this. My argument here is that Libeskind's Jewish Museum is just such an instance of originary architecture.

That the museum is originary and not metaphysical-representational could be masked if we misunderstand the design process that took place. Though it might appear that Libeskind proceeded by way of contemporary abstract conceptualization, that is not the case. Indeed, he did work out the design thoughtfully before it was built, but rather than proceeding by conceptualizations his design thinking worked out—as *phronēsis* or practical wisdom—the bringing together of what belonged together even while apart.[35] Further, the experiences engendered by the museum and its contents are powerful, but they are not experiences of the modern subject encountering objects (though they might be reduced to such in the course of contemporary production-consumption, they are not inherently so). By way of background (from which it is easy to misread the process, incorrectly taking it to be a case of what Lefebvre condemns), Libeskind came to prominence as a theoretical designer and teacher, that is, in the course of exploring architectural approaches, ideas, and pedagogy without expressly intending that his designs (at least not all of them) be built. The same was the case with Peter Eisenman, Paulo Soleri, Bruno Taut, and many other architects in the early or reflective stages of their careers. From a German Jewish family, Libeskind's own background is not European but American. His architectural education was at the University of Pennsylvania, subsequent to which he made his reputation as the director of the Cranbrook Institute, a famous design school outside Detroit. From his position as fundamentally a theoretical architect/designer and educator with a record of drawings, texts, exhibitions, and competition entries of projects that were spatial-cultural explorations he catapulted to international fame with the design for the Jewish Museum Berlin.[36] (Indeed, so rapid was the transition that when the construction began he was not a registered architect, a problem solved by having the engineering firm in Germany take responsibility for signing the necessary legal and insurance documents.)

Since Libeskind's design was different than what exists in Berlin's historical urban fabric, we can as little collapse it into architectural precedent or its urban context as we could substitute the abstract ideas of deconstruction for it. How to think, then, without rushing to vacuous generalizations in cultural, aesthetic, and speculative terms? We need to focus on what is given, that is, on the design itself. Then, beyond the design, we further need to see whether and how the thing, the building itself and the museum events occur in the city and our lives. Trying to be patient with a design means taking the time to see and read it, taking the time not to rush past it to make superficial proclamations ("Deconstruction in Berlin!") and trendy headlines ("Philosophy Professor Explains Architecture!"). A respectful response requires us to persevere in seeing how (or whether) Libeskind's design is not deconstructive architecture, that is, how or when it does not come about as a representation of deconstructive theory or philosophy. I want to show, in fact, that what calls for thinking in Libeskind's

Jewish Museum works because of its own thoughtworthiness, which in part means that Libeskind himself did not take deconstructive ideas or "concepts" and apply them as expressions in his architectural design. Nor does his work stay within a particular postpostmodern style such that it generates a new set of terms or elements to be codified or deconstructed ("the zigzag," "the sealed void," "architecturally scaled built *khora*," and so on). Rather, the design of the building was the thoughtful making of a work—as with any genuine work of art—and thus the same, in Heidegger's sense, as the composition of a poem or a symphony. Hence what we considered above with Heidegger and Trakl directly applies here. We can think about how design (in terms of *der Riß, der Aufriß, der Abriß*) belongs with actual memorials (*Gedänknis*) and recollective thinking (*Andenken*) as well as how deconstruction belongs with construction and building.

What is drawn out by the design? What was it that has been cut into and placed upon Berlin's soil and rock? What openings and gatherings for our historical, social lives are possible? We need to be patient in trying to say what the design "means" and to interpret and relate it to other designs and buildings, much less to philosophy and deconstructive theory. The question facing us is not "What does Berlin show us today?" or "What is the building like?" Since the design is a drawing, we need to ask, "What does the design draw and join?"

The Call for Design and Response

The architectural program, understood as what is called for and the design intends, is itself already a response to that which calls for a design. While the collection of artifacts for which city curators and administrators are responsible might call for some sort of display museum, the placement of these works in a museum and the mode of their setting out—which means why Libeskind designed this building the way he did[37]—are themselves already responses called for by a history.[38]

As to the formal process of the project, though an extension to the Berlin Museum was initially considered in the 1970s, the conception was formally presented at a conference at the Berlin Aspen-Institute in the spring of 1988 and approved by an international committee. Later that same year, an international competition was announced for, in the official language, "the Extension to the Berlin Museum, with the Jewish Museum Development." After the competition was closed in June 1989, Libeskind's proposed project was selected by the jury as the best among the 165 submitted.

At the simplest level, Berlin officials wanted to bring together the city's Berlin History Museum's holdings with those of the existing Jewish collections of craftwork, paintings (especially family portraits), records, and photographs that had been recovered or salvaged and brought together after the war (most of this material had been housed at two different sites, one in the Berlin City Museum and the other in the Martin-Gropius-Bau).[39] The preexisting material history museum had an unusually rich collection of fabrics because the Jewish community in Berlin was especially strong in contributing to the design and production of textiles. In addition, there were relevant materials in a theatrical department and fashion collection.

Practically, as a curatorial-political response, it was decided that the preexisting City Museum would house the collections of materials made prior to 1871 and a new building designed and built to house those after this date. More deeply, of course, the point of the project was to acknowledge and begin to repair the violent separation not just of artifacts but of the strands of Berlin's history, that is, of the lives of its Jewish and non-Jewish residents. As articulated by Eberhard Diepgen, then governing mayor of Berlin,

> the presentation of German history would be inconceivable without the history of the Jews in Germany. . . . Therefore, the vital contribution of Jewish Germans also belongs in a permanent exhibition as part of our city's cultural richness. The exterior of the *Berlin Museum* will be a home to a *Jewish Museum* which will present religious as well as secular collections. The architectural plan for the extension contains formulations and spatial elements which stimulate reflection and give the museum, in more than the usual measure, the additional character of a memorial.[40]

Hence, the social program was to reopen us to the "lost, excluded, and destroyed world of"[41] the European and Berlin Jews, which was to be accomplished through the building and exhibition programs that were to "embody the missing, the disappeared Jewish way of life and the part it played in the city's history."[42] To cite the official program:

> The exhibition rooms of the new building should present the history of the city, contain the Jewish department as well as taking on the theatrical department and the collection of fashion. The wish to ensure on the one hand that the Jewish department had the self-sufficiency which it needed while at the same time integrating it into the presentation of Berlin's history in general was central to all considerations. The idea formulated by the museum was incorporated into the text of the invitation for tenders. It said, among other

things, that "A Jewish Museum in a German city and especially in Berlin will have to keep at least three divisions in mind. The first is religion in conjunction with the traditions which religion has shaped: Judaica, the records and documents belong to this area. The second division embraces the history of the various communities which, owing to the course taken by German history, met with a cruel destiny in the persecution and murder of Jewish citizens by the National Socialists, a destiny which should not be allowed to lose its terrible significance through any form of atonement or through the otherwise effective healing power of time. Nothing in the history of Berlin has ever altered the city so much as the persecution, expulsion, and murder of its own Jewish citizens, who have had a formative effect upon the face of the city and upon its history over centuries. This alteration worked inwards, affecting the very heart of the city. The third division will consist of giving recognition to the lives and work of former Jewish citizens, who have had a formative effect upon the face of the city and upon its history over centuries. In Berlin the history of the Jews is so closely bound to that of the city that the two can hardly be separated. An autonomous Jewish Museum can not be considered without the history of Berlin just as, conversely, a museum of the civic history of Berlin would lose its significance if it did not take the Jewish citizens into consideration."[43]

Clearly, while the goal was integration of the Jewish and non-Jewish cultural components, no reduction or disappearance was to be accepted.[44] The commemoration needed to proceed by letting lie before us both the disjunction and the intersection of what belongs together even when displaced or radically absent because of exile, death, or the impossibility (for future generations) of ever coming into existence. To let lie before us so that we can take it to heart is the fitting task and mode of the museum itself, which is called upon to respond to what happened in the past and what needs to be restored as complexly belonging together in the future. The called-for social responsibility to remember and recover as best we can would be responded to insofar as the building would provide a site for the display of the works present and absent and the opening for the divergent and intersecting ways of life and history. As explained by Ulrich Roloff-Momin, Berlin's senator for cultural affairs, it also was desired that the complex function as part of the city's urban design, bringing some order to the neighboring collections of buildings.[45] All these disjunctions, intersections, and phenomena—social and physical, historical and political, for things large and small—had to be drawn and joined together by the design. The building, of course, had to be, and is, functional, with offices, archives, and library collections (on the top—fourth—floor) that enable the building to work pragmatically.[46] But in what follows these utilitarian "backstage" aspects are not covered, in deference to the more important features that are so evocative, so highly enigmatic.

The Design Itself

The manner in which Libeskind thought and planned before he began to design provides us some additional entry into what he drew and proposed for the building.[47] (Libeskind's approach was highly intellectual—"full of ideas," we would ordinarily say—but, to use Heidegger's contrast between calculative-representational and originary thinking, that does not imply that it was conceptual as distinct from the figural thought characteristic of poetry and the arts.) It turned out that Libeskind thought of "the line" as the figura that would provide the principle of unity for the project, which could unfold to bring forth the called-for built form and multiple levels of meaning. Accordingly, he named his design "Between the Lines," to indicate the (nonconceptual) formed-image,[48] by which he meant that it was a variation of the fundamental problem of how to commemorate the absent and present Jewish history of Berlin.[49] In one of the many descriptions of the figure Libeskind says, "You create two lines: the one line that is continuous and yet tortured, twisted, and angular, and the other line that is straight, orthogonal and yet disjointed, fractured, and ruptured."[50] The task, in his terms, was to relate to the life and heritage of Berlin and, more broadly, of Germany the contributions of Jews who lived there before the Holocaust, the never-to-be-realized accomplishments of those driven out, deported, killed, or never born (who will never be there because their parents, their ancestors, were murdered), and the achievements of those now again living in the city and the newly reunited country. As a built work the design physically and substantially had to respond to both the external urban context and the internal "content" of the collections and changing exhibitions; "in between," through the heart of the project, Libeskind intuited, ran a void—"a discontinuous void."[51]

> So the new extension is conceived as an emblem, where the invisible, the Void, makes itself apparent as such. The void and the invisible are the structural that have been gathered in the space of Berlin and exposed in an architecture in which the unnamed remains in the names which keep still. To put it simply, the museum is a zigzag with a structural rib, which is the void of the Jewish Museum running

across it. And this void is something every participant will experience as his or her absent presence. That is basically a summary of how the building works. It is not a collage or a collision or a simple dialectic, but a new type of organization which is organized around a center which is not, around what is not visible. And what is not visible is the richness of the Jewish heritage in Berlin, which is today reducible to archival and archeological material, since physically it has disappeared.[52]

The figure of the line occurred as, or united, multiple dimensions of the external urban context and a good deal of Berlin's history. The site was at the center of Berlin, just southeast of what had been Checkpoint Charlie when the city was divided by the wall. Libeskind utilized a complex physical and cultural realignment to the existing streets and social factors for the new buildings. The orientation had three dimensions: the preexisting City Museum was aligned in relation to the nearby Baroque intersection of Lindenstrasse, Wilhelmstrasse, and Friedrichstrasse; the violence of the war had been compounded by postwar changes the Allies made for purposes of military control during the occupation (realigning parts of the street system, modifying access to some boulevards, and changing many addresses) that interrupted or disconnected the urban fabric; finally, Libeskind's plan disconnected the new structure from both the original and from the interim urban forms and realigned it to the housing projects of the 1960s and of IBA (Internationale Bauausstellung, the major urban renewal project from the 1980s continuing to the present). Hence, in terms of generative themes, Libeskind explains, "The *Jewish Museum* is based on the invisible figures whose traces constitute the geometry of the building. The ground on which this building stands is not only the apparent one in Kreuzberg, but that other one which is both above and below it."[53]

The streets, as a paradigmatic site of public life, also provided for the direct disclosure of the violence testified to by the buildings themselves. In this regard, Berlin is to be credited with facing the memories and live issues by means of its architecture and landscape. The heritage is let stand before us to a remarkable degree. In the center of the city, the Kaiser-Wilhelm-Gedächtnis Kirche (Memorial Church) remains as a burnt ruin, which can be seen regularly against the sky because of Berlin's low skyline. Though containing a regular kind of museum, it is a memorial (*das Denkmal*; *das Andenken*) that does not so much contain objects as stand witness, facilitating the shared recollection of what happened and of what did not happen as a result of those events. In Heidegger's terms, such official and de facto memorials call for something other than a representation. They call, in Heidegger's terms, for a memorializing or recollective thinking (*Andenken, andenkenes Denken, besinnliches Denken, Erinnerung*); they call, with Derrida, for *les commerces du merci*, according to the aporias.[54]

Though I am not in any position even to comment on the accuracy of the following observation, it is striking that in 1950 while considering the "general lack of response, of emotion," in much of Germany as a case of "an escape from reality [that was also] an escape from responsibility," Arendt asserted:

> There are, of course, many Germans whom this description does not fit. Above all, there is Berlin, whose people, in the midst of the most horrible physical destruction, have remained intact. I do not know why this should be so. . . . There is no embarrassment and no guilt-feeling, but frank and detailed recital of what happened to Berlin's Jews at the beginning of the war. . . . They are remarkably well-informed and have kept their sense of humor and their characteristically ironical friendliness—apart from their having become somewhat sadder and less ready for laughter—. . . . Berlin is an exception.[55]

Indeed, throughout the city traces of the violence appear in the building façades, from the Hochschule für Kunst in the center to the Martin-Gropuis Bau (which as noted housed part of the Jewish Collection) near the museum site, which have been pockmarked with bullet holes, especially around the windows, toward which most of the firing was directed. Until recently the holes had not been cemented over or concealed but let stand as witness to the incredible violence that took place there; even after some repair many façades remain in their scarred condition.

Immediately next door to the Gropius Bau is the Topographie des Terrors, one of the headquarters of the Gestapo and a major torture center somehow "forgotten" as covered up (as was Hitler's bunker), then refound with the excavation in preparation for new building. Given how hard it would be to "forget" where Gestapo headquarters were, what needs to be accounted for is not only the violence but the oblivion—the concealment of the violence.

In the same area there was the large open, abandoned waste space of what had been Potsdamamer Platz, the once vibrant commercial heart of the city. As a positive step to help Berlin become a great civic and economic power again, the major social-political decision was to redevelop the site as a fresh commercial venture but on a larger scale than before. Subsequently, there were international design competitions, themselves of considerable interest (in terms of global capitalism and environmental sustainability, though these aspects are beyond the scope of this chapter).

To return to the line as the design's unifying figura in relation to the urban context, of course it connotes the Berlin Wall and its pathway through the city. The line also enabled the cultural program to engage the spiritual geography of the city and its Jewish population—to commemorate family lineages, genealogies. In this regard Libeskind looked up and plotted on a map the addresses of Jewish artists and intellectuals, delineating this constellation as an additional figura in the shape of a distorted yellow star, recalling the star Jews had been forced to wear—which he further thought in relationship to the description of the "Stations of the Star" contained in Walter Benjamin's book *One-Way Street*. This cultural dimension of the program was further elaborated by incorporating motifs from several musical sources, most important Schonberg's unfinished opera *Moses and Aaron*, at the end of which Moses does not sing but exclaims "Oh word, you absent word."[56] Here, the usual operatic phenomena, in which vocalization obscures words, is reversed, so that "when there is no more singing, one can understand very well the missing word which is uttered by Moses, which is the call for the deed."[57]

Nor did Libeskind think that the fracture of family lines, the absence of those absent, that resulted from the historical events could be hidden. Thus, when he generated models of the buildings to complement his drawings, he incorporated the deported Jews into the site design by placing those models on a base or ground of listings drawn from the two-volume *Gedenkbuch* (memorial book), the records, name by name, of when people were born, where they lived, when they were removed, where they were sent and died—a collection of thousands and thousands and thousands of names.[58]

In many ways, then, Libeskind's thinking involves the tangle of the visible and the invisible, of what is present and absent, of what we might experience or not, of what might be known or not. Accordingly, it is a misunderstanding to approach the museum through the usual expectations concerning aesthetics, especially insofar as this has come to connote the visible, or the tradition of well-ordered, geometrical patterns. Other words and ideas need to be employed; other experiences and interpretations deployed and appreciated. Indeed, as we next will see, the building is not symmetrical in the least: the inside and outside do not correlate with each other; the spaces on the inside are not symmetrical from floor to floor, as is usual.[59] In terms of what occurs or can be seen, "in and out," "above and below" are maximally separated and operate with a radical autonomy.

The Building

As to the design of the museum itself (the complex of buildings, grounds, and gardens), though the drawings are rather difficult to "read," they are important to consider at least briefly before focusing on the experiential quality of the spaces because the character of the experiences, as we will see, changes depending on what we "know" from the plans and intentions. Our task of seeing and reading Libeskind's design is doubly hard. In addition to the density of invisible ideas or meanings made visible, difficulty occurs because in the mode of much current architecture, plans and sections are not rendered in easily legible formats or by way of traditional conventions. The renderings are neither clear nor distinct nor even simply sequential or additive. The complexity of the design and consequently other documents required in the building process are confusing to architectural, engineering, and construction professionals themselves—indeed Libeskind observes that he could hardly read the formwork drawings necessary for the wall.[60] Rather, the drawings are densely complex and "simultaneous" or overlaid, congruent with the mode of multidimensional, collided graphics also typical of Coop-Himmelblau, Rem Koolhaus, Peter Eisenman, Morphosis, and others. (The relation of Libeskind's work to these other architects is yet another topic, of course.) Note that Libeskind's plans, sections, and models occur within his polyvalent design where not only the elements are rendered completely simultaneously but where given elements are allowed—even encouraged—to vibrate with several sorts of meaning at the same time.[61]

For those untrained in reading architectural graphics the design perhaps is easiest to comprehend through models (without here taking up the issue of the ways these are not "representational") or photographs.[62] The general model shows the dramatic zigzag form of the museum building; its apparent collision (or juxtaposition) at ground level with the preexisting, adjacent Berlin Museum; an integrating landscape scheme of the Paul Celan Court, E. T. A. Hoffmann Garden, and the Paradise Garden, plus connection with the east-west greenbelt and its relation to the fairly regular immediate urban context. As we will see, despite "appearances" the building is highly organized, though not in a visually obvious or symmetrical manner. To begin, the image of the zigzag is strong and clear but only as an imaginative projection from a bird's-eye view that you have learned about indirectly (unless you happen to be flying directly over the building)—in

Figure 2.1. The zigzag: seven sub-buildings connected to a straight but empty axis

direct experience the zigzag cannot be seen from ground level and thus does not help in orientation. I find that the best way to hold some basic gestalt in mind (which is not the intention of the architect but is important for ordinary comprehension) is to think of the building the way it was actually built and as it most simply is: as actually seven buildings connected to a straight but empty axis (twenty-two meters high and 140 meters long), with bridges here and there connecting the separate built elements.[63] This image enables me to hold in mind the overall design coherence and make more sense of the complex experience of encounter.[64]

The zigzag form, or the movement named "between the lines," of the Jewish Museum itself continues the interplay of absence and presence and the violent intersection of lines developed in regard to the external urban context as noted above. In fact, the patterns worked out here develop some of the architect's earlier explorations with the line in the 1980s, as in the competition "City Edge for Berlin" (1987), for which Libeskind won first prize.[65] Indeed, it certainly is to Libeskind's credit that he discerned and continued a strong German and European history of aesthetic linearity, of surprisingly bent and distorted lines that could provide a formal source for the design. Related to Jakob G. Tschernichow's *Study of a Multiple Fold* (1930), Paul Klee's *Transparent-Perspectival* (1921), and Wassily Kandinsky's *Now Upwards* (1931), the zigzag also developed from one of his earlier projects, *Line of Fire* (1968). The immediately obvious power of the gray zinc-tiled zigzag "lying" next to the calm, symmetrical yellow stucco Berlin Museum makes the former seem dynamic, if not alive.[66] The associations are multiple, but we need to exercise care in following those that occur to us: Heideggerian linkages would evoke Zeus's and Heraclitus's lightning bolts, Greek chthonic forces, and the *Lichtung* (lighting, clearing); Derridean fire (from his *Cinders* and *Of Spirit*); and, distressingly complicating matters, the pair of lightning bolts that were the SS rune insignia under National Socialism.[67]

Figure 2.2. Later-generation model

As normally is the case, the models are the most help in visualization (though in this instance the models helpful to nonprofessionals came only several years after the initial drawings used in the competition's decision process). Even in these late "user-oriented" models the indication of the interior volumetric spaces is so oversimplified that it appears as a mere précis of the design when compared to the detailed drawings. Those harder-to-read drawings delineate, in addition the original nineteenth-century museum building and the zigzag Jewish Museum's, the complex interior spaces. The voids within the building are not at all easy to see in the drawings, much less to interpret in terms of implied spatial character and construction. The entry proceeds through the old building, goes underground with stairs and through a corridor, then comes back up to the interior of the new building. As to the stair systems, corridors, and exhibition spaces, most are organized along two axes that cross over the other, partially below ground but not beneath the main building, then running through the new building above ground—one manifestation of the complex of lines that operates as the generative design. These linear elements were modified considerably from Libeskind's first versions, partly as a result of design changes but also in no small part because of budget considerations (since as originally designed, the slanted walls would have required elevators that ran at an incline).

The drawn design includes spaces ("rooms"?) that are present though invisible. That is, there are structural elements ("voids") extending to each story of the museum that are fragments of what would otherwise be the space between the two conflicting lines—again, a "between the lines." Some of these spaces appear as what might be called "corridor" elements, "chambers," and "towers"—though these terms that attempt translation immediately falsify and misconstrue what is occurring. Though they do give some sort of representational hint as to the quality of the spaces within, the latter need to be explicated in experiential terms—to which we will shortly turn.

First, however, there are dimensions that are available only by seeing them in the drawing (or by hearing an account of them). Specifically there are six empty spaces or "voids" (there is nothing in them) within the building that are partially sealed (the central, concrete-walled atrium, for example) and some that are entirely sealed, utterly inaccessible and not experienced by visitors—unless known to exist and thus experienced reflectively. These appear in the drawings as "voids" such that, as can be seen in section if we compare the various perspectives with the others and with the respective plans, the indicated "rooms" have no entryways on any of the six possible sides. (Not surprisingly, given their high cost and other social needs for scant resources, the proposed sealed voids were hotly debated well into 1992 and consequently reduced in number by the designer.)[68] The genuine "voids" are complemented by "voided voids," which are elements such as outer towers, apparently free-standing structures allowing the emptiness of the "voids" and the historical exclusions to be displaced and thus manifest. Originally there were more "voided voids" planned for such programmatic uses as library or reading rooms, but most were eliminated during the budgeting process. One such "voided void" appears as inserted into the old building, cutting across all of its floors and providing the entryway to the Jewish Department as discussed above. Finally, there are "varied voids," which appear at the ends of the corridors that crossed over each other and which are to be used only for special exhibitions.[69]

The Experience of the Building

On Entering The experiential character of the museum can only be hinted at in a description of what is given when you are moving through it, though it may be possible to evoke—or at least point out—some of the more powerful moments. Already at the beginning we find that there are multiple modes of experiencing the building, the differences of which will vary considerably, depending not only on direct attention to the artifacts and details of the building itself but on the "thoughtfulness of the tour." That is, significant dimensions depend on the degree to which one finds and understands what is provided by way of possible affordances of meaning since as we have seen Libeskind invested the design with a substantial number of ideas. Just as the museum's plans are very hard to read, so with the direct experience it is hard to discern or hold on to a coherent pattern, much less correlate what you have before you with the outside or with the overall building layout. This is not, however, necessarily a disadvantage. Perhaps there is no reason to correlate the different elements and dimensions; you could just have your own experiences as you go along, as the building is given to you.

In our usual mode in everyday life, we are engaged in some project and thus experience architecture inattentively: in the case of the museum, we observe artifacts on display and talk with each other about them or the topic that they stimulate in us, rather than focusing on the building itself or its details since those only provide the context, the ground for the focal interactions. Even if we come to the museum in an attentive and informed mode, we find two kinds of complications. First, the situation requires you to make constant choices. At any given point forks in the pathways force you to choose one alternative and neglect the other(s). You realize early on that the experience is not going to be one of passively following what the curators have spatially or chronologically laid out. The phenomena, in Heidegger's words, "is held," is safeguarded for us, but in an indeterminate, open manner—full of possibilities. With no directional guidance provided it is not clear where or "how" you would go, or why—just as is the case in a thoughtfully engaged lifeworld. Additionally, Libeskind has provided for an unusually wide range of physical and cognitive experiences in a very subtle manner. There certainly are layers of meaning available that are not signaled in the building itself, yet, he tells us,

> Light and the kinetic experience of the body are translated through the windows of the museum. Although this may sound intellectual or complex, the museum is meant to be experienced by people who have never read about the Holocaust or who do not know much about it. The task of the museum is to introduce light to the body in a corporeal way—to the legs and to the feet, so to speak.[70]

For example, as we will see, the alternative paths and spaces just mentioned are such that many may not be noted or paid much attention; even the three major axes and exhibition spaces are anything but linearly, much less hierarchically patterned.

Figure 2.3. Old museum (*left*); new museum (*right*)

As to the inattentive mode of experience: upon arriving, signs direct one to the museum entrance, which is to the north of the new museum, through a doorway in the older yellow building. On entering the shared foyer one may not notice anything special. You do not find a traditional large lobby or other central, symmetrical area from which the exhibition spaces branch off; rather the entry space is modest, even bland, and rather busy, if not a bit cramped. To the left there is the ticket counter, then one finds the bag check, a doorway and signage to a courtyard and café, the entrance to the new museum, and tucked away to the side of that the museum shop and the exit door. Upon going into the new museum one's ticket is taken, after which you find a flight of stairs downward to a corridor which leads to a more fully lit space. Only here have you actually arrived inside the new museum itself. Perhaps there is nothing notable here, just the experience of getting into the museum, functionally maneuvered. Or, one might note that it is a bit odd to go down a rather long stairway that is not as brightly lit as passageways normally are in public buildings.

In contrast, however, with closer attention or an understanding from the plans, a first impression is of the marked difference between the two museums. The older, traditional building in its Charlottenburg yellow is

Figure 2.4. Interior steps downward into new museum

aligned with the street it fronts, whereas the radical zigzag of the Jewish Museum, with its zinc façade and fenestration that appears as random slashes, does not. If one is aware of the ideas incorporated by the architect, you realize that the only way to enter the new museum is through the old one: on the level of cultural meaning, there is the insistence that the past cannot be fully avoided—the background history and physical fabric of the city provides the only entry point. Even if the only way in is through Berlin's history, you are at the first of a series of continuous decision points. Here you have to ask yourself: "Do I want to enter the older Berlin City Museum and see the city's story without major emphasis on the removal of the Jews (first or at all)? Or, do I want to go this other way to engage the presence and absence brought forth by the Jewish Museum and its autonomous collection?" If at the beginning you ignore altogether or skip the exhibitions in the old museum because you are focused on seeing the new museum, you have to go down rather far—ten meters[71]—not so conveniently, to and through a rather steep, darkened stairway angled sideways (to the left), with muted lighting only on the edges, so that perhaps you are glad for the handrail, and then through a corridor. Is this a sort of "journey" or "quest" in which the hero descends into the underworld, to a series of challenges before being able to rise again (perhaps a meaning reinforced by the labyrinthine character of the rest of the building)? Is it, less epically, an exercise in subtle haptic awareness of steep descent and then gradual ascent or a directive to your eyes and legs (via gravity) to go more slowly than you might otherwise, to be a bit more careful and attentive to the spaces you find?

The below-ground entry corridor opens to a larger, better-lit space, whose white, black, and gray surfaces provide a cool, calm atmosphere. Moving directly to the museum proper (going past the E. F. Ross Gallery for special exhibitions and the Rafael Roth Learning Center on the right) one encounters the network of three axes, though this is not obvious because there are display cases in or along one's path. That is, there is no single point at which one can stand and simultaneously see all three axes. The "intersection" occurs "around" a three-sided solid into which are set display windows—which are lower to the ground than usual to make it easier for children to see what is there (the museum's brochure points out the concern with being able to "speak to the family").[72] In attending to the contents of the displays in these small built solids a good deal of focus is required, largely because of the low level of lighting inside the cases and the small print of the interpretive texts. Thus the three main axes are not presented as "the" gestalt; further, the corridors themselves are neither presented nor perceived in terms of a privileged route or preferred hierarchy. Thus, my intent is not to trace all the possible combinations here but to give some idea of the major likely experiences.

The museum's master brochure wisely shows three simple axes. Indeed, Libeskind calls these "roads" that may lead us one way or another. They would be understood to beckon to us, inviting us to move as we choose. That the axes are largely underground is not clear as you go through the building. Likely one does not even think about where ground level is; it does not matter much since one is not looking out windows but along the axes and into display cases. Fundamentally the museum provides an inward, centripetal orientation.

For example, if one leaves the main corridor by first going off to the right (research shows that Americans, probably because of the convention of driving on the right side of the road but possibly because of right-hand dominance or other factors overwhelmingly tend to choose pathways that go to the right—a fact exploited in the design of amusement parks and department stores), you move along the Axis of the Holocaust, along the windows of displays of objects witnessing the sad story to the sober volume at the terminus. You retrace the path to the main intersection next to go along the second axis to the right—the Axis of Exile—the way of escape, which tells the story of possible hope that culminates in a external environment that makes "escaped" and "outside" somewhat disorienting. You then retrace that path to the intersection and again turning right take the Axis of Continuity to the exhibitions covering the full history, passing all the way through, perhaps emerging with a sense that life goes on, past the horrors of the past—in other words dealing with the hard reality without forgetting but finding an opening beyond it—to other crucial issues to be sure, but with a restored sense of moving to an open future.

A rather different experience would be likely if one first went straight along the main Axis of Continuity to the exhibitions of the overall Jewish

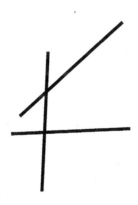

history, then after coming back down the main stairway went off to the left along the Axis of Exile, which might seem to fit into and elaborate part of the overall history, confirming and enlivening that prospect of an alternative life, though then one would be caught up short by finishing with the Axis of the Holocaust—and its dead end—facing more brutally, as it were, the Holocaust itself. Or, in another variation, if you first went up the Axis of Continuity and came back down next to explore the Axis of the Holocaust, after being sobered by the path of death and ending with the Axis of Exile you might regain a sense that mercifully the worst was not in store for everyone since a large number went on (which might loop your reflection back to the history of continuity).

To describe each of the paths in a bit more detail, I will follow the first itinerary: Path of the Holocaust, Path of Exile, Path of Continuity.

Axis of the Holocaust   The Axis of the Holocaust takes us up a rather steep incline, which though not visually emphasized is clearly noticeable and certainly is operative: we are subconsciously aware on the haptic level of a subtle sense of weightiness,[73] past the sobering exhibition of artifacts such as personal effects (suitcases, letters not sent or given for safekeeping) and the stories they bear on the way to "extermination," as Libeskind bluntly names it.[74] Of course, how much these exhibitions mean depends in large part upon what one knows, ranging from a first encounter for some (young or old alike) to bitter memories for families of Holocaust victims. At the end of the corridor is a large door, often with several people waiting outside with especially serious looks on their faces. On opening the door you find it to be unusually heavy and hard to move. It closes behind you— perhaps surprisingly—with a disconcerting thump, the heavy door weighted to swing itself shut—with the finality of a bank vault being locked. On entering, there is nothing to see.

You find yourself in a confined space with tall, bare concrete walls and a very high "ceiling" that you have to crane your neck to see—as if at the bottom of a sealed tower with only a little light coming in indirectly from a single narrow vertical slot at the top.[75] You feel small and alone, even when there are others there, because of the unusual severity of the space— intimidatingly large and confined all at once—and the silence. After few moments you can become aware of some noise from outside, perhaps traffic. It is easy to feel subject to what is given, to imagine what it is like being inside a transport boxcar, aware of the outside but not in direct contact with it, the outside world oblivious to you inside and you having no way out. At one "end" of the room, away from the door, where two walls come

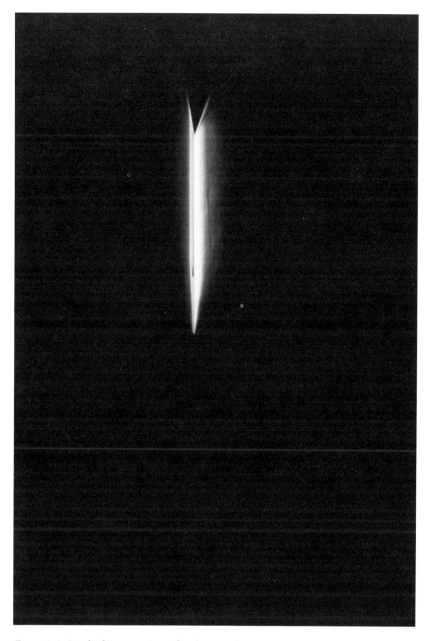

Figure 2.5. Inside the tower, Axis of Holocaust (long exposure has exaggerated the brightness)

together at a severe, oblique angle, people try out the darkest "corner," almost wedging themselves in there (since there are a few other people in the space, and since others peer in without entering, there is some small amount of noise that is distracting or disturbing in the unusually quiet and stark setting, thus interrupting the experience and reflection). If your eyes have adjusted to the low light level you can note that this spot is worn or marked by the bodies of those who have pressed themselves there, especially where they have rubbed their arms and hands. Sometimes there are a few visitors discreetly standing close to that corner so as to be next to go to that tight, not quite enclosing area. As you leave you may experience a moment of not quite panic but certainly distress when you try to open the door to leave, but it won't open—if you start to push your way out, the door doesn't budge. It takes a few seconds to hit on the solution: Move it the other way: pull it open. Whether to pull or push is not something one remembers after the entry experience (because you were focusing on what was to come and because the memorable, disconcerting slam of the door behind you likely overrode any memory of which way you swung the door to enter).

Axis of Exile The pathway along the corridor of the Axis of Exile leads past more windows of exhibited artifacts and interpretive information to a point where somewhat unexpectedly (and, quite differently, one realizes in retrospect) it ends at a rather ordinary door, through which you pass to find yourself outside the building, in a space filled with a few green plants and a large set of decidedly angled concrete "columns" or stele with trees growing from their tops.[76]

The trees are identified along the way as olive willows (and variously as willow oak), and the columns turn out to be ordered in a square. They are, however, on a somewhat steep slope, thus presenting themselves to the visitor as quite tilted. The environment again stimulates and correlates the haptic and visual dimensions. The slant is strong enough to give you the feeling of being off balance or even of tipping over as you wander among the columns. The architect explains:

> I think architecture begins simultaneously with the head and the feet. One has to experience it seeing it from afar and by walking through it. Later one might actually think about it, but I think one experiences it first with one's ankles and shoes. In my opinion, that is where it begins. It begins at the ground. The E. T. A. Hoffman Garden represents an attempt to completely disorient the visitor. It

represents a shipwreck of history. One enters it and finds the experience somewhat disturbing. Yes, it is unstable; one feels a little bit sick walking through it. But that is accurate, because that is what perfect order feels like when you leave the history of Berlin.[77]

There is not anything, however, to be found here, simply the chance to move around among the columns while feeling contained "within" their space since they are high enough and close enough together to hold you centripetally rather than encouraging any looking beyond. Conceptually you might have been informed, or figure out later, that just as this is the only outdoor space to be experienced, so there are forty-nine columns making up the square, which is the only geometrically ordered space in the project. After moving around a bit in the space, you realize that you need to go back inside through the same door and then back along the axis in reverse, back to the main intersection's "crossroads."

Axis of Continuity   Proceeding back to the crossroads and again turning right into the Axis of Continuity, you find it consists of a series of stairs, rising steeply upward and straight ahead (there is an elevator available, but this is not immediately obvious). Climbing the stairs takes some effort and a pause or two may be required. Here you encounter the strong shadows that play such a large part throughout the museum experience. The site is constituted not only of neutral spaces and light but of the robust interplay of light and dark, with all their connotations and associations, including evoked shades of the departed. Libeskind clearly considered this of major import and to be at the heart of the experience once the building was complete: "This is the moment of the built—the concrete, yet determinately spiritual testimony contained in each receding shadow of the names; in each ray of flickering light."[78]

Looking upward you are aware of a number of large shafts diagonally crossing overhead, emerging from one wall to pierce the one opposite—they seem like ominous intruders rather than comforting vertical structural supports. Here you are encountering the physical elements that instantiate the designer's lines that cut and interpenetrate one another, that cut and penetrate what is present as built and what is absent as the open space of the stairwell, as void, or in some other way (as in Heidegger's interpretation of design as cutting).

As a more subtle feature along the stairway there are a few small openings—one would not normally call them windows—which seem most likely to be simply a means of letting in a bit of outside light. But if you

Figure 2.6. E. T. A. Hoffman Garden

Figure 2.7. Stairway up the Axis of Continuity

bend your head the right way, you can see through them to the outside so that you are able to look at some of the building's exterior and part of the garden of columns and olive willows that you might have visited earlier. It is possible that you might imaginatively return in an "echo" back to the experience you had in the tower room of the Axis of the Holocaust, with its small bit of light coming in at the top and some outside traffic noise audible. Here you can catch a glimpse of what lies outside, though you remain within the story and experience of the museum. So, though looking out is not very comfortable, it certainly is possible; if you are interested, it allows you a bit of a chance to orient yourself to the outside or to try to piece together some of the organization of the building and the relationships of the spaces you have been through.

Along the way up the stairs, on the left is a doorway with no distinguishing marking indicating "special attraction." If you check to see what is through the entryway you find a space for changing exhibitions. But at first glance what is inside might not seem especially interesting and peripheral to one's goal of finding the core historical exhibitions (for example, in the summer of 2010 there was an exhibition here focusing on Argentina). If you do enter, you see that this interior exhibition space is itself quite large, subdivided according to the curators' plans, and not all observable from one spot. In the case of the Argentinean exhibition relating the terror of the military dictatorship there to that earlier in Germany, in addition to material on the walls, there was an opening cut into the floor, within which there were very small "books" with interpretive text explaining how the literary tradition in Argentina has been very important and is part of its cultural resistance to tyranny. In one of the back corners of this exhibition space there is another unmarked doorway; looking through it you see a corridor running off to the right.

In connection with the Argentinean exhibition this corridor was utilized as a "sidewalk of memory," with a series of tiles and plaques (*Bodenfliesen und Platten*) on the floor along one wall and then another space with memory cards placed there by visitors. The interpretive placards informed one that the exhibition tiles and plaques, on which were inscribed names of some of those disappeared in Argentina during the dictatorship from 1976 to 1983, was a development from a project originally generated by Gunter Demming in Köln in 1992 in which *Stolpersteine* bearing names of Gypsies and Jews murdered under the Nazis were set before the places where they lived. That movement spread, including to Argentina in 2006—and thence here to the museum. At the other end of the corridor is a space offering pieces of paper on which to write the names of anyone that a visitor would like to set down for remembrance. This easily could be taken to be the end of the project, in which case you would retrace your steps back through the larger exhibition to the Axis of Continuity.

Another subtle sensory clue, however, might beckon one on—as would the tendency to follow the flow of people (if there are others nearby at the moment). While in this corridor one hears faint sounds of metal clinking. Perhaps the sounds of the knives and forks, plates and cups being handled in the café kitchen or cafeteria? If you pursue the trail you come upon another striking scene: the Memory Void. You enter an enclosed volume, rising up several stories, the floor (which your bodily feeling might sense to be about ten meters long by three meters wide) is covered by small, oval metal plates, which on closer inspection are of many sizes and display a basic "face" of cut-out eyes and a mouth. The sound of clanking (which, now that you see the metal disks, is like that produced in a game of horseshoes when the shoes are thrown against an iron post) comes from people walking across the thousands of plates. The interpretive texts explain that this is a project by Menashe Kadishman called *Shalenkhet*: "Fallen Leaves," consisting of ten thousand metal faces. Evidently walking across the faceplates is encouraged. However, I could not bring myself to do it and strongly felt it was wrong to do so: after all, the plates clearly were faces, so how could one become so indifferent, especially in the museum's context of the dehumanization and murder of so many people, as to walk upon faces? That aversion came without thinking of Levinas's writings on the ethical injunction primally evoked by the face. But, others were treading about, though whether thoughtfully or not I did not ask any of the other visitors.

From here one needs to move back through the short corridor and larger exhibition space to the main stairway of the Axis of Continuity and continue walking upward. Upstairs, the main exhibition of Jewish history covers two floors—three thousand square meters the museum's brochure tells us—subdivided into small rooms and alternative pathways. The exhibitions are to be experienced in a continuous flow down from the upper to the lower level, which still is above the ground floor of the building (itself containing subdivisions). With surfaces dominantly in grays complemented by yellow-tans, the nonsymmetrical, trapezoidal gallery spaces are warmer than other parts of the building. Here and there small signs indicate and explain some of the voids, with small slits enabling you to peer into several of them, though there is "nothing" to see when looking in. (If you know it is the case, you understand that when the walls and ceiling are painted black, you are crossing a bridge from one of the seven "sub-buildings" to another across one of the invisible voids, but this is not part of any direct experience, which is that of moving through or along a corridor with black walls and ceiling.)[79] As you go through the main exhibition

Figure 2.8. "Fallen Leaves": ten thousand metal faces in the Memory Void

floors you also find there are strangely shaped slits (windows of a sort) that cut through the walls at odd angles, in a nonstandard way that ignores or violates the usual vertical-horizontal building grid and conventional manner of opening the façade.

In the horizontal gallery spaces we find artifacts displayed, though not so as to create further crossings of the lines in the way Libeskind originally intended.[80] The way Libeskind had explained his idea was that when a curator began to mount an exhibition, say of German textiles from 1920 to 1950, all the sorts of textiles designed by all the Germans in Berlin might be arranged chronologically up to a certain date, though then at that point the textiles designed by the Jews might go off in one direction and those by non-Jews in another. (Of course, the Jewish line soon would stop while the other line would continue.) Libeskind intended that curators use these intersecting lines to display the discontinuities, the stops and starts, in tradition. However, in 1988, at the last minute the administrative and political decision was made not to separate materials by date and then reintegrate the artifacts in the old and new buildings but instead to establish the Jewish Museum as an independent institution dealing with Jewish history not only in Berlin and Germany but on a worldwide scale.[81] Consequently, the Jewish Museum's collections and exhibitions became autonomous and the sole "occupant" of Libeskind's building.[82] (Knowing that the collections are in fact separate seemingly would bear on your interest in exploring the City of Berlin Museum, either when you made your original decisions on entering the buildings or when leaving the Jewish Museum Berlin if you started there.)

You can concentrate while moving through the exhibits to try to make sure that you loop around to see everything, or you can simply go from one set of items to another following the overall chronological story. The informed effort to cover it all unavoidably leads to some frustration as you find that a chosen pathway comes to a dead end or, in other cases, that from where you are you can't get to another part of the building you have not yet seen. Thus, for visitors of all levels of preparation and expectation, given that the exhibitions are not laid out according to a systematic or usual linear flow, because important spaces exist as fully or almost completely hidden, and since the usual physical and psychological fatigue sets in during a longish museum visit more is available than is likely to be found and pondered by anyone on a first visit or even after several.

Along the way down the two floors of material, in addition to the presentation of the detailed cultural artifacts and history, striking precedents and continuities between intolerance and harms from the distant past and the Holocaust are made explicit, such as when Jews were not allowed to live within or at times even enter cites, when persecuted medieval Jews were forced to wear yellow patches and distinctive hats, or when they were unjustly accused of bringing the pestilence to European towns and then burned alive. The story of gradual or periodic improvement—the Enlightenment's opening to partial inclusion or the fact that in 1871 German Jews were granted citizenship with equal rights in the new German Empire—provides some encouragement yet in the end perhaps makes matters seem even more discouraging in that any positive shift came crashing down before residual hatreds.

Exterior Spaces

The building has an exceptional exterior, as has been described; further, its relationship to its urban context is as consistently multiple as might be expected. The most striking aspects include the shape and material of the building and its fenestration. As noted earlier, the zigzag shape is not apparent to one approaching on ground level. Rather, what appears is a large metallic surface with confusing diagonal slots.

As to the zinc cladding, there are many stories. Libeskind, at various times, has noted, "I use, for example, zinc in the building, not the new zinc which is pre-weathered and already stabilized, but the more traditional form of zinc, which will take some years to become part of the city"[83] and that the zinc is used in reference to the Berlin buildings of Schinkel.[84] Or, more specifically, Libeskind and architectural critics have noted that zinc in fact is a common roofing material in Berlin, so the exterior also establishes a continuity with the urban context. At the same time, as Schneider points out, even if the zinc exterior refers to neighboring roofs, that connection is not likely to be noted experientially.[85]

Overall, the windows neither delineate any obvious pattern nor enable us to "make sense" of the interior (since the façade does not correlate with interior spaces or behaviors). The exceptions are that the slits on one façade may be discerned—by some—as forming a distorted Star of David and that a set of windows at the top of one side of the building, though oddly cut out, seem as if they probably serve office and administrative spaces.[86] More abstractly, Libeskind tells us, they are part of the imaginative weaving of the visible and invisible:

> The windows are the physical manifestation of a matrix of connections pervading the site. These "cuts" are the actual topographical lines joining addresses of Germans and Jews immediately around

Figure 2.9. Façade with window slits

the site and radiating outwards. The windows are the "writing of the addresses by the walls of the Museum itself."[87]

As noted earlier in discussing the design, the axes connecting the underground corridor with the Holocaust Void and the E. T. A. Hoffman Garden are largely underground. Thus, in the experience of the exterior these two spaces appear as separated, as nearby but autonomous. From the outside the building—likely *after* visiting the museum—the overall character of the garden is more apparent than when one is inside it, though as described earlier, from inside the museum one can enter the garden only after having exited from the end of the Axis of Exile. (The garden is separated from the outside by a low wall and in fact is accessible from the outside by a ramp, though that is not obvious when inside the garden.) Seen from the outside it is clear that there are a set of decidedly tilted concrete columns or stele that have plants growing out of their tops. Here we can appreciate Libeskind's description of the garden:

> It is the only orthogonal square form. It is the only perfectly right-angled form in the entire building. . . . It is an upside down garden with the earth remote inside concrete columns, roots above, hard ground below, and vegetation intertwined above—out of reach.[88]

In the museum grounds, for example, the Paul Celan Courtyard (that coincidentally provides the only above-ground access to the building), Libeskind continues the lines that drive his design in ground patterns of stones, mosaics, and other materials. Here the physical forms that demark and pragmatically implement the clear organization and conventions of our civic society (the painted stripes on our roadways, sidewalks with pedestrian and bicycle-lane systems marked by materials and colors that we know how to use) come to a crashing halt—in light of Heidegger's interpretation of design as cutting, their nonconforming orientation would seem a violence against conventional compliance, a refusal to align with what the "they" approve of and do (as critiqued in *Being and Time*).[89] There also is an open passage (a hole or short tunnel) with continuous paving that runs right through the building. The visible paving insets again display the intersection of lines that don't go anywhere. Experientially, not all the parts line up: here you can go "through" the building without going into it (the opposite of how you can't go into the new building without going through the older museum). Thus, there are a great many elements that either are strokes of genius or odd conceits.

Additionally, the building connects with more mundane neighborhood activities. For example, as one of the few critics to take note of the grounds,

Schneider observes that "rather than placing the building on a closed, defined lot, the architect was concerned with opening it on all sides to the life and activities of the city, including the children's playgrounds (the Walter Benjamin playground)" and the museum's meditation garden (the landscaping was by Cornelia Müller and Jan Wehberg)—spaces that have not gotten as much attention as the building.[90]

One building, or two, or seven? Autonomy of elements or complexly integrated whole? With all these alignments to spiritual, cultural, and physical elements and traces, to things visible and invisible, despite "appearances" the building is highly organized, though not in an obvious or superficially symmetrical manner. Clearly, Libeskind's museum involves much more than a strange, complex façade or peculiar interior volumes. Rather, as thoughtfully designed, built, and experienced it brings forth what happens "between the lines" that approach one another, in three dimensions, played out across the site. The physical and cultural dimensions, the relation to the exterior context and interior "content," and the built elements and voids that result from the generative figura of the fragmented, discontinuous line are all joined together in a building unlike any that most of us have ever experienced or imagined. As the architect tells us, in confronting what is exhibited as well as the void of the disappeared and the never-to-be, "every participant in the museum will experience [these phenomena as] absent presence"[91] and thus our past and future responsibility. In regard to the "encounter" noted above, Libeskind says: there is an emblem of hope—ethical architecture."[92]

> The task of building a *Jewish Museum* in Berlin demands more than a mere functional response to the program. Such a task in all its ethical depth requires the incorporation of the void of Berlin back into itself, in order to disclose how the past continues to affect the present and to reveal how a hopeful horizon can be opened through the aporias of time.[93]

Again, in the end, we are questioned. In our encounters today how are we disposed to deal with the other? How do the rest of us arrive at a moral response adequate to this past born of violence and appropriate for a future trajectory? Hopefully, together, by reestablishing a proper civic realm and public spaces for witness and action? How does the museum help us? By bringing the past and present together in a particular way? I would contend that the real design of the museum is that which draws us still, haunting us as we seek to respond appropriately when called to bear witness and act responsibly. How might other thinkers help?[94] Arendt and Levinas might continue to aid us in better understanding the phenomena of differences, of many voices and lives, of worlds that remain in collision.

The Testimony: Violence and Loss Cannot Annihilate Personhood or Responsibility

Dealing with presence and absence, always simultaneously to be both here and elsewhere, requires that we think nonmetaphysically, nonrepresentationally about not just the museum but also violence and testimony in order to encounter the phenomena in a mode proper to the primary level of the lifeworld. Levinas provides the guidepost when he says, "Metaphysics has the alibi that true life is absent"—but then counters, "no, we are in the world."[95] Heidegger also holds that, yes, we are in the world, where we do violence to nature and to one another. How do we make sense of this?

Earlier we saw that art works from the earliest human times and the high culture of Greece witness the continuous violence that marks our relation to the earth and its animals. Yet despite the efforts of the perpetrators of the Holocaust to reduce inmates' lives to a bare minimum, even to "dehumanize" and "objectify" them through the instrumentation of terror,[96] Levinas argues that compared to the killing that achieves a goal "as I hunt or slaughter animals" the murder of humans is a radically different phenomena and quite another kind of violence:

> Neither the destruction of things, nor the hunt, nor the extermination of living beings aims at the face, which is not of this world. They still belong to labor, have a finality, and answer to a need. Murder alone lays claim to total negation.[97]

Arendt, the great thinker of the difference between work and labor in light of political dignity, agrees with this point. Further, congruent with Heidegger's distinctions concerning how the meaning of technology changes in different historical epochs and pressing the point of the danger of conflating the functional and genuine action (a difference not explicit in what we have seen so far of Heidegger's gloss on *Antigone*), Arendt insists we take care to avoid the mistake of using the measure of *Homo Faber* for that of *Creatura Dei*.[98] That is, to see ourselves reductively only as producers (using nature's raw materials to produce our world and indeed ourselves) is to obliterate any classical sense either of our having a sacred dimension or of our political character (since "making ourselves" as social humans is a matter of action, not production). Arendt explains the distinctive features of violence against persons, that is political violence, by examining it in relation to terror, power, strength, force, and authority.

One of her central points is the difference between positive action and negative repressive violence. Violence may, in some instances, be the only way to "dramatize grievances and bring them to public attention" as a group tries to move toward reform or effectively resist "massacre and submission."[99] But, she argues, cases with such a "sense of justice" are the exception, found for instance in "the rebellion of the oppressed and downtrodden" that leads to the high political action of founding a state in order that the people are brought to be themselves.[100] Many of us hold that such positive force was exercised in the American Revolution. In contrast, unambiguously, the Holocaust was completely devoid of any positive libratory power; it was an event of incredible, murderous violence that negatively repressed the other.

But even such thoughtful analysis does not enable us to "make sense" of that to which the disappeared and their things testify. In her "Social Science Techniques and the Study of Concentration Camps," Arendt says that the Holocaust's concentration and extermination camps "are beyond human understanding" if we take that to mean using common sense, utilitarian rationality, or any conceptual ethical system.[101] Whereas any project of aggression, hostility, or exploitation, however reprehensible, nonetheless normally is intelligible in terms of self-interest at the expense of "the enemy" or victim, Arendt finds bizarre

> the non-utilitarian character of the camps themselves—the senselessness of "punishing" innocent people, the failure to keep them in a condition so that profitable work might be extorted from them, the superfluousness of frightening a completely subdued population . . . their anti-utilitarian function, the fact that not even the supreme emergencies of military activities were allowed to interfere with these "demographic policies."[102]

Only following the insane consistency with which the Nazis pursued the perverse logic of the initial assumptions brings us close to finding any "logic" at all.

The Jewish Museum and its artifacts, then, bear witness to repressive violence gone mad. But what does it mean to say that they testify to such extreme violence? What are the implications for us who, through the museum or in some other manner, witness that testimony? What would it be to comprehend the event of unimaginable loss? How could we think it? Levinas helpfully develops a nonconceptualizing position to explain what these phenomena disclose about our character as persons, our ethical responsibility, and the primal way we are engaged through testimony. In the first place, he argues, the event of witnessing does not involve a modern metaphysical subject (conceived as the being characterized by internalized consciousness and centripetal experiences) who might say "I saw it happen" to report a merely sensuous perception.[103] Second, the mode of understanding is not a matter of derivative abstractions or representations connecting any such private, interiorized consciousness and the external world.[104] Third, the ethical obligation disclosed is direct and primal, prior to any systematized ethics or set of rules and neither reducible to our psychological acts nor founded on any transcendental source.[105]

According to Levinas, the usual metaphysical mode of reporting and evaluating, however common and utilitarian, is not able, even in principle, to make contact with the primal world that matters most. Metaphysically and representationally understood:

> Testimony—the confession of some knowledge or of an experience by a subject—can be conceived only in relation to the disclosed being which remains the norm; it brings about only indirect truths about being, or about the relations man has with being. . . . The critique of testimony—by whatever method (the proliferation and comparison of testimonies, investigation into the credibility of the witness, etc.)—is necessary to draw out the truth (since the question is suppressed).[106]

Thus authentic testimony is not equivalent with a subject's experience; rather, it is the opening to the appearance of the real truth that unfolds through the witness. It occurs in the egress of the subject out of itself, out of its reserve, into a response to a summons (of and to the other)—specifically, into a responsibility to/for the other. We are given what is needed in

> the meaning of the subjectivity included in the everyday and extraordinary event of my responsibility toward other humans, that is, of my responsibility for the freedom of others, for a destiny that escapes my will. The freedom of the other will never have been able to originate in my own. . . . [107]

That is, it exceeds me. What occurs first, unfolding toward me as it enfolds me, is the responsibility for the other that is prior to all the other aspects:

> Responsibility for the other does not amount to a beginning: my relation with another freedom does not fit into a free decision. . . . Responsibility for the other precedes every decision, it is before the origin. An-archy.[108]

In the fundamental argument that a more primal, direct experience of responsibility must be acknowledged to replace what fails in representational conceptions Levinas famously contends that in direct confrontation the face of the other discloses the other as a human being and establishes our responsibility, unavoidably and prior to any theorization.[109] He takes it as uncontestable that the face presents—is—"the primordial expression, is the first word: 'you shall not commit murder.'"[110] In this event the ethical is first revealed. The face-to-face encounter between two persons does involve what we can still call subjectivity (as long as we distinguish it from the modern concept of the subject), in which the call is particularized to this situation and both the other and I are fully individualized.[111] It is precisely this other, before me here and now, as she is, who calls to me, summons me to a response. At the same time, the summons is directed to me alone, as irreplaceable.[112] We witness "the impossibility of slipping away and being replaced"; "to this command continually put forth only a 'here I am' can answer."[113]

With the museum, we have an initiatory nonconceptual response to the other (by the architect, by the gathering and holding together of the artifacts, and through the spaces that bid welcome and encourage visitors to reflect).[114] Additionally, we could apply Levinas's thoughts concerning names and calling to the testimony given by the things there and the life-worlds behind them calling to me. He holds that the name (proxy for the face) calls me: when my name is called, I cannot turn away. As Jean-Luc Marion notes in explicating Caravaggio's painting *The Calling of St. Matthew*, once the eyes of the other and mine meet, I can demure no further, initially resisting responsibility by trying to hold it off for a minute or two by querying back "Who, me?", already knowing that the answer is "Yes, you!" from which there is no further flight. In Levinas's terms, here we have an instance of the "summons of me by the other, where no one could stand in for me."[115] The force of the name to call is held and brought forth to us by the Jewish Museum, as Libeskind recognized in incorporating the *Gedenkbuch* and the life stories of the murdered into the core of his design. In this calling and response, this dialogue, no one is allowed to interrupt the direct encounter between me and the other; anyone else is, at least initially, outside and secondary. That is why the museum withdraws insofar as the things that it keeps themselves come forth to testify and call us.

Though neither any object nor any one is allowed to come between the two persons who are engaged face to face, because the persons are not subjects in the metaphysical sense of interior private consciousnesses there is no implication that the basic dialogue is hermetic or exclusionary. Quite the opposite: the fundamental person-other relationship opens to yet others and is that "by which justice arises."[116] Hence, Levinas goes further in his analysis to discuss how the face becomes—is—public because

> The third party looks at me in the eyes of the other—language is justice. . . . The epiphany of the face qua face opens humanity. . . . The thou is posited in front of a we. . . . [The response] to the epiphany of the face . . . [is] an irreducible movement of a discourse which by essence is aroused by the epiphany of the face inasmuch as it attests the presence of the third party, the whole of humanity, in the eyes that look at me.[117]

In addition to agreeing that behind the face that discloses itself there are yet others, Arendt provides a fuller account of how this primal one-to-one relationship comes into the full light of the public order. This shift does not lead to abstracting or generalizing responsibility but to appreciating the fact that it is social. The particular can become additionally individualized by many such encounters. The face that calls remains singular, the one called remains unique and irreplaceable, and the historic situation of the calling and response is shared by others yet still remains distinct with its own characteristics. "The greatest danger for a proper understanding of our recent history is the only too comprehensible tendency of the historian to draw analogies. The point is that Hitler was . . . entirely different."[118] Beyond this, it is the very particularity of the phenomena that gives it the power to open widely, to be comprehensible "to the whole of humanity."

According to Arendt, the witnessing of our public words and deeds is necessary in establishing the meaning of our actions and our identity because at any given moment and place it is "more than likely that the 'who,' which appears so clearly and unmistakenly to others, remains hidden from the person himself."[119] According to Arendt, "In contra-distinction to other elements peculiar to action—above all to the preconceived goals, the impelling motives, and the guiding principles, all of which become visible in the course of action—the meaning of a committed act is revealed only when the action itself has come to an end and become a story susceptible to narration."[120] "Action reveals itself fully only to the storyteller, that is, to the backward glance of the historian, who indeed always knows better what it was all about than the participants"; perhaps such is the case also because the significant "event illuminates its own past."[121] To be clear, however, this does not absolve us from the obligation to be communally reflective and responsible about ourselves. To the contrary, now, the entire circle of understanding comes round again: "the process of understanding [for example, totalitarian movements] is clearly, and perhaps primarily also a process of self-understanding."[122]

Insofar as Arendt is right that "who one is" is not accomplished until we are done with the course of our lives, then, in a strange way, who we have become again turns out to be a function of others, not only in that our words and deeds must be public but that only others who witness them can interpret what the testimony discloses and thus say what our life means, can say who we are. The site where I enact my life is none other than the political-ethical scene in which I am addressed in my particularity, as the unique one who is called to respond and whose mode of response or non-response establishes who am I. This Levinasian point coincides with Arendt's: who I become through public word and deed witnessed by others is who I am individually.

Accordingly, having found that the trail of testimony to the violence of the Holocaust calls on us to respond to the face of the other—of the neighbor, of those upon whom we come and who come upon us—we further need to ask, "What do we, the visitors, find in the museum's testimony about death? About the millions of deaths witnessed?"

While Arendt properly characterizes death as the most apolitical experience, in that through it we disappear from the shared world of appearances and leave the company of humans,[123] both she and Levinas insist that death is not the disclosure of nothingness but of the capacities and relationships of the human beings that we are. This is a critical point since one of the intentions common to acts of hatred and murder, and certainly prominent in the Holocaust, is to "degrade" or "eliminate" the other. There are many modes in which those filled with hatred attempt to reduce the victimized other: to an object, to the minimal organic living condition, to the totally predictable. Arendt's perceptions of murder brought about through "accumulated terror"[124] that proceeded by first bringing its victims to "the lowest common denominator of organic life itself"[125] and in "monstrous equality without fraternity or humanity" have, of course, been developed since by Agamben with his ideas concerning "bare life," which does not need to be re-covered here.[126] Her own analysis of "the use of terror to maintain domination"[127] stresses that

> The concentration camps are the laboratories in the experiment of total domination. . . . Total domination is achieved when the human person, who somehow is always a specific mixture of spontaneity and being conditioned, has been transformed into a completely conditioned being whose reactions can be calculated even when he is led to certain death. . . . The end result is the reduction

of human beings to the lowest possible denominator of "identical reactions."[128]

More radical still than dominion is the drive behind the Holocaust to eliminate the Jews (as well as many other ethnic groups, those whose sexual orientation was disapproved, and "sick persons" as specified by Hitler under the proposed National Health Bill).[129] Arendt argues that there is convincing evidence that the perpetrators of the Holocaust were not primarily concerned with control of the population by terrorizing them but instead with totally erasing the hated other, that is, with attempting literally to consign these people to oblivion. For instance, in the later phases of the war years, victims of concentration and extermination simply disappeared rather than being used as the basis "to spread horrible stories":

> From the moment of his arrest, nobody in the outside world was supposed to hear of the prisoner again; it is as if he had disappeared from the surface of the earth; he was not even pronounced dead.[130]

Opposite to operating in the public realm, as Arendt reports quoting documentation gathered after the war,

> It was strictly ordered that "third persons (are to be left) in uncertainty as to the whereabouts of prisoners." . . . This also includes the fact that the relatives may not learn anything when such prisoners die in concentration camps.[131]

Certainly "the violence of war and murder is a negativity" and in many circumstances seeks "to reduce our response [to the face] to silence," which makes all the more clear the "importance of speaking, of witness."[132]

Despite all this, both Levinas and Arendt, partially in critique of Sartre's ideas in *Being and Nothingness* and their source in Heidegger's early work on Being, death, and nothingness, argue that murder and the deaths of the victims does not lead to nothingness. Within his larger project of thinking beyond Being, Levinas sets aside the metaphysical, philosophical, and religious traditions within which we might situate our understanding of death as either a passage to another mode of being "continuing in another setting" (as covered in the first part of this chapter) or as nothingness. In the subject matter we are considering here, his relevant move in "the refusal of that ultimate alternative" is against seeing death as the opening to nothingness.[133]

Levinas's basic move is to explain how death in fact connects me to "what is against me" rather than to annihilation. In contrast to Arendt, who contended that the extreme solitude of death marked it as apolitical, Levinas argues that it is a relation to the other. In the first place, in death we come to face the menace against my living, as might occur through sickness, accident, or other means. Even more immediately than death, which he takes to lie in the future as far as our existential experience goes, we may have pain and suffering right now. Hence, focusing on our immediate experience and fear in relation to my bodily being, he says, "Thus the fear for my being which is my relation to death is not the fear of nothingness, but the fear of violence—and thus it extends into fear of the Other, of the absolutely unforeseeable."[134] In this fear and suffering we find the range of possible relations to the other. On the positive side,

> The solitude of death does not make the Other vanish, but remains in a consciousness of hostility [to my life], and consequently still renders possible an appeal to the Other, to his friendship and his medication. The doctor is an a priori principle of human mortality. Death approaches in the fear of someone, and hopes in someone. "The Eternal brings death and brings life." A social conjuncture is maintained in this menace. It does not sink into the anxiety that would transform it into a "nihilation of nothingness."[135]

Hence, Levinas finds that here, beyond what metaphysical philosophy or religion hold as explanations, even in regard to our bodily being we encounter "behind the threat [death] brings . . . , its reference to an interpersonal order whose significance it does not annihilate."[136]

Of course, the menace against me that I face and the congruent relationships with others may be darker still, more fearful than the suffering because of disease or accident. But even in the extreme phenomena of murder, Levinas holds that rather than the annihilation that metaphysical thinking would perceive, relationships with the other are sustained and manifest: "Murder, at the origin of death, reveals a cruel world, but one to the scale of human relations."[137] Despite what would appear to be the case, the ordinary assumption (which in our everyday life is still metaphysical) that death is directed toward nothingness is not confirmed.

> In the whole philosophical and religious tradition . . . as it were a priori we approach death as nothingness in the passion for murder. The spontaneous intentionality of this passion aims at annihilation. . . . The identifying of death with nothingness befits the death of the other in murder. But at the same time this nothingness presents itself there as a sort of impossibility. For the Other cannot present himself as Other outside of my conscience, and his face expresses my moral impossibility of annihilating. This interdiction is to be

sure not equivalent to pure and simple impossibility, and even pre-supposes the possibility which precisely it forbids—but in fact the interdiction already dwells in this very possibility rather than presupposing it; it is not added to it after the event, but looks at me from the very depths of the eyes I want to extinguish. . . . The movement of annihilation in murder is therefore a purely relative annihilation, a passage to the limit of a negation attempted within the world. In fact it leads us toward an order of which we can say nothing, not even being, antithesis of the impossible nothingness.[138]

Self-contradiction, then, unavoidably vitiates the intention to obliterate by murder. Everything that comes to me from the other (*autrui*) starting from being in general certainly offers itself to my comprehension and possession. I understand him in the framework of his history, his surroundings and habits. What escapes comprehension in the other (*autrui*) is him, a being. I cannot negate him partially, in violence, in grasping him within the horizon of being in general and possessing him. The Other (*Autrui*) is the sole being whose negation can only announce itself as total: as murder. The Other (*Auturi*) is the sole being I can wish to kill.

I can wish. And yet this power is quite the contrary of power. The triumph of this power is its defeat as power. At the very moment when my power to kill realizes itself, the other (*autrui*) has escaped me. I can, for sure, in killing attain a goal. I can kill as I hunt or slaughter animals, or as I fell trees. But when I have grasped the other (*autrui*) in the opening of being in general, as an element of the world where I stand, where I have seen him on the horizon, I have not looked at him in the face, encountered his face. The temptation of total negation, measuring the infinity of this attempt and its impossibility—this is the presence of the face. To be in relation with the other (*autrui*) face to face is to be unable to kill. It is also the situation of discourse.[139]

Even in murder, there is the undeniable, nondestroyable encounter of two persons, of each other to the other. Beyond his "generous" presentation of the phenomenological structure in terms of what might be my intention to the other, of course, in the Holocaust the murders are those done unto the Jews (the victims, with whom the reader no doubt identifies). In developing the hatred behind murder Levinas, without announcing it, shifts perspective and voice to match what would be the perspective of the victims and empathetic readers. Again he focuses on the immediacy of suffering and the "not quite yet" of death:

[In suffering] we still witness this turning of the I into a thing; we are at the same time a thing and at a distance from our reification. . . . The supreme ordeal of freedom is not death, but suffering This is known very well in hatred, which seeks to grasp the ungraspable, to humiliate, from on high, through the suffering in which the Other exists as pure passivity. Hatred wills this passivity in the eminently active being that is to bear witness to it. Hatred does not always desire the death of the Other, or at least it desired the death of the Other only in inflicting this death as a supreme suffering. The one who hates seeks to be the cause of a suffering to which the despised being must be witness. To inflict suffering is not to reduce the Other to the rank of an object, but on the contrary is to maintain him superbly in his subjectivity. In suffering the subject must know his reification, but in order to do so he must precisely remain a subject. Hatred wills both things. Whence the insatiable character of hatred; it is satisfied precisely when it is not satisfied, since the Other satisfies it only by becoming an object, but can never become object enough, since at the same time as his fall, his lucidity and witness are demanded. In this lies the logical absurdity of hatred.[140]

Thus, in what perhaps are their deepest insights into violence, murder, testimony, and the human person, Levinas and Arendt each come to the "conclusion" that the attempted consignment to oblivion of hatred and murder is self-defeating. The personhood of the victim is affirmed in the act that would obliterate it: "[murderous] violence can aim only at a face" and thus inherently affirms the face of the intended victim.[141]

But, in the same breath, Levinas presents us with a correlate hard truth: just as murder can only aim at a face, so too only a face is capable of committing murder. The violence that endures through the hateful act of murder "comes from the other as a tyranny": "It is produced only in a world where I can die as a result of someone and for someone."[142] In the case where I have a chance to resist my murderer, "[my] will that refuses the foreign will is obliged to recognize this foreign will as absolutely exterior": "Th[is] Other cannot be contained by me: he is unthinkable—he is infinite and recognized as such."[143] Hence, beyond the benign or needy Other whom I encounter (including the "someone" for whom I would die), there is another Other (at the hands of whom I can die), a point that Levinas emphasizes rather than downplays: "Th[is] Other, inseparable from the very event of transcendence, is situated in the region from which death, possibly murder, comes."[144] Though Levinas's reflections are able to incorporate Arendt's insistence that we cannot excuse ourselves from ethical obligation by differentiating ourselves from "the guilty"—"The reality is that 'the Nazis are men like ourselves'; the nightmare is that they have shown, have proven beyond doubt what man is capable of"[145]—his point is more shocking. Once we are over the surprise of explicitly realizing the ontological and ethical "status" of those who hate us, we find that we are called to a primal responsibility harder than might have been imagined: we need to acknowledge the undeniable, indestructible, irreducible personhood of murderers just as that of the victims. We need to find the appropriate—which is not to say identical—way to respond ethically to both of the "opposed" faces that disclose themselves in violent, oppositional events.

How we could so respond to deal with not only the core violence but this seemingly perverse "paradox" remains open. Arendt calls on us to find a way that ends the cycles of mutual hatred that though comprehensible in their reasons continue to poison us and preclude any movement to a public reconciliation or at least to a nonviolent, tolerant way forward. In what would be called a "hard saying," in dedicating a book to Karl Jaspers in 1947 she writes,

> The factual territory onto which both peoples have been driven looks something like this: On the one side is the complicity of the German people, which the Nazis consciously planned and realized. On the other side is the blind hatred, created in the gas chambers, of the entire Jewish people. Unless both peoples decide to leave this factual territory, the individual Jew will no more be able to abandon his fanatical hatred than will the individual German be able to rid himself of the complicity imposed upon him by the Nazis. . . .
>
> In the context of . . . a world still intact despite all the hostility in it, the possibility of communication between peoples and individuals remains. We are spared the blind and eternal hatred that inevitably seizes us if we accept the consequences of the facts the Nazis created.[146]

As I have argued above, with Levinas and Arendt it is the very particularity of persons involved in a given situation that is critical to ethical calling, response, and responsibility; it is just such concrete individuation that has the power to open widely, to be comprehensible "to the whole of humanity."[147] Witnessing and reflection are the means to retain the specificity and thus open the possibility of broadening matters into the public realm—as the means to engaging others toward the future.

In regard to the museum itself, I contend that whether we personally like it or not, Libeskind's building does give testimony: it stands as a memorial that bids us to think by inviting us in so that we can stand open to and consider things (and absences) that themselves genuinely bear witness. The real point of the museum is not to call attention to itself. Rather, it provides the place for the exhibitions where the things themselves evoke the experience in the individual visitor. The artifacts displayed are not objects, not dead remainders (though as noted earlier, they can be reduced to such through patterns of production and consumption); these things more robustly are part of the lifeworld. The task has been and remains to show them in such a way that they show, let vibrate, let resonate their lifeworld. Again we return to the power these things have to hold their world—a world of violation and obliteration that has been destroyed. The things still hold that world in memoriam. They bear world, as Heidegger says. They bear witness to a world that is gone, a world not going to be, and out of that a world we are called toward yet have to make. The museum then would be profound: it is a thing that gathers and holds things that in turn gather, hold, and witness worlds for us—and issues upon which we need to reflect. The museum then is a kind of call. It is a response to a situation, but it further calls us to see what we are going to do.

However we finally interpret the museum environment and experience, Libeskind himself explicitly intends us to encounter it not as an autonomous object but in terms of the particularity of German Jewish culture in Berlin, which, in turn, belongs to the relation of the Jewish tradition to German culture overall and is integrally part of the historical realm of modernity, of the nuclear and postnuclear age in which we live. He says,

> I believe this scheme joins architecture to questions that now are relevant to all humanity. What I have tried to say is that the Jewish history of Berlin cannot be separated from the history of Modernity, from the destiny of this incineration of history; they are bound together. But bound together not through any obvious forms, but rather through faith; through the absence of meaning and an absence of artifacts. Absence therefore serves as a way of binding in depth, and in a totally different manner, the shared hopes of a people. It is a conception which does not reduce the museum or architecture to a detached memorial or to a memorable detachment. A conception, rather, which re-integrates Jewish/Berlin History through the unhealable wound of faith, which in the words of Hebrews (11: II) is the "substance of things hoped for; proof of things invisible."[148]

But the architect's words already take us too far, too fast. As Heidegger might say, perhaps it is best here to break off and let things be. The design is so complex that we need to pause, staying with the design—the drawing and the incision into the city—so that it might resonate for us. The meanings and possible interpretations are so multiple that we need to continue thinking in a way that allows them to unfold so that we can take them to heart.

As Wim Wenders' marvelous film *Wings of Desire* [*Der Himmel über Berlin*] shows us, human life, ordinary things, and our built environments involve haunting failures and possibilities, breathtaking moments of lost and seized responses to what is mysteriously given to us. Though one cannot be simultaneously human and angelic, to be mortal and finite is to have the potential to realize values in the world that will not come about in any other way. Daniel Libeskind attempts the same thing as Wenders does, not by doctrinaire or ideological deconstructive maneuvers but by responding to the existential situation encountered in Berlin and the moral task of designing and building so as to hold on to the meaning of that special place and to open to our larger, shared contemporary world.

3

When the Given Is Gone
From the Black Forest to Berlin and Back
via Wim Wenders' Der Himmel Über Berlin

Givenness and Coming to Visibility

What once was given is gone. We have rehearsed the story of the loss of a coherent world many times. The order provided by cultural realms such as the Greek polis, the Roman Empire, medieval Christendom, Renaissance Europe, nineteenth- and twentieth-century nationalisms and technological inventions is long gone, replaced by the unfulfilled promise of globalism that has fractured into myriad competing localisms, even provincialisms—as if we were back before Homer with each valley a suspicious stranger of the next. Now, the last rural ways of life, which have managed to persist because of remote locations, succumb to the lures of the cities, to unfavorable economic pressures, and to the advances of large-scale agribusiness and tourism. Nor, at present, have our burgeoning metropolitan areas fared any better, as is seen in urban unemployment and homelessness, class and racial fracturing, and environmental pollution apparently beyond the point of reversal.

Further, as Heidegger and many others convincingly argue, the greatest displacement occurs in another dimension: we find ourselves without any grounding. The modern age has subordinated the metaphysical to the epistemological; along with that, dominating humanistic science has replaced God with explanations of natural elements, forces, and processes—not to mention that God was found absent by many during the Holocaust and that He is hard to discern in the hardening of hearts all too typical in resurgent fundamentalisms. With the destructive technology generated by science through two world wars and the nuclear age, with global climatic and ecological destruction wrought by the systems of the epoch of *Gestell*, with the poststructuralist undercutting of still powerful though untenable positivist criteria and procedures, and with feminist and postcolonial warnings not to essentialize, we find ourselves without any sure foundations or direction.

Hence we are well advised to attend to any clues we have as to what is happening, as to what we might do. Both Martin Heidegger and Wim Wenders offer material for reflection. Set in Germany in the aftermath of the bombing of World War II, Heidegger's modest "homey" lectures and Wim Wenders' film *Wings of Desire* [*Der Himmel Über Berlin*] address us from the midst of what still is our current situation. As Heidegger describes the physical and cultural scene,

> Many Germans have lost their homeland, have had to leave their villages and towns, have been driven from their native soil. Countless others whose homeland was saved, have yet wandered off. They have been caught up in the turmoil of the big cities, and have resettled in the wastelands of the industrial districts. They are strangers now in their former homeland. And those who have stayed on in their homeland? Often they are still more homeless than those who have been driven from their homeland. Hourly and daily they are chained to the radio and television. Week after week the movies carry them off into uncommon, but often merely common, realms of the imagination, and give the illusion of a world that is no world. . . . All that with which modern techniques of communication stimulate, assail, and drive man—all that is already much closer to man today than his fields around his farmland, closer than the sky over the earth, closer than the change from night to day, closer than the conventions and customs of his village, than the tradition of his native world. . . .
>
> What is Happening here? . . . The loss of rootedness springs from the spirit of the age into which all of us were born.[1]

Though the buildings of today's technological domain house us, they are not dwelling places. Still, since we do need to be housed,

> In today's housing shortage even this much is reassuring and to the good; residential buildings do indeed provide shelter; today's houses may even be well planned, easy to keep, attractively cheap, open to air, light, and sun, but—do the houses in themselves hold any guarantee that *dwelling* occurs in them?[2]

Figure 3.1. Angel looking down from Berlin's Kaiser-Wilhelm-Gedächtnis Kirche

Wenders shows us a parallel world. What remains given when the civilized heritage of a culture, when God himself, are gone? People and, surprisingly, according to Wenders, angels. *Wings of Desire* opens with shots of a cloud-filled sky (heavens; *Himmel*) and a bird's-eye view of postwar Berlin, with a winged angel looking down from the top of the Kaiser-Wilhelm-Gedächtnis Kirche (Memorial Church) [1003–06].[3] The camera then descends to the midst of the world of the Berliners, where a series of point-of-view shots reveal what the guardian angels see. After a series of shots of residents (notably parents and children) in the streets and of the activities in Scharoun's City Library filled with readers (though we also are given several reciprocal perceptions of children), the angels, especially Damiel and Cassiel, observe how the Berliners are weighed down by the burdens of life. Image after image unfolds of bodies bent under the daily regime, of heads bowed in fatigue and distress. In the U-Bahn riders are bored, tired, and weary. Throughout the city, and especially in their apartments, inhabitants are isolated, cut off from one another. Or, only marginally better, some stare down at nothing, "spaced out" as we used to say, while alone listening to loud music or absorbed in television [1031–34]. The angels can hear what people are thinking (as conveyed through voiceovers): parents are simultaneously fed up with and worry about their children, a man visits his deceased mother's residence, couples fight, people wonder how they will be able to pay for the things of daily life or for much-needed doctors on their meager incomes, a child feels left out of the play of three of his acquaintances, and even a circus finds itself bankrupt. In a long

Figure 3.2. Damiel comforting forlorn man

take Damiel puts his arm around a forlorn man's shoulders, comforting the latter, who is thinking of his parents who have disinherited him, his wife who has been unfaithful, his friend who has moved to another city, his children who only remember his speech defect [2003].

Along with the depression in the midst of the grayness of everyday urban life, Wenders gives us more dramatic events. Throughout the film, we are shown images of the horrors of World War II, of those dead from the bombings, of residents moving about the destroyed city. In the contemporary scene, there is an accident. A Mercedes has collided with a motorbike, whose rider, thrown to the curb, lies dying [2059–62]. In another long take, the car's passengers and some residents stand by as onlookers; Damiel holds the dying man in his arms while from the periphery one young man runs to the rescue. Later, a prostitute works under an U-Bahn bridge, finally crying at her situation [3002–06].

Though it does not quite rise to the level of functioning as a motif, given the stark postwar conditions, Wenders' recurrent use of consumer objects and spaces (BMW showrooms, Mercedes Benz automobiles and headquarters) as settings is pointed enough—these mise-en-scènes emphasize how life quietly succumbs not only to the impoverished urban environment but to the pressures of its opposite, capitalism's surplus. As the philosopher Jean-Luc Marion describes the technological challenge to any genuine dwelling:

We can also consider the phenomenon that perhaps most contradicts the phenomenality of habitation: that is, the monstrous com-

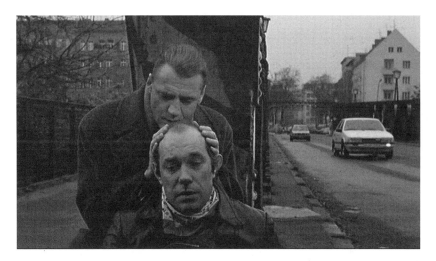

Figure 3.3. Damiel holding dying accident victim

mercial city, almost unlimited and without form, oozing its own vulgarity, awash in items for sale. I obviously do not know its dimensions or residents, nor the shipyards, shareholders, bottom line, or financial results. . . . These phenomena (and numerous others) share one exceptional property: I no longer simply remain outside them, as if faced with what is an object to me, at the distance of intentionality and manipulation; rather they happen to me or arrive over me like what successively shelters me, embraces me, distracts me—in short, imposes on me. I can enter and yield to them or withdraw and exit them; but in all cases I must inhabit them or (what amounts to the same thing) be exiled. On principle, I must habituate myself to them.[4]

But, if as Marion indicates, "inhabiting them calls less for building and thinking than for habituating oneself," how do I accomplish the latter? By withdrawing inward, into "classic" alienation? Wenders gives us many images of urban residents closed in upon themselves. A suicide perches atop the Mercedes Center. Cassiel comes to his side in an effort to comfort him, first putting a hand on the man's shoulder, then back. But the man jumps to his death anyway as his circumstances and lack of prospects prove too much [4037–39].

Yet we also see people connected to the outside world—by way of images that are decidedly more positive. Counter to the possibility that we might habituate ourselves only by self-enclosure, in the library people read and reflect, quietly focusing on works that connect them to what is outside themselves: they learn about the natural world, explore mathematics and history. As already noted, the angels and we do witness positive moments and dimensions in the city. Someone does run to the accident victim. Children play and retrieve a lost coin with a magnet, lovers meet and embrace, the circus entertains, even a weary extra laughs as Peter Falk sketches her [3057–68] while on set to make a movie, as does Cassiel when Falk tries on hats [3034–39]. In an ambulance on its way to the hospital with a pregnant woman, while her husband holds her hand, Damiel puts his hand on her rotund stomach; amid the contractions, given the coming of her child, she laughs [1042–43]. After sober reflection on the grisly photographs of the dead and a walk through the city where even familiar haunts once located in the now destroyed Potsdamer Platz can scarcely be imaginatively relocated, the long-time resident and local storyteller Homer finds a little music box in a souvenir stand (labeled Andenkenladen—ironically in regard to Heidegger's etymologies).[5] It brings a spontaneous smile to Homer's face as it plays the melody "Das ist die Berliner Luft" ("That's Berlin Air") [2088]. There are good social experiences and interchanges, then, through which together we might come to habituate ourselves to the phenomena of the city.

For their part, as traditionally, the angels are guardians. Not divine messengers they, for there are no messages, nor would we expect word from the absent God. As guardians they witness what is given: the travails of life and its small pleasures. To the pains they caringly respond, bending tenderly over the fatigued, immediately holding life's victims—the intimacy

Figure 3.4. Angel (Cassiel) listening to reader in library

of the care often is underscored by eyeline matches between the angels and the person they are comforting. Sometimes the intended help is effective, sometimes not, which pains them as we see with Cassiel: a bit later, after the suicide's jump, having failed to make a difference, he rests high above the city on the powerful arm of the angel atop the victory column, then leaps into the void in a reciprocal gesture.

Correlate with Heidegger's *Andenken*, memorializing or recollective thinking, the angels witness and remember. So does one Berliner, the aforementioned Homer, as when in the library he ponders a book of wartime photographs of the dead, including many lying in the streets after bombing raids. The angels, however, remember it all, from before even the beginning of time. After an opening shot of an almost leafless tree surrounded by the flooding waters of the Wannsee, Cassiel and Damiel recall what they have seen in this place: from before history had begun, through creation, the ice age, and the greening of the earth and appearance of fish, animals, and birds, and the laughable coming of humans from whose shouts and calls the angels learned to speak—a long history after which stones flew and another history began—the history of war, from the Napoleonic era through World War II to the dreary city today—even as the first history of sun, grass, and air continues on [4001–4914].[6]

Importantly, despite their role as witnesses and guardians, whether the care is felt or not, the angels themselves—though given—are not visible to the Berliners (save to some children). The angels do not rise up into phenomenality for the inhabitants as they do for us or for each other. As Jean-Luc Marion describes the gift that is given as phenomena, it is the crossing of the invisible to the visible that "produces the phenomenality of the phenomena": "the arising into appearing of what gives itself in appearing always bears the mark of the ascent to the visible"—"a free and autonomous coming forward" that is not anything we create but arises from elsewhere.[7] Insofar as Marion is correct about the power of the visual arts and of our own genuine seeing (where in the critical event in experiencing a phenomenon, what matters is "seeing its coming up into visibility"), Wenders' film presents a substantial disparity between the Berliners on the one hand and the angels and viewing audience on the other (BG, 48). In *Wings of Desire*, though the angels are immediately "in contact" with the Berliners—often while positioned directly between two of them whom they see, overhear, and care for—the former themselves are not seen by the latter. None of the angels at the library are seen, nor is Damiel as he rides in the ambulance between the woman in labor and her man, hand on swollen belly, as he attends the victim at the accident scene, or watches Marion, the trapeze artist at the circus (the one-way vision is underscored by the conceit of

Figure 3.5. Damiel and Marion in her trailer: only one-way vision

Damiel watching Marion through her makeup mirror, while of course she sees only her own reflection).

Yet even given the constant solicitude of the angels and the light-hearted moments, overall, life appears grim. It is not just that the Berliners do not see the angels; they often fail to see the world around them. To a substantial extent, it too lies before them as invisible. As if *Wings of Desire* were an exploration of *Being and Time*, many Berliners are sunk in average everydayness and the objects about them; even their very existence is shrouded in its fog. In Jean-Luc Marion's terms, what comes to their consciousness is so low in intuition that it barely registers as experience. Little that is not negative (life threatening) rises to a significant level of intensity for the urbanites, resulting in the pervasive empty life as depicted by the shot of the Turkish woman at the laundromat, alone, her back to us, facing the cycling machines [5016–18].

Such is not the case for the angels. They do see everything with increasing appreciation as the film unfolds. Again Jean-Luc Marion is helpful here in explaining how things come to phenomenality insofar as the given washes over consciousness. The facticity of the given comes by way of "unpredictable landings" of phenomena. Crashing upon the receiver, "according to discontinuous rhythms, in fits and starts, unexpectedly, by surprise, detached from each other, in bursts," the given forces its way toward phenomenality—to visibility. "Our initiative is limited to remaining ready to receive the shock" (BG, 131–132). Obviously, in the case of the most saturated, the phenomena are not just "there to be looked at" but must be *re-*

ally seen, which is facilitated insofar as they almost, or actually, overwhelm one by crashing in as does a tornado hitting a building or a thunderstorm passing sublimely across a mountain valley.

The angels, not surprisingly, do not require such stimulation as we do. They are able to find that everything happening as a fait accompli, unpredictably and contingently in the course of life in the city, comes to them vividly (BG, 131–140). Hence, they become witnesses to a swath of what arrives to consciousness broader than any finite human is able to, and to a more substantial degree or depth. What might not appear to be saturated enough with intuitions to commandeer attention in the course of our self-absorption in the problems of everyday life may nonetheless have the power to do so if falling upon a more sensitive, more open consciousness. Since the constitution of phenomena requires both givenness and its complement—reception—the latter also needs to be brought to visibility. Wenders clearly portrays differences in receptive capacities by contrasting the degrees of sensitivity of consciousnesses of humans and angels (though there also appear to be significant differences among individuals of either group).

Thus, though some of what once was given is gone, givenness continues. Not only in the case of the angels, who are given to us while remaining invisible to the Berliners, but as the world itself (given to the inhabitants though not really seen by those sunken in ordinary everydayness), which falls upon the angels with increasing intensity. Already early on in the film, as they sit in the BMW showroom, Damiel and Cassiel discuss how they wish they could be in the realm of embodied experience and to feel, rather than remain spirits [1048–69]. More and more comes to visibility under the angels' eyes. Pushing itself forward, nothing other than the ordinary appears to Damiel, but, in Jean-Luc Marion's terms, in showing itself, what gives itself begins to shine.

The Gaze, Call, and Response

What is given becomes visible in the film, both as it is given and then as variously received by the characters and by us. What is given is received for the most part by the inhabitants in their being downcast as a result of its impact; some dimensions of the given come to phenomenality in lighter moments of play (by the children, at the circus) and of intimate embrace. Still other dimensions, as we have seen, are given but not received—and thus do not come to be visible in the lives of the Berliners, though they are shown to the angels by the way they fall upon and are successfully received and responded to by Damiel and Cassiel.

As the angels witness our lives, the ordinary rises to visibility as they and some Berliners receive it. But that is not all. As Jean-Luc Marion contends, parallel to Heidegger's emphasis on "What calls for thinking?," what befalls us calls us.[8] As already noted, the Berliners appear weighed down with troubles. The difficulty of the burdens, even the problem of having problems, calls to the angels, who respond. Even if their intended assistance is not always efficacious, they do respond. Is that what it is to be a guardian angel? To hear the call in the very seeing of the trouble and to respond (without need of further mediating prods or processes)? With Damiel the situation is somewhat different. He evidently is given the same as the Berliners and the other angels but is able to receive it differently—to receive more adequately the high saturation or intensity of the ordinary so that it is let come. With Damiel's receiving the given, a difference happens, a difference from the others and from his former self.

Damiel sees that humans lack something, that they want something even if they now are oblivious for the most part to the fact that they want it (as with Heidegger, they are oblivious to being oblivious). What do they desire? To be happy? To . . . ? As we have seen, there are some positive events and experiences in which Berliners laugh, smile, and embrace. Is this what they want more of? In the case of the angels—without quite understanding what he is missing since he is not embodied—Damiel himself comes to want that to which the Berliners are oblivious—the ordinary, specifically as humanly experienced. In this way, the given is received by Damiel in a special manner. In his case the given is received so as to exert a special call, a call directed peculiarly to him, while not upon the Berliners or Cassiel. He experiences a call that he does or cannot resist. In Jean-Luc Marion's terms, it crashes over him; he neither creates nor controls it.

As Marion points out in his phenomenology of phenomenality, giving and receiving often take the form of a call and response, especially when a situation is provoked—evoked—by a gaze. In his analysis of Caravaggio's *The Calling of Saint Matthew*, a scene in many ways very similar to one in *Wings of Desire*, Marion points out that what is given as a call in the gaze is directed specifically to Matthew. While the gaze itself remains invisible, the call rises to visibility insofar as Matthew feels its force strike him (alone) and responds, quizzically, "Who? Me?"—acknowledging that the gaze has hit home in a double manner, wherein he becomes conscious of the fact of being called and of having an obligation to respond. His reception, however, is laced with one of the usual human cautions (out of self-protection or selfishness?): "Maybe not me? Maybe I don't need to respond?"

Hence even in recognizing the givenness of the call, there is a delay, not only because the response can only come after the call but because the response is not immediately, not necessarily, a "yes" full of acceptance, affirmation, and commitment. Though several others at the table see the outstretched arm of Christ, they do not feel the gaze—it is neither directed toward them nor shown to them. An exception, St. Peter does apparently witness it, by seeing the two "poles"—the outstretched arm that sends and the complementary hand of Matthew, fingers bent back toward his breast, that completes the intentional direction at the other end of the arc (the viewer "fills in" the invisible charge that sparks across the gap, as happens between God's outstretched hand and reclining Adam in Michelangelo's *Creation*).

With an awareness of the importance of the gaze as the site of call and response it is easy to see *Wings of Desire* as a dense network spun of little else, dense with variations of failure and success. People look at things but do not see; couples manage to complete mutual gazes and responses; children see the angels; angels see everything including each other. In this stronghold of expectant gazes (fulfilled and unfulfilled), we are shown the mutual coming together of Damiel and the trapeze artist, Marion. But in all the looking, only some appear as call and response.

Witnessing the gazes of the Berliners, the film shows that for a great deal of the time they gaze at nothing (perhaps they notice, but they do not really see), that they seldom gaze at each other. But some gazes are both directed at others and *are* successfully exchanged.[9] Beyond the mere noticing of the gaping onlookers at the accident scene, one person runs forward, gaze fixed on the victim. Two sets of lovers gaze into each other's eyes and embrace. Husband and pregnant woman in the ambulance exchange gazes. At the circus rehearsal and performances, with care "the same as" the angel's, the circus troupers (and seemingly the audience too) gaze upon one another, and especially at Marion who performs high above the ground. Of course, the angels' gazes upon those to whom they attend remain invisible; necessarily unrequited. In this atmosphere of blank looks, of expectant, fulfilled and unfulfilled gazes, we are led to and shown the central complex of gazes of Damiel and Marion, which unfold from initially being one-sided to becoming mutual.

As the next sections of the film shift to show us the making of the movie in which Peter Falk is starring and to Damiel taking Cassiel to the circus, we are given a bridge to the development of the giving and calling. In both situations, laughter—perhaps as the audible equivalent of the gaze—works its "opening magic."[10] The woman extra laughs as Falk sketches her; Cassiel laughs with Falk as the latter tries on hats from the production's wardrobe.

And we find that Falk appears to be aware of Cassiel, as if he feels, then traces back the gaze of the angel [3040]. Similarly, at the circus performance, Cassiel laughs along with the crowd, and the little girl sitting next to him not only clearly sees him but repeatedly directs comments to him (while in the film it is not unusual for a child to see an angel, in this instance the look is presented as an unusually explicit and strong contact, and the address is genuinely exceptional) [3081–90].

Beyond any mere noticing objects, much less not seeing at all, in the genuine gaze, she who looks upon the other calls him, calls on him to respond. The gaze gives a call, gives and calls. The multiple gazes in *Wings of Desire*, then, call forth and are differently received and responded to. The response is critical in at least two ways. First, without reception, givenness is not let come, is not finally given. Thus the call only comes to be a call, only shows itself as a call, if it is responded to. For example, as Jean-Luc Marion contends in agreement with Levinas,

> it is self-evident that the face gives itself as a call and shows itself (phenomenalizes itself) only to the degree that the gifted responds to it. For, what of the Other shows itself, puts on a good or bad face, depends precisely on the response that I address to his living call: depending on whether I see him or not, kill him or love him, he changes his face. (BG, 293)

Second, as Marion also explains, only in response does the receiver come to be who she is. In his general arguments that "after the subject" we can discern the centrality of the "gifted," that is of "the recipient where what gives itself shows itself," of "he whose function consists in receiving what is immeasurably given to him, and whose privilege is confined to the fact that he himself is received from what he receives" (BG, 322). Receiving the given and thus herself, the receiver herself is the site of givenness, of letting phenomenality occur, of letting arise the coming into one's own (or, as Heidegger puts it, letting both, at the same time, in their mutual belonging together, come to their own).

The complex, indeed self-intensifying, positive feedback between givenness and the modes of reception plays out in the film as the basic Berlin world continues, while in its midst moments or pockets become unusually "charged" (for lack of a better term). The film develops this motif beyond the accumulation of scenes in which the angels witness pain and pleasure, or thinking, playing, and hugging. The call of the givenness of the world goes out to Damiel, though not through a gaze directed to him. The world shows itself so that the angels can see and appreciate it in a such way that many Berliners do not. It also shows itself to them in a way that while apprehending what is given, they simultaneously, abstractly comprehend that since they are not embodied they themselves do not understand or experience the sensual dimensions that humans do. They understand that the dimension remains inaccessible to them. Even more crucially, as just noted, the givenness of the world that comes to the angels does "not exactly come through a gaze directed" at them, no matter how strong the indirect call of things and human life witnessed.

As there are differences between humans and angels in regard to what is given and received and between modes of call, so too there are differences in response. There is a response to the call appropriate for angels, as we have seen: to be guardians, that is, to witness as faithfully and to care as effectively as possible. Yet another response is proper for humans—not to witness abstractly at some sort of distance but as embodied—to appear and testify, in person, as in court, face to face; to care by physically responding—to the hurt, to the things of the world, to human existence itself. Indeed, Wenders shows us that in the response there is given, there happens "becoming human"—as occurs in the central dramatic moments when Damiel responds to the call of mortal existence in a no-longer-angelic mode and with wonder and gratitude for the first time "comes to his senses."

As a further complication, because angels are not seen, they are not addressed, person to person. Hence Wenders has the problem of how to have the gaze experienced and felt as a call by the angels. A significant concern of *Wings of Desire*, then, is to show Damiel's experiences and responses to the call of the world (as well as how these differ from Cassiel's). Damiel is well aware of what is given and received and that much is not; most important, he becomes increasingly sensitive to what does not rise to phenomenality for him and to the fact that he does not rise to phenomenality for the Berliners, that he remains invisible. Gradually, he not only wants to experience what he is missing but also wants to be seen. But, as Jean-Luc Marion shows, the response (even desire) never initiates anything; it is delayed—it cannot be a response or respond—until after the call is given.

Wenders makes visible the gaze that calls to Damiel through a double movement, by way of the powerful draft that the circus performer Marion exerts upon Damiel even though she can neither see him nor directly call him, complemented by the mediation of the former angel, Peter Falk, who, even though not able to see Damiel, speaks straightforwardly to him, issuing the invitation. The film shows how, of all that is in the world, it is primarily Marion who calls out to Damiel, not by addressing him or gazing at him but by being herself.

After watching Marion and her colleagues complete a dress rehearsal (her costume complete with angel's wings, foreshadowing their appropriateness for each other, as does the fact that this is the first scene shot in color in the film), Damiel reappears next to her in the following scene. Having just learned at the rehearsal that the circus has gone bankrupt, Marion faces the unhappy prospect of returning to being a waitress. She also is fearful about being up on the trapeze and breaking her neck, especially in her forthcoming final performance. Full of anxiety and emptiness she has retreated to her trailer, where she attends to her thoughts and examines some of her belongings. Overall she is keenly aware of her condition, which predominantly is one of anxiety and emptiness: "I feel nothing." In a gesture of comfort, Damiel touches her shoulder as he has many others'. Next, however, the situation turns more intimate—improperly so, as he becomes a voyeur? Or acceptably insofar as he is an unsexed, disembodied angelic being? As she starts to take off her costume, he remains, touching her shoulder, though not in the same manner as when comforting the depressed and sick. Rather, more as a tentative lover, his fingers trace her neckline in a caress [2054–56]. Clearly there is an erotic charge passing through this invisible exchange—whether he is perceived or not.[11] Though "she looks into the camera, into Damiel's eyes" [2044], the latter projection is only apparently so. She cannot see him. The script (though not the final edit of the film) tells us that it was "as if it hurt him that she cannot see him" [2045]. We hear for the first time that he misses something specific, wants something. He attends "the exclusion," as we have noted, with a caress, a gesture that meets with a first reciprocation: at that same moment she touched her shoulder as if she had felt his touch [2058].

Later on, Damiel again watches Marion in her trailer as she dresses for her circus act, still worrying about her performance on the trapeze and fearful of death, crying. This time she does feel better (thanks to his comforting?), though she is not aware of his presence. During her performance (which goes on for some time) Damiel exhibits the increasing intensity of his concern: he spontaneously rises to his feet watching her up on the ropes, then anxiously holds his hands to his stomach—sharing the watchful point of view with her coach. After the evening's acts, Damiel accompanies her to the troupe's final, farewell gathering [4084–4149]. While relaxing with her friends Chico and Loorie, Marion asserts, "I have a history. And I am going to keep having one." In contrast, we simultaneously find that Damiel has neither a personal history nor the experience of the lucky moment.[12]

Finally, when she goes to a nightclub, he experiences a dramatic episode of not "being able to be there." While she dances, he comes close and is so bold as to "hold her hand"; "for a moment it seems as if he 'dances' with Marion," that she "feels his hand." But, again, nothing happens (in the script she looks at another woman dancing nearby, though that does not appear in the final edit) [5004–15].

The scenes where Damiel is not recognized as being there because he neither is given nor received as visible, in phenomenality, and where he is hurt at what is not consummated are followed by opposite situations—alternative possibilities in life. In one, a Turkish woman sits all alone in a laundromat [5016–18]. In the other, Damiel and Marion are joined through dream images [5019–30]. Finally, as she is asleep in her trailer, a bird's wing is briefly superimposed over her face, after which she opens her eyes to see Damiel in angelic armor. They look into each other's eyes and join hands, holding fast before Marion again closes her eyes and falls back to sleep. Here, at least in a dream, they have been given to each other and have received each other in a mutual calling and responding.

But since the "exchanges" between Damiel and Marion are in fact not face to face, there is no existential exchange of gazes, no experienced and received address that actually calls. Wenders needs to close the gap, to make the potential and invisible visible. He does this by means of Peter Falk's character, who lives between the two worlds: though now human, he was an angel and retains the ability to be aware of other angels even though now he no longer can see them. Through this conceit, Falk is able specifically to call Damiel, biding him to come to mortality. Hence, after the preparatory dream sequence between Damiel and Marion, the film shifts to waking life, to show us an explicit interchange between the visible and invisible. Falk is aware of Damiel's presence and addresses him, finally extending a hand to him (Falk's bodily posture with right hand extended in receptive and invitational greeting and left hand curled back to his heart, no doubt unintentionally, synthesizes and echoes both Christ's outstretched hand of invitation and Matthew's hand to breast—asking and acknowledging me?—depicted in Caravaggio's *The Calling of St. Matthew*). The image is completed by the dialogue: Falk begins by telling Damiel that though he can not see him, he knows he is there, going on,

I wish I could see your face,

just look into your eyes and tell you how good it is to be here. Just to touch something!

Here, that's cold! That feels good!

Figure 3.6. Falk addressing Damiel, bidding him to come to mortality

Here, to smoke, have coffee. And if you do it together it's fantastic. Or to draw: you know, you take a pencil and you make a dark line, then you make a light line and together it's a good line. Or, when your hands are cold, you rub them together, you see, that's good, that feels good! There's so many good things! But you're not here—I'm here. I wish you were here. I wish you could talk to me.

'cause I'm a friend.

Compañero! [5038–5044]

Falk's words and actions not only celebrate the givenness of what shows itself for human sensory satisfaction but intensify and make fully explicit the call itself. The call of existence and of a person as well as the angel's response and thus desire come to visibility before us. The call calls for response, and response is necessary for the call to appear phenomenally as a call. Wenders shows us that response is evoked by the very character of the things and humans of this world and that it is further provoked by Falk's address to the yet-angelic Damiel (and confirmed as already possible by Falk's later admission that many former angels have passed over). In the conversation between Damiel and Cassiel that follows, as the two pause in their walk, intensely looking into each other's eyes, Damiel explains to Cassiel what has come to him and all the earthly things he intends to do now that he is ready to plunge into the flow of time—the history of the world—including what he has just now come to understand from what old men say, that from within time he must engage the moment of fear of time, of death [5046–52]. Though earlier in the BMW showroom Cassiel had joined Damiel in discussing the attractions of earthly as distinct from spiritual experience, finally Cassiel does not believe that such "daydreaming" might become reality. But Damiel does.

Wenders renders visible Damiel's "crossing to embodied existence" not only by showing the given flooding over and into him but as an event in which he crashes into himself—no longer an ethereal medium of the flow of givenness between visible and invisible realms but solidified so that what befalls him throws him down to earth. In a point-of-view shot, Cassiel sees footprints in the sand; he then actually does intervene physically in events, carrying Damiel through the wall to the West Berlin side. The culmination, now all in color, has Damiel crashing to earth at the wall—thrownness [*Geworfenheit*] into being-in-the-world indeed.[13] Nearby soldiers guarding the wall are aware that something has come about, has been brought to appearance. Cassiel carries Damiel safely to the West side of the wall. Damiel now is given the whole range of sensory experience and embodied existence. He feels a cut on his head (made by his falling armor) and, finding the blood, discovers that it has a taste and is red (after which he happily asks a passerby to name colors for him). In subsequent following shots he hears the clanking of the armor he carries under his arm as he walks down the street to a pawnbroker's shop (you need money in Berlin) and then an ambulance's siren; he smells and tastes coffee and a cigarette [5068–76]. His entry into time is underscored by his proudly acquiring a watch.

From this point, the film's still complex ending centers about Damiel and Marion actually coming together. First pictured individually and alone, in an establishing shot in the nightclub bar they find each other. Finally, in an unusually long sequence of medium shots and medium close-ups (3 minutes, 44 seconds) that culminates in extreme close-up, shot/reverse shots, they exchange gazes, discovering and committing themselves to the other, and then truly embrace [7033–35]. After this, there is a minor role inversion, in which Damiel, fully grounded, is able to hold the pole upon which Marion practices her rope-turning routine aloft—not in the heavens, but in the earth's air [*Luft*] [7042]. Here we see the full crashing of phenomena onto consciousness and a response that has emptied itself of the need to try to control, that has opened itself so as to let the lived experiences give themselves, so they can come forward as meaningful (BG, 216). Clearly, the things of the world and especially Marion herself affect Damiel powerfully enough to knock him far "off course"—so far in another direction that a change in identity, in mode of being, follows.

Figure 3.7. Damiel and Marion embrace in the flesh

The mutual dynamic of the given and the "resistance" that occurs when it lands upon the receiver increasingly brings things and characters to visibility. As both Heidegger and Marion remind us, such is precisely what art achieves in the world. That is, Wenders' *Wings of Desire* renders visible this rising to visibility by showing the giving and receiving, the gazes that call and respond across Berlin. Transposing what Marion says about painting, we come to see that "[film] is the visible deposited by the [filmmaker]."[14]

Centripetal and Centrifugal Vision

The film, in sum, depicts at least four sorts of givenness and gaze in regard to the Berliners and the angels: (1) the weary, burdened gaze of average everydayness, where people "look down," not really seeing anything vividly; (2) the keener, attentive gaze of the angels caring for those in the first mode; (3) the less frequent but still occurring dynamic mutual gaze among some Berliners; and (4) the implication of the possibility of angels being thus addressed by the eye, in person and able to respond to the call of the givenness of things or even of another person.

It is not so clear what it means for the possibility of the sensory things of this world or a mortal being not only being given to an nonembodied angel but addressed so as to call and generate a lure or desire for what is given "in person," as Jean-Luc Marion says. It would seem that since the angels are not visible and not seen, that what is given in the form of the human look—eye to eye, person to person—is not addressed to them. But this does not entail that the givenness of the human look, much less that of things or of the observed human experience of things, does not call to them. How often are we drawn to what is given, but not given to us? Even if we otherwise might be perfectly content without it? Do not we all, at one time or another, set aside our toys for the one in the store window, for the one another child is playing with right now? No matter how many toys we already have?

But if the difference between staying an angel and becoming human were to be considered in terms of temptation it would be important that such an interpretation not mindlessly spring from an unquestioned humanistic-anthropocentric view that "human life is the ultimate evolution of the universe." The differences between angels and humans surely are much more complex than that. After all, we are told in Genesis that the original temptation at the beginning of creation was manifest when Satan attempted to leave his angelic nature and "rise upward" to the place of God—a temptation in the opposite direction than in *Wings of Desire*. It is not surprising that whereas the Old Testament reports the temptation to try to be godlike, in our age when God is gone, the anthropocentric measure, value, and temptation would be to become like us—human. Thus, we would have to inquire about the extent to which (or the manner in which) the angels, who are so much more aware of the power of the given than are the Berliners, might be called—tempted—to things. The film delineates that and how they are attracted, or at least how Falk was and Damiel is, to the experience of cold, to the smell of coffee and its warmth in one's hands on a cold morning, and finally to person-to-person exchange and intimacy—to being seen and looked at, to becoming directly engaged with another mortal.

Similarly, we need to reflect on the issue of what could constitute a proper angelic response. It would not seem "proper" for angels as angels to be thus called or respond, for thereby they would lose their angelic nature for a human one (at least in Heidegger's sense of "ownness" [*eigen*] where that word articulates the dynamic (once termed "essence") whereby one is gathered with the rest of the constituents of the world so as to come into what is particularly and properly one's own). Perhaps, though, the opening is appropriate for Damiel and Falk, who made such a choice and change? It would not follow though that the latter's' change is better than what happens with Cassiel, who is at least partially observant of and interested in the same worldly phenomena as Damiel, who may or may not be addressed in the same way, and who, in any case, remains true to his angelic character. Here we obviously need to further consider the differences of both what is given to and received by Damiel and Cassiel.

Though he does not seem to be drawn to things or a person as Damiel is, Cassiel is issued the same direct call by Falk but does not respond. Emphasizing Falk's mediatory role, Wenders follows the scene in which the now mortal Damiel and Falk converse [6010–46] with a series of other encounters: the entry of Marion and some circus colleagues [6047–59]; an encounter between Damiel and Cassiel in their new relationship, in which Cassiel can hear Damiel's thoughts but Damiel now cannot see Cassiel (though as a former angel Falk is able to feel his presence) [6071]; a meeting of Falk and Marion at the *imbiss* (snack bar), and Falk feeling the presence of Cassiel and making the same offer in words and gestures that he did to Damiel. In the first scene of the sequence, the now embodied Damiel addresses Falk as "*compañero*" (a coded word from their earlier meeting), and Falk, looking him over, engages in conversation and explains that he too had been an angel, further welcoming Damiel and validating his decision by affirming that "There's a lot of us" that have gone over to the other side [6010–45]. In the ending scene, Falk makes the same overture to Cassiel, "because there are so many things I want to tell you," but Cassiel does not respond (does not "shake" his hand as did Damiel), leaving Falk unsure whether contact was made or not [6084–87]. While the same is given to both Damiel and Cassiel, we witness different responses, different choices of what givenness to receive and let rise to phenomenality, including what self-identity—immortal or mortal. *Wings of Desire* leaves both possible trajectories open.

At the least, the film (without appealing to current posthumanistic arguments) presents us with a story in which the human is not the only good, measure, or goal. Whether a call or response to mortal finitude would be good for angels is not for us to debate; how could we (dare) try to answer for angels? As mortals, we are (generally throughout history, and certainly in the dominant modern era in the West) unaware of angels' presence; should they appear to us we cannot read their minds, much less make judgments on their behalf. The end of the film reminds us of all these limitations: we have become used to hearing both what people think to themselves—through the perspective of Damiel and Cassiel—and what the angels themselves say and think. But, with Damiel now become human, listening to and through him, we humans, in fact, cannot hear what Cassiel thinks [7029].

As the story tells us in multiple variations, so that we have to consider the phenomena from a plurality of perspectives, and as Damiel himself writes at the end, humans see as angels do not. So? Insofar as the movement of the reflection has taken us from considering the modes of givenness and gaze of the Berliners and angels in the film, to the point where we speculate about what to make of the angels' possibilities, and then, as we consider that question, we are moved yet once more to the "fact" that we do not, and will not be able to, experience things the way angels do. We seem to be led to the obvious. But do we adequately receive what we have been shown? As its tropological meaning—indicating the way to live, since understanding entails action—the film finally points to us, the audience, and to our moral obligations.[15]

There is, then, a fifth mode of givenness and gaze in *Wings of Desire* that leads us to try to understand that the call to the things of this world and to other people is a call to us, a call to see how we might respond and come to receive ourselves. Do we not come to appreciate the value of what we have been given, of who we are—even as finite mortals living amid pain and distress—in seeing it so valued by an immortal being that he would freely choose to become mortal that he might have the embodied consciousness and experience of humans? While Cassiel makes his choice affirming his current immortal condition and identity as an angel, Damiel moves in the opposite direction, giving up immortality for mortal existence. But if, as just noted, we do not implausibly take the film as a hyper-anthropomorphic paean, it would appear that *Wings of Desire* presents an inverse version of the story of choice and identity already found in (the other) Homer's *Odyssey*. In the latter, Odysseus declines the possibility of remaining on Circe's island forever, which means giving up his chance to become immortal. Instead he chooses the lot of a mortal, continuing his tiring journey home, including heading toward dreaded death, because only thus can he be who he really is.

Who? Us?

The film is given to us, all flickerings of light and shadows that impinge on our consciousness and that we receive as images of the heavens over Berlin and of angels, of earthly Berlin and its mortal inhabitants. Further, what is *so shown* finally addresses us, calls to us and calls for a response. Of course, what is given by and in the film is not given to any angel or inhabitant but only to those of us engrossed in Wenders' *Wings of Desire*. What is given? What are we shown? What do we, the audience, each and all of us together, see? We have the capacity, as do the angels, to see and understand empathetically the hardships and joys of life in the city. As do the angels, we may see more than many Berliners and understand that they (and we perhaps) do not see much of anything because of being lost within the fog of average everydayness; we also may see, as do the angels and some inhabitants too, that care is called for, that what is given even—or especially?—ordinarily is to be received gratefully, with a sense of wonder. Comforted by Damiel, Marion feels better enough to move from her anxiety to affirm, "I just lift my head and the world appears before my eyes, and fills my heart" [2033]. Cassiel and Damiel show us that angels see everything but that what is disclosed in their ability to receive so much is attended by concealment, since, as unembodied, they cannot experience the sensuous—a present absence that may evoke a response to the call of the world, to desire for full human existence.

Here we need be mindful of Heidegger's contention that the gathering of the fourfold into world depends on mortals contributing their part since, even though we neither create the meanings of things nor ourselves bring about the gathering, we are responsible for crafting the things (poems or temples or political acts) necessary to precipitate as it were the gathering together of what belongs together into place and history. Echoing Heidegger in his own way, Jean-Luc Marion places our responsibility for an adequate response squarely before us:

> Here the gifted, finite by definition and originarily a posteriori, finds itself in charge of receiving or denying the given, that is, the a priori of givenness. It is inasmuch as it remains negatively indifferent (by deficiency of sight) that it receives the burden of positive indifference (to bring it about·that what gives itself shows itself, or not). The gifted, inasmuch as finite, has nothing less than the charge of opening or closing the entire flux of phenomenality. (BG, 306–307)

Wings of Desire also shows us, then, that the question most immediately facing us would be how we might be capable of receiving the given that still is given. Can we see as angels? No. Because we are embodied, we see differently, both less and more, not everything, nor for all time, yet capable of receiving the sensory. Can we pass beyond being incapable of receiving what is given, which blocks its coming to phenomenality, to become more fully human, as Damiel would, joining the mortals who do manage to be adequate to receive what is immanently given, thus letting it come to phenomenality and significant experience—which would mean that from receiving what we are given, we finally might receive ourselves too?

From Berlin to the Black Forest

What does Berlin have to do with the Black Forest? Wenders with Heidegger? A great deal. In the first place, this essay gets to Berlin from the

Black Forest. That is, it is substantially because of what we have received from Heidegger's thinking and writing that we are able to try to encounter and ponder Wenders' film as we do, that we are able to benefit in the project from the insights of Jean-Luc Marion, who follows the same path himself in regard to givenness and the power of art. Second, because Heidegger comes to be who he is, which includes becoming the witness and guardian of that which calls to him for thinking, while twice declining the academic call to move to Berlin to teach from a much more prestigious position. He remains in his homeland (occasionally visiting the big cities), knowing that it is only in the rural that he would be able to receive what is given, that is, to share what is given to many there but that is sent as an address specifically to him, to which he is obliged to respond and though which he would be able to become himself. Thus, after the war, from Freiburg where he lives and teaches, from Messkirch, his birthplace, where he often works with his brother Fritz, and from Todtnauberg, where he has his ski hut and does most of his writing, Heidegger continues to follow the path of originary thinking. The task, he tells us in his "Memorial Address," delivered in Messkirch on the occasion of the 175th birthday of the town's famous composer, Conradin Kreutzer, is "to dwell on what lies close and meditate on what is closest; upon that which concerns us, each one of us, here and now; here, on this patch of home ground; now, in the present hour of history."[16]

One of the most pressing questions to be faced by Heidegger and his fellow citizens is whether a new rootedness is possible. That is why, as I posited at the beginning, many of the concerns Heidegger voices from his rural home, especially in his local commemorative and festival addresses, are the same as those addressed by Wenders in his film. And, parallel to the atmosphere of a hushed audience's reception of a film, the local festivals at which Heidegger speaks also bring a moment of quiet and reflection: "Over and against the alien which comes towards us we must balance off what comes to us from our origin. So we bring to the noisy and the frantic, stillness and restraint."[17] Even for Messkirch, which "will become woven into the network of the age of technology" and its displacements, where "perhaps the relationship to homeland, the attraction to homeland will disappear from the existence of modern man," Heidegger is able to retrieve from "the hidden, unadmired, deflected . . . homesickness" the "still unavoidable attraction to our homeland." From there he can demonstrate that "in the alienation of the modern technological world there is at the same time homeland" and can reaffirm that "the attraction to homeland is still alive," that there is "at the same time homeland" (700YM, 236).

Heidegger too is bringing the given to visibility, opening reception by means of retrieval and recollective thinking and saying as he meditates on the importance of retrieving, keeping, and guarding though care and renewal of what has been—still is—given. For his part, Heidegger focuses on what comes, for instance through art works and dialect, into local community to illuminate ways of belonging to natural and once-sacred worlds. Having dedicated himself to thinking from within the region of his birth, throughout his life he affirms the continuity between his work and that of his rural neighbors in the continuation of their lifeworld. Even while in Freiburg, focally the scene of his relations with students and colleagues as well as family, Heidegger experiences the force that still comes and is received through the place itself. At a 1954 presentation of a version of his Hebel lectures in nearby Zähringer (in which he allows himself to slip into local dialect) he describes "how from his study room on Rotebuck Street in Freiburg, when he lifts his gaze from the work table and lets it run out over the *Fillebach* (brook), across the meadows and plowed fields, then up the steep slope, it comes to rest on the tower of Zähringer Castle." What matters, however, is not a beautiful view but experiencing the "secret forces at work on the work of thinking: the waking land, the quiet of the wooded mountain, the rooted power of the neighborly people"; that is, he "firmly insists on the belonging together of his work and that of his farming neighbors, and of both of them to the landscape in which they are commonly gathered."[18]

In fact, Heidegger is very clear about what is most importantly given and what the appropriate, even necessary, reception needs to be if our response is to be adequate to what must be let come again to visibility. Speaking in the town in which he was born and where his brother still lives, Heidegger says,

Homeland is most possible and effective where the powers of nature around us and the remnants of historical tradition remain together, where an origin and an ancient, nourished style of human existence hold sway. Today for this decisive task perhaps only the rural counties and small towns are competent—if they recognize anew their unusual qualities, if they know how to draw the boundaries between themselves and life in the large cities and the gigantic areas of modern industrial complexes—if they present themselves not as models and criteria but as a holding on to what is eminently their own, as the guard of feeling at home. For this two things are necessary. First, we must recognize alienation, recognize where it is actively determinative; secondly, that we do not let decay and decline the still essentially unpretentious powers of the homeland.

To become equal to both these demands—this centennial could be a good "occasion" for this, the right festival for it. . . . (700YM, 234)

As Jean-Luc Marion contends, still following Heidegger even while intending other things besides, the source still comes. In Heidegger's originary terms, the power of the ordinary can yet be heard and responded to: "the simple preserves the enigma of what abides and is great" ("The Pathway," 70; HH 423–424). Not in the least, it is dialect, the way local place speaks through us, that holds what has been given and that thus may allow it still to rise up to us ("dialect" is a common translation for *Mundart*; however, in Heidegger's region, the latter word more deeply says "fruit or product of the mouth"). To respond to dialect requires Heidegger to receive and pass along its continuing force, not what he makes up or creates but what falls upon him through what the dialect says and shows. He retrieves the way Hebel's language sets into work the world he inhabited and draws forth the meanings that continue to come for our understanding of the natural world and our local communities (in many essays, such as "*Die Sprache Johann Peter Hebel*," "Hebel—Friend of the House," and "*Sprache und Heimat*," though there is not space to consider those essays here).[19] I can at least note that Heidegger himself, while spending time among his rural neighbors and speaking with them in dialect, says that he most deeply learned to listen to, let come, and experience dialect and home by thinking and saying along with the poet who most powerfully "unfolds the giving and gathering of world that specifically happens only in dialect": Hebel.

In his own time, Hebel "provided a way to remain in and reflect upon the strange as it appears in the challenge of the Enlightenment's science and technology" that surrounded him; the task required that he hear and use dialect to "articulate a specific place, people, time, and set of events," that is "to bring forth the composition of 'the earth and works of mortals upon it, under the heavens'" (HH, 335, 338, 340, 344; "*Sprache und Heimat*," 45). From continuity with the poet, then, Heidegger is able to receive and resonate with the local dialect, to learn to hear and retrieve what is given, though fading, in what they say and in their customs. Through Hebel Heidegger learns how to respond to what is given in his own time, "to face the tasks that still remain and that are nearest to us," that is, the problems of our homelessness (HH, 353).

Accordingly, by remaining in the rural world and by continually attending to dialect (whether at his cabin in Todtnauberg, his house in Freiburg, or when traveling or writing in standard German), Heidegger does not retreat into romanticism or nostalgia for the past. Quite the opposite, he remains close to and draws from what he calls the still-coming source, which arrives through local place and dialect. Further, in the face of contemporary dislocations (parallel to Wenders' film), he argues that isolating withdrawal will not work for the rural world. If the rural is to receive what is given and only thereby finally receive itself, it needs to respond adequately to the technological world and great cities that clearly are chief among what is given to us today. Thus, perhaps surprisingly, he

> contends and proposes that one such task is to rescue and accept, into the midst of the village, the stunned and tired people of the great cities and industrial districts and to prepare them for a place and stay "where they suddenly can hear silence, where they can find rest in this silence, where they can experience what is a forest and an alpine meadow, what is a rocky slope and a lively flowing creek, what is a high sky and a sparkling starry night, what the following things mean—to dwell in such a landscape where humans still speak the strange expressive mother tongue." (HH, 427)[20]

In other words, the rural world would have the responsibility of bringing to visibility for the urban residents the natural world and the traditional cultural worlds that are slipping away into concealment, that are disappearing as phenomenal. Just as important, the task is to help keep and pass on—let continue to rise to us—what is given to them, including the modes of reception that remain preserved in the rural, that is, the modes of language, of rhythms of day and seasons, of memory through which lifeworlds are let come. The deepest task is to continue to try to be adequate to what is still given, so that it is not refused its emergence to phenomenality. This amounts to helping or "letting" the giving continue to come, efficaciously as a generative force, thus enabling both rural and urban inhabitants to continue to receive the ways of life and identity that make them who they are.

Heidegger speaks in the same language of giving and receiving that later emerges in *Wings of Desire* and Jean-Luc Marion's writings. He contends that such receiving, "such opening up would only be possible if the indigenous Todtnaubergers can offer a gift in the correct understated manner to the guests," which in turn would be possible only because the Todtnaubergers themselves must shelter their uniqueness and protect it from the urban manner of living and speaking. That is why the indigenous villagers require a special sense of tact and inner security that knows wherein everything finds its limits—another instance where "small towns and rural counties recognize their unusual qualities and know how to draw [specify] the boundaries" so as not to deny their proper way of life.[21]

As an aid to receive what still is given, Heidegger finds and retrieves from Hebel one of "the poet's key words: 'on the other side, over there.'" Spoken from the situation of the homecoming that occurs in Todtnauberg and is passed on by Heidegger, this hint

> says that we need to experience and deal with, on the other side, over there, the homelessness of the metropolitan, technological-industrial world. It says, from the condition of homelessness in which we all find ourselves, that we need to recover and shelter what is on the other side, over there: the source that still comes, albeit weakly, in dialect, in region, in local ways of life—that is, the possibility of homecoming. (HH, 429)

Heidegger contends that "together, all are nourished and become who they are; all flourish only if they properly bide their time." Beyond Heidegger's personal homecoming (which is important), he is celebrating the village's thoughtful and poetic dwelling in this story-shaped, abiding place that is "the 'something' which 'entirely simple and unpretentious came to appearance'" (HH, 430).[22] Thus, a double reception is necessary for all that crashes over us. We need to receive what is given by both "conserving and holding on to the enduring significance of places, people, and events and through learning to practice releasement to things and openness to mystery leading to a new grounding" (HH 393–394, cf. 700YM). Such advice echoes what the angels see in *Wings of Desire*: caring outreach to others and the things of the world is critical if we are to habituate ourselves to the world we are given in order to learn to dwell again today, and desire leads not to clutching and controlling behavior but to letting go, to responding out of finitude to the call of immanence that addresses one specifically, in a particular time and place.

Yet Again: Who, Us?—Yes: Still the Given, Still Called

It is not the 1950s. We are not characters inhabiting a film. It is almost a shame to have to remind ourselves that there are no angels here, nor any Berliners. What is shown is shown only to us. Here and now, in our lifeworlds, what are we given? Among much else, *Wings of Desire* renders visible our capacity to understand, as do the angels, the hardships and joys of life in the city—that the ordinary is to be received gratefully, with a sense of wonder, and that it calls to us, calls for a responsible response. The film also witnesses the givenness of a perhaps not previously understood possibility—that gift and reception can be actualized within the sphere of immanence.

As to the latter, *Wings of Desire* and the visualized phenomenon of the gaze delineate an immanent counter to the transcendental, which we clearly can see by contrasting its originary thrust with that of the metaphysical alternative masterfully portrayed by Dürer's *Melancholia*. The engraving's central figure, half man, half angel, can be seen as a prototype to the double lives of Falk and Damiel or to the composite persona wherein Damiel, still angel and on his way to becoming a man, engages with Falk, who was an angel and now lives as a man. Once again, Jean-Luc Marion provides a promising reading that would facilitate the interpretation. According to Marion, in *Melancholia* we find:

> Heavy, sitting down, his head weighing on his left hand, a man gazes. Not a man, but an angel, as his wings indicate; a man nevertheless, as other characteristics demand: human finitude is betrayed by the silver, which swells a purse at his belt, by the crown of leaves that circles his forehead, as a poet's, and by the time shown by the hourglass situated directly above his thoughtful and frozen head. Neither angel nor man—can one imagine it?[23]

But, according to Marion, this hollow and hollowing gaze "looks at everything without seeing anything, perceives everything without recognizing itself in anything or recognizing anything other than its own absence."[24] The spectacles and splendors of the world do not stop the gaze of melancholy, nor, beyond the finite, does a portrayed actual angel (from the domain that incites the transgression of the finite); rather, the melancholy figure directs his gaze out of the engraving toward a point at which the flight lines of figures within it converge. Marion contends that "melancholy gazes at nothing other than this absent vanishing point—absence from any escape, flight from any flight."[25] (Interestingly, Marion the trapeze artist voices the same assessment of her situation: that one really can't get lost because in West Berlin one can't go anywhere, always and unavoidably coming back to the wall [2041].)

Clearly, Heidegger, Marion, and Wenders present an alternative to *Melancholia*, proceeding from some of the same recognitions of what is given to a different possible mode of response. Heidegger generatively moved against transcendence, beginning the deconstruction of metaphysics that opened to the continuing exploration of immanence by figures as diverse as Derrida, Deleuze, and Jean-Luc Marion, the latter of whom explores how by way of immanence theology can think what comes in revelation—even God, nontranscendentally, without being. At the same time, of course, Heidegger recognizes the vanity of the subject and the boredom attendant with mere objects in the shroud of average everydayness (see *Being and Time*) in the modern age as well as the end of the subject and disappearance of objects into standing reserve in the contemporary era of *Gestell*. Wenders too critiques consumerist objects and absorptive technologies; he also eschews the transcendental, not only for the humans in Berlin but also for the angels in the heavens over the city, thinking of them and portraying them as "bound to this world," that is, as immanent. Though Wenders' comments on the film do not describe the way it actually turned out, what he says about the placement of the angels in the heavens over Berlin clearly is antitranscendental:

If I were to give my story a prologue, it would go something like this:

When God, endlessly disappointed, finally prepared to turn his back on the world forever, it happened that some of his angels disagreed with Him and took the side of man, saying that he deserved to be given another chance.

Angry at being crossed, God banished them to what was then the most terrible place on earth: Berlin.

And then he turned away.

All this happened at the time that we today call: "the end of the second world war."

Since that time, these fallen angels from the "second angelic rebellion" have been imprisoned in the city, with no prospect of release, let alone of being readmitted to heaven. They are condemned to be witnesses, forever nothing but onlookers, unable to affect men in the slightest, or to intervene in the course of history. They are unable to so much as move a grain of sand.[26]

Both Heidegger and Wenders bring forth an alternative to *Melancholia* in that while also eschewing any "escape" to the transcendental or to mere human inventiveness or commodity production, contrary to the Dürer engraving, their works delineate the positive saturation of things that not only can come to phenomenality but that can be gathered into worlds—into fourfold originary worlds for Heidegger and the quietly joyful urban life of Damiel and Marion that opens up by the end of *Wings of Desire*. The gathering together of this specific couple is not incidental to one of the basic motifs of this chapter and of Heidegger's and Wenders' work: the homelessness of our times that spans the arc from the end of World

War II to today. Damiel, as an angel whose lot is cast into the heavens over Berlin, is neither at home with a transcendent God nor as a mortal (human: made from *humus*, soil) on earth. Marion is without a home, as signaled by her speaking French amid a motley circus crew while in Berlin: "I'm someone who has no roots, no story, no country" [6061–62]. But together Damiel and Cassiel arrive at a new site where they begin to move to a next stage of life—where becoming gathered together with those/that to whom one belongs is as close to a definition of homecoming as we are likely to get. Significantly, as they find each other, Marion says to Damiel that it is time to be earnest, to end acting on the basis of coincidence, now taking responsibility for a deliberate decision—a further contrast with the child in the poem that is read as a voiceover at the beginning of the film who acts unselfconsciously, simply participating in the flow of what goes on [7032–37].

I further contend that both Cassiel and Damiel make visible more positive figures of possibility than melancholia: the angelic Cassiel would figure a holding true to the abiding dimension of divinities; Damiel's trajectory (and that of the film's human characters who embrace both the painful and satisfying aspects of existence) would be heuristic for us mortals. Counter to the boredom of melancholia, both Wenders and Heidegger bring to visibility "the splendor of the simple"—which is catalogued in "The Call to the World," the dying motorcyclist's poem of all he remembers and values (. . . the sun . . . bread and wine . . . the quiet of a Sunday, the horizon . . .) [2060–61].

Returning to the first gift of *Wings of Desire*—the ordinary and our responsibility for a response—we are called into question. How will we respond to the mortal existence that calls to us? Will we fail to respond because we are lost in the midst of our busy everydayness, or will we manage to answer in a thoughtful and caring but abstract, disembodied manner (proper only to angels), or perhaps properly as embodied consciousnesses, that is, as the persons we can come to be by way of more adequate response, by learning to habituate ourselves to what is given? Following the trajectory from the beginning of the film, we are called to be as open as the children, who are the only humans to see the angels but who have arrived neither at self-consciousness nor of responsibility for who they are. This "directive" is underscored by the film's circling around at the end, back to the poem that appeared as the opening image, which we now understand as being written by Damiel with his become-human hand [1001, 7049–50]): ("*Als das Kind Kind war, / wüste es nicht, daß es Kind war, alles war ihm beseelt*"). But there is more: while we are called to be as *open* as children, we are called to do so as—to become—mature mortals, in an embodied and sensory consciousness not available to angels (*"Ich . . weiss . . jetzt, / was . . . kein . . . Engel . . . weiss"*). In this doubled capacity, as open and as fully human, we would be able to witness and decisively respond to the world and life in all its painful and joyful dimensions, to its awesome and ordinary things, to the calling of and caring for human existence itself.[27]

Heidegger also would move us from the spell of average everydayness amid "mere objects" to releasement (*Gelassenheit*) from the challenges of the contemporary *Gestell* by laying before us, that we might take it to heart, the giving of that which continues to come and which calls for a thoughtful, two-track response. We need to witness and live in a world of multiple dimensions wherein we deal with the increasing challenge of technology and calculative, representational thinking and at the same time respond in a releasement to things that says both "yes" and "no" to the technological realm.[28] The necessary response entails a particular orientation to givenness, since that which still gives gives in the complex dance of simultaneous unconcealment and concealment. Heidegger tells us, "That which shows itself and at the same time withdraws is the essential trait of what we call the mystery. I call the comportment which enables us to keep open to the meaning hidden in technology, *openness to the mystery*."[29] We are given, then, and specifically addressed by mystery; at the same time, we are called to respond responsibly by learning to think, by learning releasement to things.

As we have seen, both Heidegger and Wenders eschew "escape" toward the transcendental, showing instead the complex play of pain and joy, despair and hope, that constitute finite life. Yet, Jean-Luc Marion explains, even with the necessity that we mortals receive the given in order for it to rise to phenomenality, this very "investiture"—wherein we are "set up as gatekeepers for the ascent into visibility of all that gives itself—can and should be troubling" (BG, 307):

> Nothing establishes that the gifted always can or wants to receive *all* that is given. We can never exclude some cases in which a given would not succeed in showing those unpredictable landings in which the gifted fails before the excess of the given or remains idle in its shortage. (BG, 310)

Wenders too renders the positively still-given giving as bivalent. Remember that in retrieving their memories of all they had seen in the place that came to be called Berlin, Damiel and Cassiel noted that they had witnessed two histories, that of the emergent world (*phusis*, Heidegger would say) and that of humans and war, and that despite the second, the first of grass, sun, and air still lingers [4001–4015].[30] As treated above, *Wings of Desire* rehearses both dimensions at once in the scene in the dying motorcyclist's poem naming all that he remembers and values—". . . the sun . . . bread and wine . . . the quiet of a Sunday, the horizon" [2060–61]. Heidegger says the same in commending to us that which "entirely simple and unpretentious came to appearance" in rural life, the giving of which continues to come and to call for a releasement to things.[31]

Though some of what once was given is irretrievably gone, as happens unavoidably given mortal finitude and over the course of the historical epochs of the world, we remain gifted and called by what continues to be given. You and I thereby are brought into question and called on to answer for ourselves and our world. Can we today, here and now, see what Wenders gives us, passes on to us as gift and call? Can we today, here and now, hear what Heidegger gives us, passes on to us as gift and call from Todtnauberg, Messkirch, and Freiburg—a call, that in the same way today, remains addressed to us from the giving that is not gone but still originarily comes?

Notes

Preface

1. Jean-Luc Marion, *Being Given* (Stanford, Calif.: Stanford University Press, 2002), 132. For a fuller treatment of Marion's insights, see my "The Double-Gift: Place and Identity," in *Back to the Things Themselves: Architectural Experience, Memory, and Thought*, ed. Iris Aravot (Haifa: Technion University Press, 2014) and "Call of the Earth: Endowment and Response" in *Heidegger and the Earth: Essays in Environmental Thought*, ed. Ladelle McWhorter and Gail Stenstad, new ed. (Toronto: University of Toronto Press, 2009), 70–99.

2. Marion, *Being Given*, 139–141.

3. Marion, *Being Given*, 151.

4. Jean-Luc Marion, *In Excess: Studies of Saturated Phenomena* (New York: Fordham University Press, 2002), 34.

5. Marion, *In Excess*, 35; cf. Heidegger, *Being and Time*, on average everydayness.

6. Marion, *Being Given*, 222. Marion discusses mathematical abstractions "where intention of meaning, in order to be fulfilled in a phenomenon, requires only a pure or formal intuition (for example, empty tautology in logic); mathematics and formal logic offer, precisely, only an ideal object—that is, strictly speaking, an object that does not have to give itself in order to appear, in short, a minute or zero degree of phenomenality." "The Saturated Phenomena," in Dominique Janicaud et al., *Phenomenology and the "Theological Turn"* (New York: Fordham University Press, 2000), 188.

7. Marion, *Being Given*, 222–224.

8. Marion, *In Excess*, 51.

9. For examples of Marion's analysis of particular painters and paintings, see *Being Given* on visibility and saturation in Kandinsky (49) and in cubism (201–202); bedazzlement in Claude and Turner (205–206). On Caravaggio and the call see *Being Given*, 282–287; on Cezanne and on Picasso on faces, see *Being Given*, 267. For discussions of extremes in which the object tends to disappear in favor of sensory experience or where the constitutive experience is minimalized, see *The Crossing of the Visible* (Stanford, Calif.: Stanford University Press, 2004), 13–16 on Monet, 16 on Pollock and 17–19 on Hantaï's *Tabula*, Albers, and Malévitch; and *In Excess*, 52, 72–81 on Rothko and 66–68 on Klee, about whose *Ad Marginem* Marion says, "This redoubling of the frame [making it smaller, compressing it] . . . renders visible, almost foreseeable, even inevitable, that the clash of the elementary forces of the sun and of the magma, both in fusion, ends in the implosion of enormous energy—attains the highest saturation possible."

10. Marion, *In Excess*, 60, quotation modified to read smoothly in context.

11. Claude Romano, *Event and World* (New York: Fordham University Press, 2009), 69.

12. Romano, *Event and World*, 107.

13. Romano, *Event and World*, 52.

14. Kelly Oliver, *Witnessing: Beyond Recognition* (Minneapolis: University of Minnesota Press, 2001).

15. Oliver, *Witnessing*, 7, 11.

16. I address these important dimensions of retheorizing the phenomena of embodied consciousness, perception, and action in "Anatomy of Life and Well-Being: A Framework for the Contributions of Phenomenology and Complexity Theory," *International Journal of Qualitative Studies of Health and Well-Being* (July 2010); "Northern Lights: Embodied Perception and Enacted Vision," in *Hyperborean Wind: Design and the City*, ed. Matti Ikonen (Reykjavik: University of Iceland Press, 2012).

17. Oliver, *Witnessing*, 15.

18. Oliver, *Witnessing*, 16.

19. Oliver, *Witnessing*, 15.

20. Oliver, *Witnessing*, 19–20.

21. Oliver, *Witnessing*, 19.

22. Martin Heidegger, "Memorial Address," in *Discourse on Thinking*, trans. John M. Anderson and E. Hans Freund (New York: Harper and Row, 1966), 43–57.

23. Northrop Frye, *Anatomy of Criticism* (New York: Atheneum, 1968), 97.

24. See, for example, Jonathan Crary, *Techniques of the Observer: On Vision and Modernity in the Nineteenth Century* (Cambridge, Mass.: MIT Press, 1993).

25. For a detailed description and analysis of Heidegger's life in his historical local realm via what I call his late, plain-speaking "homey works," see my *Heidegger and Homecoming* (Toronto: University of Toronto Press, 2009), 478–541.

1. The Hermit's and the Priest's Injustices: Reading Cormac McCarthy's *The Crossing* with Hcidcggcr and Anaximander

1. Translated at the front of Randall Collins, *The Sociology of Philosophies* (Cambridge: Harvard University Press, 1998).

2. I want to thank my colleague Professor Monika Kaup for pointing out the parallel between Wallace Stevens's poem "Sunday Morning" and the theme I am developing here. Stevens opens the relation of humans to divinity and nature in a domestic scene where a religious service gently pulls against the tug of natural things. In the first verse we encounter a figure in a "peignoir" comfortable with ". . . late / Coffee and oranges in a sunny chair / And the green freedom of a cockatoo / . . . The pungent oranges and bright, green wings. . . ." The middle sections of the poem peacefully resolve the dilemma of whether to yield to church or nature by exfoliating a version of the great American mythos: natural divinity, in which, as many Americans report, we often have our most religious feelings, our deepest spirituality, out in the natural world, for example, while moving about in kinds of "wilderness." This is possible, according to tenets of natural divinity, because through our experience of nature we experience our creator. The tradition, which runs from *Genesis* and the Book of Job to the modern conventions of the natural sublime, provides the means for Stevens to dissolve the tension: by yielding to nature, we give ourselves to God and thus can satisfy both impulses by going in one direction with calm soul and mind. In such a Christian life world, our lives can be unified because we are in an ordered cosmos. On natural divinity, see J. Gray Sweeney's *Themes in American Painting* (Grand Rapids, Mich.: Grand Rapids Art Museum, 1976) as well as our previous work together in *Environmental Interpretations* (Austin: University of Texas Press, 1997).

Yet, sensitive and complex thinker that he is, Stevens does not let us rest complacently in this beautiful order. Even in orthodox Christianity there is pain, pain due to us as mortals. We face death, as we know from the story of Genesis, and pain, which we hear is due to us for our place in the cosmos in relation to divine beings, for example between Yahweh and Satan as related in Job. Though it may comfort us that heaven lies as a possible, final home beyond our transitory stay on this earth, we are too discomforted and motivated by the experience of the falling away and down, that is by the death of the beings around us, not only of our family and friends but of all natural creatures. Pascal put it starkly when he said that we are as a series of chained prisoners who watch each other die in turn. Thus, the poem's second stanza's "Shall she not find in comforts of the sun / In pungent fruit and bright, green wings, or else / In any balm or beauty of the earth, / Things to be cherished like the thought of heaven? Divinity must live within herself" gives way to a sadder, more somber image. The latter, though it substitutes for the biblical readings and sermon we might have heard had we gone to the religious service, provides, now written large and in our own chosen terms, the same lesson upon which we must meditate.

The final stanza ends:

And, in the isolation of the sky,
At evening, casual flocks of pigeons make
Ambiguous undulations as they sink,
Downward to darkness, on extended wings.

As do all living creatures, humans face death, and the hope for everlasting life with a Christian God in heaven carries with it the "opposite" or "complement" of accepting the painful death of what we love, of that to which we have become emotionally attached—the death, really, of all of nature.

3. Pages 137–158. Hereafter, page citations to the novel will be given in the text. All references to *The Crossing* are to the hardbound edition (New York: Knopf, 1998).

4. As Wendell Berry so eloquently points out, in *King Lear*, which appeared at the beginning of our modern-technological era, the Earl of Gloucester's blindness is connected to his hubris, for he believed that he could control a world stabilized through knowledge and power (keynote address at the Association for the Study of Literature and the Environment, Kalamazoo, Summer 1999). Note that the Earl's second prayer presents the alternative to his first view; as he cedes to the mystery, asking the gods to "take my breath." This reversal is strikingly parallel to Heidegger's reading of the Anaximander fragment (considered here), not only in its shift and opening to cosmic order but in yielding to his fated time and not insisting on lingering in the present in an untoward way.

5. These translations are from the standard work, Kathleen Freeman, *Ancilla to the Pre-Socratic Philosophers* (Cambridge, Mass.: Harvard University Press, 1948).

6. Northrop Frey, *Anatomy of Criticism* (New York: Atheneum, 1968), 115–128.

7. "Anaximander," in *Early Greek Thinking*, trans. David Krell and Frank Capuzzi (New York: Harper and Row, 1975), 19. Hereafter references to this collection of essays will be cited in the text as EGT.

8. Heidegger, *Introduction to Metaphysics* (New York: Doubleday, 1961), 123ff.

9. Martin Heidegger and Eugen Fink, *Heraclitus Seminar 1966/67* (Tuscaloosa: University of Alabama Press, 1970), 12. I generally but not always note which of these two seminar leaders made a particular comment, because both Heidegger and his colleague Fink make similar remarks, often completing one thought together. Hereafter references to this text will be cited in the text as HS.

10. Weaving in yet another poetic strand, Heidegger and Fink add that the German poet Hölderlin says much the same in his "Peace" and other poems (HS, 32). In "Peace" we find lines 13–18:

Unyielding and unvanquished, you strike alike
The lion-hearted, Nemesis, and the weak,
And from the blow your victims tremble

Down to the ultimate generation.
You hold the secret powers to goad and curb
For thorn and reins are given into your hands.

11. On the fourfold of mortals and divinities, heavens and earth, all gathered by things, see Heidegger, "Building Dwelling Thinking" and "The Thing" in *Poetry, Language, Thought* (New York: Harper & Row, 1971), 145–186.

12. Note that this also is very close to Heidegger's ideas on truth as unconcealment (*aletheia*), which always is bound up and given simultaneously with its counter, concealment (*lethe*).

13. On the forgetting and remembering of the natural and elemental, see Luce Irigaray, *The Forgetting of Air in Martin Heidegger* (Austin: University of Texas Press, 1999).

14. On the contrary possibility, that when no name is given, things no longer retain their meaning, see Martin Heidegger's analysis of Stefan George's poetic line, "Where word breaks off, no thing may be," in "Words," in *On the Way to Language* (New York: Harper & Row, 1971), 139–156; and Gabriel Garcia Marquez's amazing account of people forgetting the names of things in *One Hundred Years of Solitude* (New York: Harper & Row, 1970), 48–49.

15. Heidegger calls poems "things." Also notice the parallel between what is said below in this passage about the tale having its abode in the telling and Heidegger's famous phrase about "Language is the house of Being" in "Letter on Humanism," in *Basic Writings*, ed. David Krell (New York: Harper and Row, 1977), 213–265.

16. On technology and the West, see especially Martin Heidegger, *The Question Concerning Technology* (New York: Harper & Row, 1977).

17. For a helpful explication of Heidegger's unorthodox no-longer-metaphysical translation of *to chreon* into "to use" (via "*cheir*: hand," "*chrao*: hand over"), see Charles Bambach, *Thinking the Poetic Measure of Justice* (Albany, N.Y.: SUNY Press, 2013), 136, 167–171; cf. what Heidegger does in *What Is Called Thinking?* with *chre*: via "hand, handle" to an originary (nonutilitarian) sense of "use"/"usage"/"it is useful" (parallel to the impersonal "it gives"), 186–193. The rest of Bambach's book is commendable for its treatment of Heidegger's reading of the Anaximander fragment and for the overall reading back and forth from the Greek to contemporary poetry on the issue of justice.

18. At the same time that Job was delivered over to Satan, he was kept in the hands of God. Such a countermove and meaning within delivery also is noted by Heidegger in the sentence immediately following the one quoted above: "But such delivery is of a kind which keeps this transfer in mind, and with it what is transferred."

19. The entire novel and social-psychological issue of the passing of violence from one person and group to another is profoundly reflected upon by the Swiss psychiatrist Alice Miller in *The Drama of the Gifted Child* (New York: Basic Books, 1994).

20. Originally, I had intended to develop what McCarthy and Heidegger say about the blind seer, our oblivion, and the importance of the tales of men that all are one by explicating the second and parallel second story within the story in *The Crossing* (that of the Sepulturero—blind man, 274–294). Obviously that has become beyond the scope of this already-too-long chapter and will need to wait for another occasion.

21. McCarthy and Heidegger as well as the Greeks have much to say on boundaries. Heidegger notes how we are bound within our mother tongue (EGT, 19); with Anaximander, he develops at some length how we are bound within temporality, between the absence of what is not yet come and that of what has passed by (EGT, 41–42, 48–49) and by the jointure of the while (EGT, 53–54); and with Heraclitus, he thinks of mortals and gods by way of day and night, that is, in terms of Helios's boundaries as set in the heavens (HS, 37–60). It also is worth noting that the Greeks and Heidegger delineate the jointure across boundaries in a manner that images the tensed stringing of opposed forces, as in the bow and lyre.

22. Hans-Georg Gadamer points out that genuine reading, in which the horizon or context of the reader is fused with that of the text because of a shared question, leads to the text calling the reader into question. See *Truth and Method* (New York: Continuum, 1989).

23. "Theory of Symbols," in Frye, *Anatomy of Criticism*, 71–128.

24. Frye, *Anatomy of Criticism*, 77.

25. On this technique in which Heidegger teaches by reflexive referral of what is said, see my *Heidegger's Language and Thinking* (Atlantic Highlands, N.J.: Humanities Press, 1988), pp. 147–183.

2. Art, Architecture, Violence: Daniel Libeskind's Jewish Museum Berlin

1. In contrast to the dominant metaphysical tradition in which thinking has come to mean exclusively representation, Heidegger articulates how the counter, originary mode is thinking that recalls (*Andenken*), that is, properly re-collective—"memorial" thinking in that it remembers and holds on to what has been given and needs to be safeguarded and taken to heart. Thus thinking (*denken*) is thought through the interplay of remembrance (*Andenken*) and memory (*Gedächnis*). All this is connected to *Denkmal*, the word for a monument or memorial.

2. See Robert Mugerauer, *Heidegger and Homecoming* (Toronto: University of Toronto Press, 2009).

3. Hannah Arendt, *On Violence* (New York: Harcourt Brace and Company, 1970), 4, 41–42, 46.

4. Sophocles, *Antigone* (Garden City, N.Y.: Anchor, 1961), lines 332–356, pp. 123–124.

5. Martin Heidegger, "The Way to Language," in *On the Way to Language* (New York: Harper and Row, 1971), 121.

6. For a detailed treatment of this tradition, see my "Hermeneutical Retrieval, American Nature as Paradise," in *Interpreting Environments: Tradition, Deconstruction, Hermeneutics* (Austin: University of Texas Press, 1995), chap. 3; J. Gray Sweeney, *Themes in American Painting* (Grand Rapids, Mich.: Grand Rapids Art Museum, 1976).

7. Martin Heidegger, "Building Dwelling Thinking," in *Poetry, Language, Thought* (New York: Harper and Row, 1968), 145–161.

8. See my *Interpretations on Behalf of Place* (Albany, N.Y.: SUNY Press, 1998).

9. See Robert Mugerauer, "Openings to Each Other in the Technological Age," in *Global Norms and Urban Forms in the Age of Tourism: Consuming Tradition, Manufacturing Heritage*, ed. Nezar AlSayyad (New York: Routledge/Spon, 2001).

10. Sigfried Giedion, *The Eternal Present: The Beginning of Art* (New York: Bollingen Foundation, 1962).

11. See Nold Egenter on the origins of human dwellings in the nest building of the great apes and the primal traditions and symbolism of bamboo and reeds: *Gottersitze aus Schilf und Bambus/Sacred Symbols of Reed and Bamboo* (Bern: Peter Lang, 1982); *The Present Relevance of the Primitive in Architecture*, Architectural Anthropology Research Series 1 (Lausanne: Structura Mundi, 1992).

12. For a general overview of Egyptian practices see chapter 2 of my *Interpreting Environments*; Mircea Eliade, *Patterns in Comparative Religion*, trans. Rosemary Sheed (New York: World, 1968), e.g., section 43; H. Frankfurt, *Kingship and the Gods* (Chicago: University of Chicago Press, 1948).

13. Julius Guttmann, *Philosophies of Judaism: The History of Jewish Philosophy from Biblical Times to Franz Rosenzweig*, trans. David Silverman (New York: Holt, Rinehart, and Winston, 1964).

14. Schopenhauer was the exception in applying the ideas of the sublime to architecture, specifically working out the idea of the mathematical sublime: "We receive this impression of the mathematical-sublime, quite directly, by means of a space which is small indeed as compared with the world, but which has become directly perceptible to us, and affects us with its whole extent in all its three dimensions, so as to make our own body seem almost infinitely small. An empty space can never be thus perceived, and therefore never an open space, but only space that is directly perceptible in all its dimensions by means of the limits which enclose it; thus for example a very high, vast dome, like that of St. Peter's at Rome, or St. Paul's in London. The sense of the sublime here arises through the consciousness of the vanishing nothingness of our own body in the presence of a vastness which . . . exists . . . in our idea." *The World as Will and Idea* (New York: Doubleday, 1961), 219.

15. Hannah Arendt, *The Human Condition* (Chicago: University of Chicago Press, 1958), 194–195.

16. Alberto Perez-Gomez, *Built Upon Love* (Cambridge, Mass.: MIT Press, 2008*)*, 132.

17. Of course, though it cannot be done here, Heidegger, Derrida, and others' thinking on the dynamic between absence and presence is important to help us deal with death, with our social ways of attempting to deal with loss.

18. Emmanuel Levinas, *Otherwise Than Being* (Pittsburgh, Penn.: Duquesne University Press, 1988), 144; Emmanuel Levinas, "Is Ontology Fundamental?" in *Basic Philosophical Writings* (Bloomington: Indiana University Press, 1996), 8.

19. The specification that "the other has the face of the poor, the stranger, the widow, and the orphan" appears throughout Levinas's writings: to cite just one instance, for example, *Totality and Infinity* (Pittsburgh, Penn.: Duquesne University Press, 1969), 77.

20. This position is shared by feminist ethics of care. From the huge literature see especially J. C. Tronto, *Moral Boundaries: A Political Argument for an Ethic of Care* (New York: Routledge, 1993); Margaret Urban Walker, *Moral Contexts* (New York: Rowan and Littlefield, 2003).

21. Levinas, *Totality and Infinity*, 39. Note that in this passage Levinas goes on to immediately add, "But the Stranger also means the free one. Over him I have no power."

22. Levinas, *Totality and Infinity*, 235.

23. Martin Heidegger, "Language in the Poem: A Discussion on Georg Trakl's Poetic Work," in *On the Way to Language* (New York: Harper and Row, 1971), 196.

24. Martin Heidegger, "Language," in *Poetry, Language, Thought* (New York: Harper and Row, 1971), 200.

25. Heidegger, "Language," 195.

26. Heidegger, "Language," 204; cf. Martin Heidegger, "Words," in *On the Way to Language* (New York: Harper and Row, 1971), 153.

27. Heidegger, "Language," 204–205.

28. Libeskind himself notes and plays with the multiple meanings of "draw": "The word 'drawing' has so many connotations: You draw water out of a well; you draw a drawing; you draw cards in a game of cards; and you can also draw a gun. It is somehow the same word in each case. I think that in English the word 'drawing' has a magnetic center to it, which is not just a sign but is the measure of the buildings." G+B Arts International, *Jewish Museum Berlin: Architect Daniel Libeskind* (Berlin: 1999), 43.

29. Heidegger, "Language in the Poem," 181; cf. 183.

30. For example, Bruno Latour makes a case for considering things as "actants" since they play a major part in the constitution of networks of meaning and action. See his *Reassembling the Social: An Introduction to Actor-Network-Theory* (Oxford: Oxford University Press, 2007).

31. Martin Heidegger, *What Is Called Thinking?* (New York: Harper and Row, 1968).

32. Libeskind's design simultaneously developed in the context of Berlin's built (and partially still destroyed) urban fabric, in the thinking and writing of our time (such as Derrida's and Heidegger's), and in our need for an adequate moral and public stance or response to past and future historical deeds. But he was not then reading Heidegger and had his first encounter with Derrida and continentally oriented philosophers only in April 1991 at the conference "*Das Unheimliche*: Philosophy, Architecture, the City," held at De Paul University in Chicago. Derrida and Libeskind had not met before this conference, and Derrida made his remarks after only a brief meeting with Libeskind and then hearing the general presentation of the project. At the same time, however, "proceeding in the other direction," philosophers had gotten glimpses of initial versions of his design, which had been printed in architectural journals beginning in 1989, and had begun discussing the material in phenomenological and deconstructive terms. The main point here is that for the most part, or perhaps altogether, Libeskind had been independently exploring presence and absence.

33. Martin Heidegger, *On Time and Being* (New York: Harper and Row, 1972), 1.

34. Henri Lefebvre, *The Production of Space* (Oxford: Blackwell, 1991).

35. Heidegger's famous recovery of Aristotle's potent ideas concerning *phronēsis* (practical wisdom) from Book VI of Aristotle's *Nicomachean Ethics* has recently had an increasing impact in the retheorization and implementation of practice and political action in a variety of disciplines ranging from planning to nursing. See Heidegger's 1924/25 lecture course *Plato's Sophist* (Bloomington: Indiana University Press, 1997), and especially the 1922 "Phenomenological Interpretations with Respect to Aristotle: Indication of the Hermeneutical Situation," in *Man and World* 25 (1992): 355–393 and the 1924 lecture course *Basic Concepts of Aristotelian Philosophy* (Bloomington: University of Indiana Press, 2009). William McNeill's analyses of Heidegger's modulations of Aristotle are exceptionally helpful: *The Glance of the Eye: Heidegger, Aristotle, and the Ends of Theory* (Albany, N.Y.: SUNY Press, 1999); *The Time of Life: Heidegger and Ēthos* (Albany, N.Y.: SUNY Press, 2006). On the current reappreciation and applications, see Bent Flyvjberg, *Making Social Science Matter* (New York: Cambridge University Press, 2001) and *Real Social Science: Applied Phronesis* (New York: Cambridge University Press, 2012); Lenore Sandercock, *Cosmopolis II: The Mongrel Cities of the Twenty-First Century* (New York: Continuum, 2003).

36. El Croquis, *Daniel Libeskind: 1987–1996* (Madrid: 1996), 21–22.

37. Seth Paskin, personal correspondence of July 22, 1995. I want to thank Seth for discussions about how important it is to articulate the details of the ways in which the museum-memorial is a response to a particular design competition that, in turn, is a response to part of the history of the Jews and the events of the Holocaust.

38. Cf. Levinas below, and Jean-Luc Marion's insights on call and response in *Being Given: Toward a Phenomenology of Givenness* (Stanford, Calif.: University of Stanford Press, 2002).

39. Kristin Feireiss, ed., *Daniel Libeskind: Extension to the Berlin Museum with the Jewish Museum Department* (Berlin: Ernst & Sohn, 1992), 33.

40. Feireiss, *Daniel Libeskind*, 11.

41. Roth Bothe in Feireiss, *Daniel Libeskind*, 44.

42. Bothe, in Feireiss, *Daniel Libeskind*, 48.

43. Bothe, in Feireiss, *Daniel Libeskind*, 33–34.

44. On this point, also see Bothe in Feireiss, *Daniel Libeskind*, 34.

45. In Feireiss, *Daniel Libeskind*, 15.

46. Bernard Schneider, *Daniel Libeskind: Jewish Museum Berlin* (New York: Prestel, 1999), 45.

47. The architectural program, as discussed above, usually provides the context for or directive to the designer's intentions—so that their connection raises once again the somewhat hoary issue of the "author's intention." Though this topic may remain worth exploring for architecture, even if "resolved" for literature, it is not considered here because in this essay I follow Heidegger's and Gadamer's mode of seeing the design, and program too, in terms of the fusion of horizons, hermeneutically interpreted to include, but extend beyond, the author's/designer's intentions. Also see G+B Arts International, *Jewish Museum Berlin*, 32.

48. Heidegger uses *Gebild* to indicate the originary sense of disclosing image, in distinction from the usual historical sense of representational picture, as is nicely conveyed when Hofstadter translates the word as "image formed" to differentiate it adequately from the usual connotation of *Bild*:

> Only image formed keeps the vision.
> Yet image formed rests in the poem.
> [*Erst Gebild wahrt (d.h. verwahrt) Gesicht.*
> *Doch Gebild ruht im Gedicht.*]

"The Thinker as Poet," ["From Out of the Experience of Thinking"], in *Poetry, Language, Thought*, 7.

49. See Libeskind's statements, which elaborate his comments at the 1991 De Paul conference, in Peter Noever, ed., *Architektur im Aufbruch* (München: Prestel Verlag, 1991), 67–78, which are somewhat longer and different that the first English account he gave in Architectural Monographs 16 (*Daniel Libeskind: Countersign* [London: Academy Editions, 1991]). The most elaborate version available (based on the exhibition of project design materials in September 1992 in the Israel Museum, Jerusalem, is in Feireiss, *Daniel Libeskind*.

50. El Croquis, *Daniel Libeskind*, 9.

51. Daniel Libeskind, "The Extension to the Berlin Museum with the Jewish Museum, 1989," in Architectural Monographs 16 (*Daniel Libeskind: Countersign*), 86.

52. El Croquis, *Daniel Libeskind*, 45.

53. Libeskind, in Bernhard Schneider, *Daniel Libeskind: Jewish Museum Berlin* (New York: Prestel, 1999), 17.

54. From the many possibilities, see, for example, what Heidegger says about recollective or memorializing thinking or meditation in "Memorial Address," in *Discourse on Thinking*, trans. John M. Anderson and E. Hans Freund (New York: Harper and Row, 1966), 43–57; and Jacques Derrida, *Aporias*, trans. Thomas Dutoit (Stanford, Calif.: Stanford University Press, 1993), e.g., 13. Also, of course, see Jacques Derrida, *Of Spirit*, trans. Geoffrey Bennington and Rachel Bowlby (Chicago: University of Chicago Press, 1989); and *Cinders*, trans. and ed. Ned Lukacher (Lincoln: University of Nebraska Press, 1991).

55. Hannah Arendt, "The Aftermath of Nazi Rule: Report from Germany," in *Essays in Understanding: 1930–1954* (New York: Schocken, 1994), 250, 255.

56. The English version, in Architectural Monographs 16 (*Countersign*) inexplicably translates and cites only part of the quotation, "Oh word, thou word," omitting the crucial reference to the fact that the word is absent, missing. The longer account in Noever's *Architecktur in AufBruch* provides, "*O Wort, du Wort, das mir gefehlt!*" where "*das mir gefehlt*" would mean "absent, missing, wanting, or lacking," indicating a key development of Libeskind's ideas here and his treatment of the idea of textuality.

57. Libeskind, Architectural Monographs 16 (*Daniel Libeskind: Countersign*), 86.

58. *Gedenkbuch—Opfer der Verfolgung der Juden*, 2 vols. (Koblenz: Bundesarchiv, 1986).

59. When Libeskind did claim that the project was symmetrical on one occasion, he was clearly referring to the function of the spine or axial void, the linear feature that in itself is not connected to symmetries other than there being two heterogeneous "sides" so separated. Daniel Libeskind, *Traces of the Unborn: 1995 Raoul Wallenberg Lecture* (Ann Arbor: College of Architecture, University of Michigan, 1995), 31.

60. In Libeskind, *Traces of the Unborn*, 41.

61. Evidently Libeskind was aided in elaborating the complexity of the design by being able to work on the smaller, exceptionally similar Felix Nussbaum Museum in Osnabrück, Germany, at the same time. He won the Berlin competition in 1989 but because of many complications that museum was not completed until 1999, whereas he won the Osnabrück completion but managed to complete that project in 1998. To compare the two projects for yourself, see Thorsten Rodiek, *Daniel Libeskind: Museum ohne Ausgang—Das Felix-Nussbaum-Haus des Kulturgeschichtlichen Museums Osnabrück* (Berlin: Ernst Wasmuth Verlat, 1999).

62. A decent set of basic exterior images is available on the museum's website: http://www.jmberlin.de.

63. Libeskind notes, "The building is built in the same way as it is conceptually constructed in that the bridges are the last thing to be put into the building. They are lightweight elements, and only when they are installed will one be able to walk through the different fragments in a unified way." *Traces of the Unborn*, 35.

64. For Libeskind's comments on the elements as independent buildings and the cement pouring, see his *Traces of the Unborn*, 32, 34–35, 38.

65. Architectural Monographs 16 (*Daniel Libeskind: Countersign*), 65.

66. The zinc tiles, in fact, have a long history in Berlin building history.

67. The development from the core figure continues in other forms. For example, in the stage of becoming more visitor friendly, the museum's staff designer, Marion Meyer, combined the zigzag with the symbol of three pomegranates to generate the museum's new logo. *Jewish Museum Berlin: Opening Issue* (Berlin: Stiftung Jüdisches Museum Berlin, 2001/5761): 8.

68. G+B Arts International, *Jewish Museum Berlin*, 114.

69. There are multiple attempts (more or less successful) by Libeskind and others to explain the voids. For example, Schneider, *Daniel Libeskind*, 51; Libeskind, *Traces of the Unborn*, 32, 34.

70. Libeskind, *Traces of the Unborn*, 35.

71. Libeskind, *Traces of the Unborn*, 32.

72. Jewish Museum Berlin, "Museum Booklet," 7, 9.

73. See my "Northern Lights: Embodied Perception and Enacted Vision" in *Hyperborean Wind: Design and the City*, ed. Matti Ikonen and G. Backhaus (Reykjavik: University of Iceland Press, 2012), 75–111.

74. Libeskind, *Traces of the Unborn*, 33.

75. This is the Holocaust Void, one of the "voided voids."

76. We learn from the commenting literature that the plantings are irrigated from below; thus, this may be seen as an upside-down garden (e.g., Schneider, *Daniel Libeskind*, 40).

77. Libeskind, in Schneider, *Daniel Libeskind*, 41.

78. Libeskind, in Schneider, *Daniel Libeskind*, "Preface."

79. For example, this is "explained" in Schneider, *Daniel Libeskind*, 57–58.

80. A fruitful study could be made of the "chiasm"—the intertwining enacted across the flesh in the touching–being touched of which we are capable (as when "my hand, while it is felt from within, is also accessible from without, itself tangible, for my other hand, for example" [133]); or, the "double and crossed situating of the visible in the tangible and of the tangible in the visible" (134)—to the doubling-up, the reversibility, the crossing-over fundamental to contemporary architecture by working out the implications of Merleau-Ponty's *The Visible and the Invisible* (Evanston, Ill.: Northwestern University Press, 1968). A beginning is made in regard to Steven Holl and museums in my "Embodied Perception—Enacting Color Vision," presented at a special session, "Chiasmatic Encounter with Stephen Holl: His Work Architectural and Written," at his new museum, Kiasma, at the annual conference on the International Association for Philosophy and Literature, Helsinki, June, 2005; a revised and expanded version appears as "Northern Lights: Embodied Perception and Enacted Vision."

81. Schneider, *Daniel Libeskind*, 24.

82. For a detailed account see Helmuth F. Braun, "The Jewish Museum in Berlin: Past-Present-Perspectives, *G+B Arts International* (1999): 100–116.

83. Libeskind, in Schneider, *Daniel Libeskind*, 41.

84. Libeskind, *Traces of the Unborn*, 40.

85. Schneider, *Daniel Libeskind*, 33, 45.

86. Libeskind notes the distorted Star of David in his *Traces of the Unborn*, 30.

87. Libeskind, in Schneider, *Daniel Libeskind*, 27.

88. Libeskind, in Schneider, *Daniel Libeskind*, 41; and Libeskind, *Traces of the Unborn*, 33.

89. This needs to be thought in regard to, and versus, the "they" (*das Man*) as fundamentally analyzed by Heidegger in *Being and Time*, throughout, but see for example Division 1: Section IV, "Being-in-the-World as Being-with and Being a Self: The 'They,'" 107, 122 (Albany, N.Y.: SUNY Press, 1996).

90. Schneider, *Daniel Libeskind*, 40.

91. Architectural Monographs 16 (*Daniel Libeskind: Countersign*), 87.

92. Libeskind, *Traces of the Unborn*, 42–43.

93. Libeskind, in Schneider, *Daniel Libeskind*, 19.

94. Of course, in the end, a more spectacular deconstruction might be called for.

95. Levinas, *Totality and Infinity*, x.

96. That violence is instrumental is one of the major theses and points of analysis in Arendt's *On Violence*; cf. G. Agamben who develops these themes explicitly starting from Arendt's contribution in *Homo Sacer* (Stanford, Calif.: University of Stanford Press, 1998).

97. Levinas, *Totality and Infinity*, 198; cf. 222 and "Is Ontology Fundamental?," section 5, titled "The Ethical Significance of the Other (*Autrui*)," 9.

98. Arendt, "The Eggs Speak Up," in *Essays in Understanding*, 23.

99. Arendt, *On Violence*, 53,79.

100. Arendt, *On Violence*, 63–64, 79. The strategies and tactics of resistance in everyday life are subtly described by Michel de Certeau, *The Practice of Everyday Life* (Berkeley: University of California Press, 1984); and de Certeau with Luce Giard and Pierre Mayol, *The Practice of Everyday Life—Volume II: Living and Cooking* (Minneapolis: University of Minnesota Press, 1998). On the ways of "making do" in the face and aftermath of violence, see my "Insinuating a Better Way of Life: 'Making Do' in the Everyday Spaces of Buenos Aires" (Berkeley, Calif.: IASTE—Traditional Dwellings and Settlements Working Paper Series, 2010).

101. Hannah Arendt, "Social Science Techniques and the Study of Concentration Camps," in *Essays in Understanding*, 215, 232–236, 241–242.

102. Arendt, "Social Science Techniques and the Study of Concentration Camps," 233.

103. Levinas, *Otherwise Than Being*, 146–147.

104. Levinas, *Otherwise Than Being*, 100, 104, 143, 150.

105. Levinas, "Truth of Disclosure and Truth of Testimony," in *Basic Philosophical Writings*, 102, 104; *Otherwise Than Being*, 144. Again, there is substantial common ground with feminist ethics of care. See note 20, above.

106. Levinas, "Truth of Disclosure and Truth of Testimony," 100.

107. Levinas, "Truth of Disclosure and Truth of Testimony," 101.

108. Levinas, "Truth of Disclosure and Truth of Testimony," 103.

109. Perhaps Levinas's major theme. It appears many places, for example, "Is Ontology Fundamental?" in *Basic Philosophical Writings*, 1–10; "The Face to Face—An Irreducible Relation," and Section III, "Exteriority and the Face," both in *Totality and Infinity*, 79–81 and 187–219; "Meaning and Sense," in *Basic Philosophical Writings*, 33–64.

110. Levinas, *Totality and Infinity*, 199.

111. Levinas, "Truth of Disclosure and Truth of Testimony," 106; *Otherwise Than Being*, 148. Levinas goes on to another aspect of testimony since he holds that the entire phenomena under discussion here, the giving of responsibility and response to the other, itself "testifies to Infinity."—"This witness is true, but with a truth irreducible to the truth of disclosure." *Otherwise Than Being*, 145–146. Developing how "this testimony belongs to the very glory of the Infinite," to God, is beyond the current discussion. Levinas says "entering me by the simple effect of traumatism, by breaking and entering," *Otherwise Than Being*, 144; cf. how Marion describes how the other, the neighbor, comes crashing over me, *Being Given*, 103, 105.

112. Levinas, "Truth of Disclosure and Truth of Testimony," 102.

113. Levinas, *Otherwise Than Being*, 142, 145.

114. To interpret museums themselves as already a nonconceptual response is to begin to try to understand them as originary rather than still metaphysical and representational; it neither implies any irrationality nor precludes parallel scientific conceptualization, as Heidegger consistently argues (with special clarity in the accessible "Memorial Address," where he treats "two-track" thinking).

115. Marion, *Being Given*, 102.

116. Levinas, "Truth of Disclosure and Truth of Testimony," 106.

117. Levinas, *Totality and Infinity*, 213.

118. Arendt, "Social Science and Concentration Camps," 243.

119. Arendt, *The Human Condition*, 179.

120. Hannah Arendt, *Men in Dark Times* (New York: Harcourt, Brace, World, 1968), 21.

121. Arendt, *The Human Condition*, 192; "Understanding and Politics," in *Essays in Understanding*, 319.

122. Arendt, "Understanding and Politics," 310.

123. Arendt, *On Violence*, 67.

124. See Tilman Allert, *The Hitler Salute: On the Meaning of a Gesture* (New York: Metropolitan, 2005).

125. Hannah Arendt, "The Image of Hell," in *Essays in Understanding*, 198.

126. There also is a large body of work exploring "the abject," which I do not take up here: see especially Julia Kristeva, *Powers of Horror* (New York: Columbia University Press, 1982). Kelly Oliver provides a useful overview and analysis of the subject in Part Three, "The Ethics of Maternity," of *Womanizing Nietzsche: Philosophy's Relation to the Feminine* (New York: Routledge, 1995), 130–193.

127. Arendt, *On Violence*, 54–55.

128. Arendt, "Social Science Techniques and the Study of Concentration Camps," 240, 242.

129. Arendt, "Social Science Techniques and the Study of Concentration Camps," 237–239, 245.

130. Arendt, "Social Science Techniques and the Study of Concentration Camps," 240.

131. Arendt, "Social Science Techniques and the Study of Concentration Camps," 240n20 on 246, citing reports from *Nazi Conspiracy and Aggression* (Washington, D.C., 1946), VII:84ff.

132. Levinas, *Totality and Infinity*, 225.

133. Levinas, *Totality and Infinity*, 232–233.

134. Levinas, *Totality and Infinity*, 233–235.

135. Levinas, *Totality and Infinity*, 234.

136. Levinas, *Totality and Infinity*, 234.

137. Levinas, *Totality and Infinity*, 236.

138. Levinas, *Totality and Infinity*, 232–233.

139. Levinas, "Is Ontology Fundamental?," section 5, titled "The Ethical Significance of the Other (*Autrui*)," 9.

140. Levinas, *Totality and Infinity*, 238–239.

141. Levinas, *Totality and Infinity*, 225.

142. Levinas, *Totality and Infinity*, 239. Levinas goes so far as to say, "There is responsibility for the other right up to dying for the other! This is how the alterity of the Other—distant and near—affects, through my responsibility, the utmost present." *Time and the Other*, 114.

143. Levinas, *Totality and Infinity*, 230.

144. Levinas, *Totality and Infinity*, 233.

145. Hannah Arendt, "Nightmare and Flight," in *Essays in Understanding*, 134.

146. Hannah Arendt, "Dedication to Karl Jaspers," in *Essays in Understanding*, 214–215.

147. There recently has been new appreciation as to how local connection to place bears on the modes in which our knowing, acting, and "identity" concretely emerge. In this regard it is worth remembering the stress Heidegger places on Hebel's figure of the plant: "Johann Peter Hebel once wrote: 'We are plants which—whether we like to admit it to ourselves or not—must with our roots rise out of the earth in order to bloom in the ether and to bear fruit."

Works, ed. W. Altwegg (Frauenfeld: Verlag Huber, 1935), III:314. "The poet means to say: For a truly joyous and salutary human work to flourish, man must be able to mount from the depth of his home ground up into the ether. Ether here means the free air of the high heavens, the open realm of the spirit." "Memorial Address," in *Discourse on Thinking*, 47, 48.

148. Libeskind, in El Croquis, *Daniel Libeskind*, 45 (an earlier citation circulating, for example, in Architectural Monographs 16 [*Daniel Libeskind: Countersign*], 87) was incorrect, evidently because it cited Aquinas—an intermediate source.

3. When the Given Is Gone: From the Black Forest to Berlin and Back via Wim Wenders' *Der Himmel Über Berlin*

1. Martin Heidegger, "Memorial Address," in *Discourse on Thinking*, trans. John M. Anderson and E. Hans Freund (New York: Harper and Row, 1966), 48–49.

2. Martin Heidegger, "Building Dwelling Thinking," in *Poetry, Language, Thought* (New York: Harper & Row, 1971), 145.

3. The references in brackets are to the numbered shots in *Der Himmel Über Berlin: Ein Filmbuch von Wim Wenders und Peter Handke* (Frankfurt am Main: Suhrkamp Verlag, 1987).

4. Jean-Luc Marion, *Being Given* (Stanford, Calif.: Stanford University Press, 2002), 129–130. Hereafter cited in the text as BG.

5. Heidegger uses the word "*Andenken*" to connote recollective or memorializing thinking, his originary mode of meditation explicitly contrasted to the dominant metaphysical representational, calculative thinking.

6. In another interpretive approach than I am undertaking here, obviously the angels can be fruitfully understood via Benjamin's angels of history, especially in regard to the angel's explaining that they have witnessed two histories, that of the unfolding of the natural world and that which has happened since humans have appeared—the history of war [4011]. Wenders himself notes that his idea for angels came from several sources, including the "Angel of Peace" (once the "Triumphant Angel of War") atop the Victory Column, Rilke's *Duino Elegies*, Paul Klee's paintings, and Walter Benjamin's *Angel of History*, as well as a song by the Cure. Wim Wenders, *The Logic of Images: Essays and Conversations* (Boston: Faber and Faber, 1991), 77. Also see note 11 below on the difference between Damiel and Marion (the trapeze artist) on having or not having a history and on Jean-Luc Marion on historicity resulting from our responses to excess givens.

7. Jean-Luc Marion, *The Crossing of the Visible*, trans. James K. A. Smith (Stanford, Calif.: Stanford University Press, 2004), 5; Marion, *Being Given*, 122.

8. Using the same terms of call and response, a political critique of Heidegger's originary calling and Jean-Luc Marion would come from Louis Althusser, who develops the way "Ideological State Apparatuses" draw us into

the dominant system of values so that, as we endorse them, a society is able to reproduce itself and endure. The ISAs "hail individuals as subjects"; when we recognize ourselves as being called (usually only unconsciously) and respond by consenting to the relationships or conditions, we become transformed, molded as subjects of the dominant order. Marion acknowledges Althusser as an influential teacher but otherwise does not cite him on the use of call and recognition as leading to identity constitution, though Althusser famously says that "the hailed individual . . . becomes a *subject* . . . because he has recognized that the hail was 'really' addressed to him, and that 'it was *really him* who was hailed' (and not someone else)." Louis Althusser, "Ideology and Ideological State Apparatuses," in *Lenin and Philosophy and Other Essays*, trans. B. Brewster (New York: Monthly Review Press, 2001), 118.

9. There are many images of characters with eyes closed (Damiel in the public library in his Christ-like pose against the railing [1079] and Homer in a chair [1087]). But, clearly, the majority of these occur when the person or angel is sunk deeply in thought (as we are explicitly told in the case of one of the extras, the old woman who *"ganz in Gedanken versunken in die Ferne schaut"* [3049, cf. 3079]), or when the person or angel has closed his eyes in order to concentrate on something outside himself (as when Damiel listens in the library in a long take of almost a minute's duration [1073] or when he and Homer are head to head, both with eyes closed [2075]). This bodily attitude provides closure to anything external that otherwise would be distracting at the moment in order to let something more important come to thought or memory. The closed eyes, then, do not in the least indicate that the characters are closed off or self-absorbed in any negative sense.

10. Wenders himself emphasizes the importance of laughter, a human ability admired by the angels. Wenders, *The Logic of Images*, 82.

11. In addition to whether Wenders overromanticizes the relation between Damiel and Marion, there is the issue of whether Damiel's attention to Marion in her trailer is intrusive voyeurism rather than angelic propriety. Of course, insofar as he is asexual and immaterial, it may just be that we are prudishly responding in thinking that he is acting improperly, yet it certainly appears that he is beginning to have some sort of "erotic" stirrings, so that, rather than comfortingly touching her, he goes further, caressing her shoulder and neckline. The way he picks up the stone in Marion's trailer [2052–54] has its precedent in his picking up a pen in the library, or more properly his picking up and carrying around its essence rather than the physical object, which remains where it was [1078–81]. A critique of Wenders' portrayal of erotic desire in the film and of Damiel's "act[ing] out his male desire through a most remarkable realization of a male fantasy," looking "on in a scene that borders on sexual invasion," though in an "ineffective and humiliating mode of male voyeurism" is provided by Robert P. Kolker and Peter Beicken, *The Films of Wim Wenders: Cinema as Vision and Desire* (New York: Cambridge University Press, 1993), 155–156, who also cite bell hooks's essay on the film.

At the same time, in the director's comments on the extended DVD version of the film, Wenders points out that Damiel leaves the trailer as Marion begins to undress: his disappearance is signaled by the shift from black and white to color, that is, to the mode of human experience beyond his own (the convention of the film is that human-lived experience is emphasized by color, while the angels' essential, nonphysical comprehension is portrayed in black and white) [2017]. Insofar as Damiel is the unseen between Marion and the audience, it is a more subtle question as to how the erotic is involved in the passage of the exchange of gazes—or rather through the impossibility of seeing the invisible gazes themselves—that pass through the eyes of the intermediate icon (as distinct from the idol), "in effect by crossing the invisible" to open "up to an extremely erotic face-to-face relation." Marion, *The Crossing of the Visible*, 21.

12. "*Damiel wird Ernst, as er Marion Gedanken hort. Er hat keine Geschichte, und er kennt auch den glucklichen Augenblick nicht.*" While Marion says, "*Ich habe eine Geschichte! Und ich werde weiter eine haben!*" [4149]. That the angels, who, though there from the beginning of time and having seen everything, do not themselves exactly have a history, because they are out of the flow of time, in contrast to mortals, who are intimately defined by their placement and actions in time, needs to be thought via Heidegger on historicity, human life, and what once was called "being"—Damiel tells Cassiel, just before dropping from the heavens to the earth, from "divinity" to "mortality," that he wants to enter the flow of time [5046].

Of course, there is not space here to develop the connection of Damiel's *Augenblick* (just noted) with Heidegger's work on time and *kairos*: the decisive moment. Whether there is a poetic play here on *Geschichte* (history) and *Gesicht* (face), as there is with Heidegger's between *Geschichte* and *Geschickt*—the epochal sending-giving from *Ereignis* (Martin Heidegger, *Four Seminars*, trans. A. Mitchell and F. Raffoul [Bloomington: Indiana University Press, 2003], 61), I do not know, though it is possible since Damiel, without a history as an angel, perhaps begins to inhabit a sending-destiny as he enters the flow of time, taking on historicity as he begins to respond finitely to the excess of what is given. He "does not" have a face insofar as he is not seen by mortals, though simultaneously he does insofar as he is a "character" and is seen by us. Thinking along these lines also would benefit from Jean-Luc Marion's discussion of history as resulting from our inability to respond to the excess of what is given, that is, to the need to finish saying all the way what we are able to bring to phenomenality, which generates our engagement over time and thus our characteristic as mortals: "The call precedes the responsal, which continually confesses and fulfills its delay by multiplying responses, whose series opens nothing less than a historicity proper to the gifted" (BG, 295).

13. Cf. Martin Heidegger, *Being and Time*, trans. J. Stambaugh (Albany, N.Y.: SUNY Press, 1966), 135 and §38, "Falling and Thrownness."

14. Marion, *The Crossing of the Visible*, 21.

15. On the tropological and other levels of meaning, see my *Heidegger's Language and Thinking* (Atlantic Highlands, N.J.: Humanities Press, 1988), 204–228.

16. Heidegger, "Memorial Address," 47.

17. Martin Heidegger, "Seven Hundred Years of Messkirch," translated as "Homeland" by Thomas O'Meara, *Listening* 6, no. 3 (Autumn 1971): 238. Hereafter cited in the text as 700YM.

18. Robert Mugerauer, *Heidegger and Homecoming* (Toronto: University of Toronto Press, 2009), 398–999; Martin Heidegger, "*Johann Peter Hebel: Zähringer Rede*" (1954), in *Gesamtausgabe*, vol. 16: *Reden und Andere Zeugnisse Eines Lebenswebes*, item 222 (Frankfurt: Klostermann, 2000), 491. Some of the cited materials in the following sections are quotations from or paraphrases of my *Heidegger and Homecoming*, hereafter cited as HH.

19. For a detailed presentation of this subject matter, see my *Heidegger and Homecoming*, the section of Chapter 6 titled "The Homey Works," 478–541.

20. The Heidegger quotation is from Martin Heidegger, "*Festansprache Beim Heimatfest Todtnauberg*" (1966), in *Gesamtausgabe*, vol. 16: *Reden und Andere Zweugnisse Eines Lebenswebes*, item 251 (Frankfurt: Klostermann, 2000), 648.

21. Heidegger, "*Festansprache Beim Heimatfest Todtnauberg*," 648. Cf. my *Heidegger and Homecoming*, 427–428; Heidegger, "Seven Hundred Years of Messkirch," 234.

22. The Heidegger quotation is from Heidegger, "*Festansprache Beim Heimatfest Todtnauberg*," 644.

23. Marion, *God Without Being*, 132.

24. Marion, *God Without Being*, 132.

25. Marion, *God Without Being*, 134.

26. Wenders, *The Logic of Images*, 78.

27. This might be the point of the intriguing fact in *Wings of Desire* that whereas angels see each other, of humans only children see angels. In addition to the rather banal point that children are innocent and thus might see as adults do not, the more significant idea might be that though some do see, some do not. Those of us who are adult moviegoers are invisible since no film character sees us, neither angel nor Berliner, though they may call us by giving and showing themselves as phenomenal. If we are to pass beyond understanding ourselves as subjects, we need to give up our roles as voyeurs or detached aesthetic observers. Nor can we remain witnesses only, invisible to most of the world as angels are, for we must act—and if witnesses we need be, that embodied testimony rises as political, affecting what is to come to phenomenality and is received by those involved, bearing on the social outcome.

As the angels are invisibly among and often literally between the Berliners, and because of that situation and their characteristics are called to respond as best they can, so we the audience members are invisibly between the angels and the Berliners and because of our situation and character also are called to act as best we can. Seemingly, at first, that would mean we are called to become aware of being called and to question what would be "the best we can do."

We are between possible trajectories, between the children who are embodied but know themselves not and angels who are more fully conscious of themselves but are not embodied. We are between in that we are able to lapse into becoming one of those who does not receive what is given, or we can rise up to be among those who come to see, in the sense of finding themselves addressed by the call of the world, by the gaze of others, and who try to respond responsibly to what we receive.

28. Heidegger, "Memorial Address," 54.

29. Heidegger, "Memorial Address," 55.

30. Translated as "lingering," the script has "*dauert*"; cf. Heidegger's originary reinterpretation of *wesen* by way of *währen*, lasting or enduring, and *weilen*, whiling—which "is indeed the old sense of the word being, *sein*, so that 'whiling' names both: being and ground"—and thus is another name for what later shows itself as granting-giving-opening, *Ereignis*. And note that *wären* [to endure] should be thought together with *gewären* [to grant]. See my *Heidegger and Homecoming*, 256, 261; Martin Heidegger, "The Question Concerning Technology," in *The Question Concerning Technology and Other Essays*, trans. W. Lovitt (New York: Harper & Row, 1977), 30; cf. *wära*, in Martin Heidegger, "Science and Reflection," in *The Question Concerning Technology and Other Essays*, 164–165; Martin Heidegger, *The Principle of Reason*, trans. R. Lilly (Bloomington: Indiana University Press, 1991), 127.

31. See Heidegger, "Memorial Address," 54; Mugerauer, *Heidegger and Homecoming*, 430; Heidegger, "*Festansprache Beim Heimatfest Todtnauberg*," 644.

Bibliography

Agamben, Giorgio. *Homo Sacer.* Translated by Daniel Heller-Roazen. Stanford, Calif.: Stanford University Press, 1998.

Allert, Tilman. *The Hitler Salute: On the Meaning of a Gesture.* New York: Metropolitan, 2005.

Althusser, Louis. "Ideology and Ideological State Apparatuses." Translated by Ben Brewster. In *Lenin and Philosophy and Other Essays* [1969], 85–126. New York: Monthly Review Press, 2001.

Architectural Monographs no. 16. *Daniel Libeskind: Countersign.* London: Academy Editions, 1991.

Arendt, Hannah. *Essays in Understanding: 1930–1954.* New York: Schocken, 1994.

———. *The Human Condition.* Chicago: University of Chicago Press, 1958.

———. *Men in Dark Times.* New York: Harcourt, Brace, World, 1968.

———. "Nightmare and Flight." In *Essays in Understanding*, 133–135. New York: Schocken, 1994.

———. *On Violence.* New York: Harcourt Brace and Company, 1970.

de Certeau, Michel. *The Practice of Everyday Life I.* Translated by Steven Rendall. Berkeley: University of California Press, 1984.

de Certeau, Michel, Luce Giard, and Pierre Mayol. *The Practice of Everyday Life—Volume II: Living and Cooking.* Translated by Timothy Tomasik. Minneapolis: University of Minnesota Press, 1998.

Collins, Randall. *The Sociology of Philosophies.* Cambridge, Mass.: Harvard University Press, 1988.

Crary, Jonathan. *Techniques of the Observer: On Vision and Modernity in the Nineteenth Century.* Cambridge, Mass.: MIT Press, 1993.

Derrida, Jacques. *Aporias.* Translated by Thomas Dutoit. Stanford, Calif.: Stanford University Press, 1993.

———. *Cinders.* Translated and edited by Ned Lukacher. Lincoln: University of Nebraska Press, 1991.

———. *Of Spirit.* Translated by Geoffrey Bennington and Rachel Bowlby. Chicago: University of Chicago Press, 1989.

Egenter, Nold. *Gottersitze aus Schilf und Bambus/Sacred Symbols of Reed and Bamboo.* Bern: Peter Lang, 1982.

———. *The Present Relevance of the Primitive in Architecture.* Architectural Anthropology Research Series 1. Lausanne: Structura Mundi, 1992.

El Croquis. *Daniel Libeskind.* Madrid, 1996.

Eliade, Mircea. *Patterns in Comparative Religion.* Translated by Rosemary Sheed. New York: World, 1968.

Feireiss, Kristin, ed. *Daniel Libeskind: Extension to the Berlin Museum with the Jewish Museum Department.* Berlin: Ernst & Sohn, 1992.

Flyvbjerg, Bent. *Making Social Science Matter.* New York: Cambridge University Press, 2001.

———. *Real Social Science: Applied Phronesis.* New York: Cambridge University Press, 2012.

Frankfurt, H. *Kingship and the Gods.* Chicago: University of Chicago Press, 1948.

Freeman, Kathleen. *Ancilla to the Presocratic Philosophers.* Cambridge, Mass.: Harvard University Press, 1948.

Frye, Northrop. *Anatomy of Criticism.* New York: Atheneum, 1968.

G&B Arts International. *Jewish Museum Berlin: Architect Daniel Libeskind.* Berlin, 1999.

Gadamer, Hans-Georg. *Truth and Method.* New York: Continuum, 1989.

Garcia Marquez, Gabriel. *One Hundred Years of Solitude.* New York: Harper & Row, 1970.

Gedenkbuch—Opfer der Verfolgung der Juden. 2 vols. Koblenz: Bundesarchiv, 1986.

Giedion, Sigfried. *The Eternal Present: The Beginning of Art.* New York: Bollingen Foundation, 1962.

Guttmann, Julius. *Philosophies of Judaism: The History of Jewish Philosophy from Biblical Times to Franz Rosenzweig.* Translated by David Silverman. New York: Holt, Rinehart, and Winston, 1964.

Hebel, Johann Peter. *Works.* Edited by Wilhelm Altwegg. Frauenfeld: Verlag Huber, 1935.

Heidegger, Martin. "The Anaximander Fragment." In *Early Greek Thinking*, 13–58. New York: Harper & Row, 1975.

———. *Basic Writings.* Edited by David Krell. New York: Harper & Row, 1977.

———. *Being and Time.* Translated by Joan Stambaugh. Albany: SUNY Press, 1966.

———. *Discourse on Thinking.* Translated by J. M. Anderson and E. H. Freund. New York: Harper & Row, 1966.

———. *Early Greek Thinking*. Translated by David Krell and Frank Capuzzi. New York: Harper & Row, 1975.

———. "Festansprache Beim Heimatfest Todtnauberg." 1966. In *Gesamtausgabe*, vol. 16: *Reden und Andere Zweugnisse Eines Lebenswebes*, item 251, 641–649. Frankfurt: Klostermann, 2000.

———. *Four Seminars*. Translated by Andrew Mitchell and François Raffoul. Bloomington: Indiana University Press, 2003.

———. *Gesamtausgabe*, vol. 16: *Reden und Andere Zeugnisse Eines Lebenswebes*. Frankfurt: Klostermann, 2000.

———. *Introduction to Metaphysics*. Translated by Ralph Manheim. New York: Doubleday, 1961.

———. "Johann Peter Hebel: Zähringer Rede." 1954. In *Gesamtausgabe*, vol. 16: *Reden und Andere Zeugnisse Eines Lebenswebes*, item 222, 491–497. Frankfurt: Klostermann, 2000.

———. "Letter on Humanism." In *Basic Writings*, 189–212. New York: Harper & Row, 1977.

———. "Memorial Address." In *Discourse on Thinking*, translated by John M. Anderson and E. Hans Freund, 43–57. New York: Harper & Row, 1966.

———. *On the Way to Language*. Translated by Peter Hertz and Joan Stambaugh. New York: Harper & Row, 1971.

———. *On Time and Being*. Translated by Joan Stambaugh. New York: Harper & Row, 1972.

———. "The Pathway." Translated by Thomas Sheehan. In *Heidegger: The Man and the Thinker*, edited by Thomas Sheehan, 69–71. Chicago: Precedent, 1981.

———. *Poetry, Language, Thought*. Translated by Albert Hofstadter. New York: Harper & Row, 1971.

———. *The Principle of Reason*. Translated by Reginald Lilly. Bloomington: Indiana University Press, 1991.

———. *The Question Concerning Technology*. Translated by William Lovitt. New York: Harper & Row, 1977.

———. "Seven Hundred Years of Messkirch." Translated as "Homeland" by Thomas O'Meara. *Listening* 6, no. 3 (Autumn 1971): 231–238.

———. "Sprache und Heimat." In *Hebbel Jahrbuch*, ed. Ludwig Koopmann and Erich Trunz, 27–50. Heide in Holstein: Westholsteinische Verlagsanstalt Boyens, 1960.

———. *What Is Called Thinking?* Translated by Fred Wieck and J. Glenn Gray. New York: Harper & Row, 1968.

Heidegger, Martin, and Eugen Fink. *Heraclitus Seminar 1966/67*. Tuscaloosa: University of Alabama Press, 1970.

hooks, bell. "Representing Whiteness: Seeing Wings of Desire." In *Yearning: Race, Gender, and Cultural Politics*, 165–171. Boston: West End, 1990.

Irigaray, Luce. *The Forgetting of Air in Martin Heidegger*. Austin: University of Texas Press, 1999.

Jewish Museum Berlin. "Museum Booklet." n.d., collected September 2010.

Jewish Museum Berlin: Opening Issue. Berlin: Stiftung Jüdisches Museum Berlin, 2001/5761.

Kolker, Robert P., and Peter Beicken. *The Films of Wim Wenders: Cinema as Vision and Desire.* New York: Cambridge University Press, 1993.

Kristeva, Julia. *Powers of Horror.* New York: Columbia University Press, 1982.

Latour, Bruno. *Reassembling the Social: An Introduction to Actor-Network-Theory.* Oxford: Oxford University Press, 2007.

Lefebvre, Henri. *Production of Space.* Oxford: Blackwell, 1991.

Levinas, Emmanuel. *Basic Philosophical Writings.* Edited by Adriaan Peperzak. Bloomington: Indiana University Press, 1996.

———. *Otherwise Than Being: Or Beyond Essence.* Translated by Alphonso Lingis. Pittsburgh: Duquesne University Press, 1988.

———. *Time and the Other.* Translated by R. A. Cohen. Pittsburgh: Duquesne University Press, 1987.

———. *Totality and Infinity.* Translated by Alphonso Lingis. Pittsburgh: Duquesne University Press, 1969.

Libeskind, Daniel. *Traces of the Unborn: 1995 Raoul Wallenberg Lecture.* Ann Arbor: College of Architecture, University of Michigan, 1995.

McCarthy, Cormac. *The Crossing.* New York: Knopf, 1998.

Marion, Jean-Luc. *Being Given: Toward a Phenomenology of Givenness.* Translated by Jeffrey Kosky. Stanford, Calif.: Stanford University Press, 2002.

———. *The Crossing of the Visible.* Translated by James K. A. Smith. Stanford, Calif.: Stanford University Press, 2004.

———. *God Without Being.* Translated by Thomas Carlson. Chicago: University of Chicago Press, 1991.

———. *In Excess: Studies of Saturated Phenomena.* Translated by Vincent Berraud and Robyn Horner. New York: Fordham University Press, 2002.

———. "The Saturated Phenomena." Translated by Thomas Carlson. In *The Visible and the Revealed,* by Jean-Luc Marion, 18–48. New York: Fordham University Press, 2008.

Merleau-Ponty, Maurice. *The Visible and the Invisible.* Evanston, Ill.: Northwestern University Press, 1968.

Miller, Alice. *The Drama of the Gifted Child.* New York: Basic Books, 1994.

Mugerauer, Robert. "Anatomy of Life and Well-Being: A Framework for the Contributions of Phenomenology and Complexity Theory." *International Journal of Qualitative Studies of Health and Well-Being* (July 2010).

———. "Call of the Earth: Endowment and Response." In *Heidegger and the Earth: Essays in Environmental Thought,* edited by Ladelle McWhorter and Gail Stenstad, new ed., 70–99. Toronto: University of Toronto Press, 2009.

———. "The Double-Gift: Place and Identity." In *Back to the Things Themselves: Architectural Experience, Memory, and Thought,* edited by Iris Aravot. Haifa: Technion University Press, 2014.

————. *Heidegger and Homecoming*. Toronto: University of Toronto Press, 2009.

————. *Heidegger's Language and Thinking*. Atlantic Highlands, N.J.: Humanities Press, 1988.

————. "Insinuating a Better Way of Life: "'Making Do' in the Everyday Spaces of Buenos Aires." Berkeley: IASTE—Traditional Dwellings and Settlements Working Paper Series, 2010.

————. *Interpretations on Behalf of Place*. Albany: SUNY Press, 1994.

————. *Interpreting Environments: Tradition, Deconstruction, Hermeneutics*. Austin: University of Texas Press, 1995.

————. "Northern Lights: Embodied Perception and Enacted Vision." In *Hyperborean Wind: Design and the City*, edited by Matti Ikonen and G. Backhaus, 75–111. Reykjavik: University of Iceland Press, 2012.

————. "Openings to Each Other in the Technological Age." In *Global Norms and Urban Forms in the Age of Tourism: Consuming Tradition, Manufacturing Heritage*, edited by Nezar AlSayyad. New York: Routledge/Spon, 2001.

Noever, Peter, ed. *Architektur im Aufbruch*. München: Prestel Verlag, 1991.

Oliver, Kelly. *Witnessing: Beyond Recognition*. Minneapolis: University of Minnesota Press, 2001.

————. *Womanizing Nietzsche: Philosophy's Relation to the Feminine*. New York: Routledge, 1995.

Perez-Gomez, Alberto. *Built Upon Love*. Cambridge, Mass.: MIT Press, 2008.

Rodiek, Thorsten. *Daniel Libeskind: Museum ohne Ausgang—Das Felix-Nussbaum-Haus des Kulgturgeschichtlichen Museums Osnabrück*. Berlin: Ernst Wasmuth Verlag, 1999.

Romano, Claude. *Event and World*. New York: Fordham University Press, 2009.

Schneider, Bernhard. *Daniel Libeskind: Jewish Museum Berlin*. New York: Prestel, 1999.

Schopenhauer, Arthur. *The World as Will and Idea*. New York: Doubleday, 1961.

Sweeney, J. Gray. *Themes in American Painting*. Grand Rapids, Mich.: Grand Rapids Art Museum, 1976.

Wendel, Barry. "Keynote Address." Association for the Study of Literature and the Environment, Kalamazoo. Summer 1999.

Wenders, Wim. *The Logic of Images: Essays and Conversations*. Boston: Faber and Faber, 1991.

Wenders, Wim, and Peter Handke. *Der Himmel Über Berlin: Ein Filmbuch von Wim Wenders und Peter Handke*. Frankfurt am Main: Suhrkamp Verlag, 1987.

————. *Wings of Desire*. Road Movies Filmproduction GMBH, Berlin and Argos Films, Paris, 1987. DVD with audio commentary by the director Wim Wenders and Peter Falk, MGM Home Entertainment, 2003.

Index

absence/absent, xx, 12, 14, 21, 32–33, 58,
68–70, 72, 74, 80, 85, 95–96, 107,
109, 114, 130, 136, 146n21, 148n17,
149n32

action, xiv, xvi–xvii, xxiii–xxiv, 2, 4,
37–38, 48–50, 54, 57–58, 64, 95–102,
124, 129, 143n16, 148n30, 149n35,
158n12

address, xvi, xviii, 21, 70, 72, 92, 94, 101,
110, 120–31, 135, 139–40, 157n8

aesthetics, xiv, xix, 52–53, 65, 72, 74,
159n27

allotment, 9, 18, 36, 39

Anaximander, x, xvi, xix, 11–25, 27,
29–32, 35, 37–39, 41–45, 144n4,
144n7, 145n17, 146n21, 155n125,
155nn127–31, 155nn145–46

angels, xxiii, 108, 111, 114–18, 124,
126–30, 135–39, 156n6, 157n9,
157n11, 158n12, 159n27

animal(s), 2, 7–9, 12–16, 19–24, 29–34,
48–51, 55, 96, 104, 115

apportion(ment), 9, 19, 22, 32, 40, 45.
See also measure

architecture, xvi–xiv, 47–70, 73–74, 77,
80, 84, 92, 95, 99, 107, 147n11,
147n14, 150n47, 152n80

Arendt, Hannah, xvi, 48–50, 57, 59, 62,
71, 95–97, 100–2, 105–6

art(works), xv–xxii, 8, 47–56, 61, 64, 66,
69, 72, 96, 115, 126, 131–32

Bambach, Charles, 145n17

Benjamin, Walter, 72, 95, 156n6

Berlin, xvi, xix, xxiii, 47–48, 62, 65–7,
80, 85, 91–92, 107–8, 110–21,
125–31, 135–39, 149n32, 151n61,
152n66, 159n27

between, xv, xix, xxi, xxiii, 8–9, 12,
14–15, 32, 36–37, 45, 49, 52, 57–63,
69, 74. *See also* middle

body/embodiment, xvi, xxi, xxiii, 34, 56,
58, 64, 67, 77, 84, 89, 102–3, 111,
117–18, 121–30, 138–39, 142n16,
147n14, 152n73, 152n80, 157n9, 159n27

Buddhism, 53, 146n21

building, xvi, xxiii–xxiv, 6, 30, 48–49,
52–57, 61–95, 106, 108, 110, 113, 117,
145n11, 147n11, 148n28, 151n63,
152n64, 152n66

call(ed), xiv, xvi–xvii, xx, xxiii, 1, 10,
13–14, 16, 35, 37, 41, 44–48, 52, 57,
59, 62, 64–72, 95, 99–101, 106–7,

call(ed) (*continued*)
113, 115, 118–31, 134–40, 142n9,
146n22, 149n38, 156–57n8, 158n12,
159n27
Caravaggio, 99, 118, 123, 142n9
care, 2–6, 10, 16–23, 30, 43–45, 50, 56,
74–80, 96, 115, 119, 121–22, 130–32,
146n20, 148n20, 154n105
chaos, 1–2, 4
churches, xxiii, 3–4, 6, 10–11, 14, 18–19,
22, 24, 38, 57, 64, 70, 111, 143n2
city, xxiii, 4, 10, 20, 57, 65–72, 74, 80,
91–92, 95, 107, 111–17, 129, 135, 137,
149n32
community, xvi, xx, 19–20, 42, 57–59,
67–68, 106, 110, 132–33
cosmos, xxii, 1–7, 11, 15, 23–26, 29,
31–32, 37, 41–45, 52, 58, 143n2

danger, 2, 26, 38, 40, 49, 53, 59, 96, 100
death, xx, xxiii, 1–3, 7–11, 14, 18, 25,
29–31, 35, 37, 39, 45–46, 50, 53–57,
60, 64, 68, 82, 101–5, 113, 122, 125,
129, 143n2, 148n17
deliver, 29, 32, 35–36, 131, 145n18
design, 48–57, 61–77, 81, 85, 91, 94–95,
99, 107–8, 149n32, 149n37, 150n47,
150n49, 151n61, 152n67
destiny, 31, 33, 44–45, 68, 98, 107,
158n12. *See also* fate
destruction, xiv, xix, xxiii, 2, 4, 6, 13–14,
16, 18–19, 22–23, 29, 36, 42–45, 50,
53, 71, 96, 106, 110
dialogue, xv–xvii, xxii–xxiv, 8, 99, 133
disaster, xx, 4, 6, 41, 54
displace, xvii, xx, 64, 68, 76, 109, 131
divinities, xxiii, 7, 37, 52–53, 56, 138,
143, 145, 151
Dürer, Albrecht, 136–37

earth, xxiii, 7–11, 14, 18, 21, 35, 37, 41,
49–56, 60, 62, 94, 96, 102, 110, 115,
124, 125, 129, 133, 137–38, 143n2,
145n11, 155n147, 158n12
encounter, xiv, xxiii, 3, 13, 24–28, 34,
44–45, 48, 52, 55, 60, 62–63, 65, 74,
80, 82, 85, 95–96, 99–100, 103–8,
128, 131, 143n2, 149n32

environment, xviii–xix, xxiii, 16, 36, 38,
42, 49, 54–55, 63, 72, 81, 89, 107–9,
112, 144n4
ethics/ethical, xviii–xx, xxiii, 49, 89, 95,
97–99, 101, 105–6, 148n20, 149n35,
153n97, 154n105, 155n126, 155n139
exile, 5, 68, 81–82, 84, 94, 113

face, the, 2, 14, 48, 59–60, 68, 82, 89,
96, 99–101, 103–6, 113–14, 120–23,
142n9, 148n19, 154n109, 158nn11–12
fate, xxii, 30–33, 38–41, 45, 58, 144n4.
See also destiny
figure, xxii–xxiii, 9, 28, 49, 52, 56, 62,
69–70, 72, 85, 95, 136, 138, 143n2,
152n67, 157n147
fourfold, xxiii, 7, 130, 137,145n11
freedom, xxii, 43, 51, 9, 105, 143
Frye, Northrop, xxii, 7, 43, 142n23,
146nn23–24

gathering, xvi, xix, xxii–xxiii, 6–8, 13–14,
18–22, 29–33, 42–47, 55–58, 61–63,
69, 99, 107, 122, 127, 130, 132–33,
137–38, 145n11
gift(ed), xiv, 17–18, 21–23, 115, 120, 130,
143, 136, 138–40, 141n1, 145n19,
158n12
God, 2, 4, 52–53, 56–57, 109, 111, 114,
119, 127, 137–38, 143n2, 145n18,
154n111
gods, 1, 3, 8–10, 12, 14, 23, 25, 27–34,
36, 38–39, 42, 44–45, 50, 55, 58, 127,
144n4, 146n21
grant, 17, 19, 22, 40, 42, 92, 160n30
guardian, 59, 77, 111, 114–15, 118, 11,
125, 131–32, 146n1

hatred, 92, 101, 104–6
hear(ing), xviii, 2, 4–11, 15, 17, 20, 23,
25, 28–45, 48, 55, 59, 63, 76, 89, 102,
108, 111, 115, 118, 122, 125, 128,
133–34, 140, 143n2
heavens, xxiii, 7, 9, 18, 37, 55, 111, 125,
129, 133, 137–38, 145n11, 146n21,
156n147, 158n12
Hebel, Johann Peter, 132–33, 135,
155n147, 159n18

novel, xvi–xviii, xxii–xxiv, 2, 5–7, 10, 13, 17, 19, 20–24, 26, 28, 31, 33–36, 40–41, 43, 49, 145n19

oblivion, 7, 12, 27, 29, 35, 37–42, 51, 56, 71, 102, 105, 146n20
Oliver, Kelly, xviii, 142n14, 155n126
open(ing), xiv–xviii, xxi–xxiii, 19–28, 35, 45–46, 49, 51, 53, 57–58, 62, 66–68, 71, 77, 80–85, 88, 91–95, 98–108, 110–11, 115, 117, 119, 123, 125–39, 143n2, 144n4, 147n9, 147n14, 156n147, 158nn11–12, 160n30
order/disorder, xiii, 1, 10–31, 36–38, 41, 44–46, 52, 59, 68, 100, 102–5, 109, 143n2, 144n4, 157n8
other(s), 1, 69, 110, 113–29, 135, 138, 143n2, 147n9, 148nn17–19, 154n11, 155n142, 159n27

pain, xx, xxiii, 7, 11, 18, 45, 60–62, 103, 114–15, 120, 129, 138–39, 143n2
painting, xiv, xvi, xx–xxii, 50– 52, 55, 63, 67, 99, 126, 142n9, 143n2, 147n6, 156n6
Parmenides, 30–32, 35–36, 40–41
particular(ity), xvi, xix–xx, xxii, 32, 37, 47, 52, 55, 62, 64, 66, 95, 99–101, 106–7, 127, 135, 139, 142n9, 144n9, 149n37
person(s), xvi, xviii, 10, 41, 48, 55, 60, 64, 82, 96–97, 99–106, 115, 119, 121–28, 135–38, 145n19, 157n9
phenomena, xiii–xiv, xvii, xx, xxiv, 47, 49, 50–54, 61–62, 68, 72, 77, 95–97, 100, 103, 112–30, 134, 137, 139, 141n4, 141n6, 142n16, 154n111, 158n12, 159n27
place, xxiii, 2, 9, 11, 17, 19–21, 24, 30–39, 42–45, 54–59, 64, 66, 68, 71, 76, 88, 97, 99, 100, 103, 107–10, 115, 127, 130–39, 143n2, 155n147, 158n12
Plato, xiv, 56, 149n35
poem, xxii, 28, 59, 61, 66, 130, 138, 140, 143n2, 145n15, 150n48
poetry, xxii, 7, 34, 47–49, 69, 145n17

political, xviii, xx–xxiii, 4, 40, 47–51, 54, 57–58, 62, 67–68, 71, 91, 96–97, 101–2, 130, 149n35, 154n121, 156n8, 159n27
possible/possibility, xiv–xiii, 2, 10, 16, 19, 23, 26–28, 30, 33, 35, 37, 39, 44–51, 55, 57–60, 66, 68, 70, 77, 81, 88, 99, 102–8, 113, 121, 124, 126, 128–38, 142n9, 143n2, 145n14, 151n54, 158nn11–12
power, xiii–xiv, xxiii, 10–11, 18, 27, 36–39, 42, 44, 49–56, 62–65, 68, 71, 74, 76, 96–97, 100, 104, 106–7, 110, 115, 117, 121, 125, 127, 131–33, 144n4, 145n10, 148n21
present/presence, xx, 5, 9, 11–28, 30–33, 36–44, 55, 60, 67–70, 72, 74–75, 80, 84–85, 95–96, 99–100, 103–5, 109, 122–23, 128, 130–32, 144n4, 147n10, 147n14, 148n17, 149n32, 155n142
priest, the, 2–10, 15, 17–22, 24–30, 33–35, 38–44
production, xix, 49, 51, 64–67, 96, 107, 119, 137, 149

question, xix–xxiii, 2, 9, 15–16, 38, 41, 44–45, 48, 52, 55, 59, 63, 66, 95, 98, 107, 127, 129–31, 138, 140, 146n22, 158n11

receive, xiii, xvi–xviii, 15, 49, 116–23, 126–39, 147n14, 159n27
recollect(ion), 7, 34, 47, 63, 66, 70–71, 115, 132, 151n54, 156n5
releasement, 135, 139–40
response, xiv–xxiii, 25, 38, 58, 64–67, 71, 95, 98–102, 106–8, 118–21, 124–32, 136, 138–39, 149n32, 149nn37–38, 154n111, 154n114, 156n6, 156n8, 158n12
responsibility, xviii, 16, 48, 59, 62, 65, 68, 71, 95–100, 106, 130, 134, 138, 154n111, 155n142
rural, xxiii, 109, 131–35, 140

Schopenhauer, Arthur, 1, 53, 147n14
singularity, xvii, xx–xxi, 55, 100
Sophocles, 50, 52–53, 60–61, 146n4

space, xviii–xix, xxiii, 2, 22, 49, 51, 53, 55, 57–59, 63–64, 69, 71–85, 88–95, 99, 111–12, 133, 147n14, 158n12

specific/specificity, xvi–xvii, xx, xxii, 1, 16, 22, 41, 99–101, 106–7, 117, 125, 157n8

Stevens,Wallace, 41, 143n2

story, xxii, 2–4, 13–14, 17–20, 24, 28–29, 33–40, 43, 50, 55, 58, 63, 76, 80–81, 88, 91–92, 100, 109, 114, 128–29, 135, 137–38, 143n2, 146n20

subject(ivity), xviii, 1, 52, 62, 65, 98–99, 105, 120, 137, 155n126, 157n8, 159n27

technology, xxi–xxii, 2, 8, 35–42, 47–56, 96, 109–12, 131–39, 144n4, 145n16, 147n9, 160n30

testimony, xvi, 11, 14–15, 19, 24, 26, 28, 34–35, 41–48, 50, 55, 58–59, 62, 85, 96–101, 105–6, 154n105, 154n111, 159n27

thing(s), xxiii, 1, 3–50, 54–55, 58, 60–63, 68, 95–99, 105, 107–8, 111, 116, 119, 121, 124–40, 143n2, 143n11, 143nn14–15, 148n30, 151n63

time, xiv–xxiii, 4–6, 9–39, 45, 48–50, 54–56, 61–62, 65, 67–68, 73, 84, 92, 94–96, 99, 103, 105, 109, 114–16, 119–27, 130–39, 144n4, 145n18, 149n32, 158n12

Trakl, Georg, 59–62, 66, 148n23

transitory, 1–2, 11–15, 29, 55, 143n2

trauma, xvi, xx, xxiv, 59, 154n111

truth, 7, 27–28, 35, 38, 44, 59, 61, 98, 105, 145n12, 146n22, 154n105, 154n111

unsubstitutability, xvi–xvii, 65, 143

urban, xxiii, 49, 65, 68–74, 92, 109, 112–13, 116, 134, 137, 149n32

violence, xvii, xx, xxiv, 1–5, 8, 17–18, 30, 42, 47–62, 70–71, 94–97, 101–6

visibility, xiv, xvii–xviii, 115–18, 124, 126, 132, 143, 138–39, 142n9

void, 66, 69–70, 75–76, 85, 89, 94–95, 115, 151n59, 152n69, 152n75

war, xvi, xx, xxiii, 3, 9–10, 29–30, 32, 36, 41–42, 49, 54, 67, 70–71, 102, 110–12, 115, 131, 137–39, 156n6

weaving, 3, 33, 41, 49, 92, 144n10

witness(ing), xiv–xviii, xxiii, 2, 5–15, 19, 25–30, 34–37, 41, 45–48, 50–59, 62, 70–71, 81, 95–102, 105–7, 114–21, 128, 131, 136–39, 154n111, 156n6, 159n27

world, xiv, xvi–xvii, xix–xxiii, 1, 4–16, 21, 24, 27, 29–30, 33–37, 40–67, 77, 80, 83, 91, 96, 98–117, 120–40, 143n2, 144n4, 147n14, 156n6, 159n27

Perspectives in Continental Philosophy
John D. Caputo, series editor

John D. Caputo, ed., *Deconstruction in a Nutshell: A Conversation with Jacques Derrida.*

Michael Strawser, *Both/And: Reading Kierkegaard—From Irony to Edification.*

Michael D. Barber, *Ethical Hermeneutics: Rationality in Enrique Dussel's Philosophy of Liberation.*

James H. Olthuis, ed., *Knowing Other-wise: Philosophy at the Threshold of Spirituality.*

James Swindal, *Reflection Revisited: Jürgen Habermas's Discursive Theory of Truth.*

Richard Kearney, *Poetics of Imagining: Modern and Postmodern.* Second edition.

Thomas W. Busch, *Circulating Being: From Embodiment to Incorporation—Essays on Late Existentialism.*

Edith Wyschogrod, *Emmanuel Levinas: The Problem of Ethical Metaphysics.* Second edition.

Francis J. Ambrosio, ed., *The Question of Christian Philosophy Today.*

Jeffrey Bloechl, ed., *The Face of the Other and the Trace of God: Essays on the Philosophy of Emmanuel Levinas.*

Ilse N. Bulhof and Laurens ten Kate, eds., *Flight of the Gods: Philosophical Perspectives on Negative Theology.*

Trish Glazebrook, *Heidegger's Philosophy of Science.*

Kevin Hart, *The Trespass of the Sign: Deconstruction, Theology, and Philosophy.*

Mark C. Taylor, *Journeys to Selfhood: Hegel and Kierkegaard.* Second edition.

Dominique Janicaud, Jean-François Courtine, Jean-Louis Chrétien, Michel Henry, Jean-Luc Marion, and Paul Ricoeur, *Phenomenology and the "Theological Turn": The French Debate.*

Karl Jaspers, *The Question of German Guilt*. Introduction by Joseph W. Koterski, S.J.

Jean-Luc Marion, *The Idol and Distance: Five Studies*. Translated with an introduction by Thomas A. Carlson.

Jeffrey Dudiak, *The Intrigue of Ethics: A Reading of the Idea of Discourse in the Thought of Emmanuel Levinas*.

Robyn Horner, *Rethinking God as Gift: Marion, Derrida, and the Limits of Phenomenology*.

Mark Dooley, *The Politics of Exodus: Søren Kierkegaard's Ethics of Responsibility*.

Merold Westphal, *Overcoming Onto-Theology: Toward a Postmodern Christian Faith*.

Edith Wyschogrod, Jean-Joseph Goux, and Eric Boynton, eds., *The Enigma of Gift and Sacrifice*.

Stanislas Breton, *The Word and the Cross*. Translated with an introduction by Jacquelyn Porter.

Jean-Luc Marion, *Prolegomena to Charity*. Translated by Stephen E. Lewis.

Peter H. Spader, *Scheler's Ethical Personalism: Its Logic, Development, and Promise*.

Jean-Louis Chrétien, *The Unforgettable and the Unhoped For*. Translated by Jeffrey Bloechl.

Don Cupitt, *Is Nothing Sacred? The Non-Realist Philosophy of Religion: Selected Essays*.

Jean-Luc Marion, *In Excess: Studies of Saturated Phenomena*. Translated by Robyn Horner and Vincent Berraud.

Phillip Goodchild, *Rethinking Philosophy of Religion: Approaches from Continental Philosophy*.

William J. Richardson, S.J., *Heidegger: Through Phenomenology to Thought*.

Jeffrey Andrew Barash, *Martin Heidegger and the Problem of Historical Meaning*.

Jean-Louis Chrétien, *Hand to Hand: Listening to the Work of Art*. Translated by Stephen E. Lewis.

Jean-Louis Chrétien, *The Call and the Response*. Translated with an introduction by Anne Davenport.

D. C. Schindler, *Han Urs von Balthasar and the Dramatic Structure of Truth: A Philosophical Investigation*.

Julian Wolfreys, ed., *Thinking Difference: Critics in Conversation*.

Allen Scult, *Being Jewish/Reading Heidegger: An Ontological Encounter*.

Richard Kearney, *Debates in Continental Philosophy: Conversations with Contemporary Thinkers*.

Jennifer Anna Gosetti-Ferencei, *Heidegger, Hölderlin, and the Subject of Poetic Language: Toward a New Poetics of Dasein*.

Jolita Pons, *Stealing a Gift: Kierkegaard's Pseudonyms and the Bible*.

Jean-Yves Lacoste, *Experience and the Absolute: Disputed Questions on the Humanity of Man*. Translated by Mark Raftery-Skehan.

Charles P. Bigger, *Between* Chora *and the Good: Metaphor's Metaphysical Neighborhood.*

Dominique Janicaud, *Phenomenology "Wide Open": After the French Debate.* Translated by Charles N. Cabral.

Ian Leask and Eoin Cassidy, eds., *Givenness and God: Questions of Jean-Luc Marion.*

Jacques Derrida, *Sovereignties in Question: The Poetics of Paul Celan.* Edited by Thomas Dutoit and Outi Pasanen.

William Desmond, *Is There a Sabbath for Thought? Between Religion and Philosophy.*

Bruce Ellis Benson and Norman Wirzba, eds., *The Phenomenology of Prayer.*

S. Clark Buckner and Matthew Statler, eds., *Styles of Piety: Practicing Philosophy after the Death of God.*

Kevin Hart and Barbara Wall, eds., *The Experience of God: A Postmodern Response.*

John Panteleimon Manoussakis, *After God: Richard Kearney and the Religious Turn in Continental Philosophy.*

John Martis, *Philippe Lacoue-Labarthe: Representation and the Loss of the Subject.*

Jean-Luc Nancy, *The Ground of the Image.*

Edith Wyschogrod, *Crossover Queries: Dwelling with Negatives, Embodying Philosophy's Others.*

Gerald Bruns, *On the Anarchy of Poetry and Philosophy: A Guide for the Unruly.*

Brian Treanor, *Aspects of Alterity: Levinas, Marcel, and the Contemporary Debate.*

Simon Morgan Wortham, *Counter-Institutions: Jacques Derrida and the Question of the University.*

Leonard Lawlor, *The Implications of Immanence: Toward a New Concept of Life.*

Clayton Crockett, *Interstices of the Sublime: Theology and Psychoanalytic Theory.*

Bettina Bergo, Joseph Cohen, and Raphael Zagury-Orly, eds., *Judeities: Questions for Jacques Derrida.* Translated by Bettina Bergo and Michael B. Smith.

Jean-Luc Marion, *On the Ego and on God: Further Cartesian Questions.* Translated by Christina M. Gschwandtner.

Jean-Luc Nancy, *Philosophical Chronicles.* Translated by Franson Manjali.

Jean-Luc Nancy, *Dis-Enclosure: The Deconstruction of Christianity.* Translated by Bettina Bergo, Gabriel Malenfant, and Michael B. Smith.

Andrea Hurst, *Derrida Vis-à-vis Lacan: Interweaving Deconstruction and Psychoanalysis.*

Jean-Luc Nancy, *Noli me tangere: On the Raising of the Body.* Translated by Sarah Clift, Pascale-Anne Brault, and Michael Naas.

Jacques Derrida, *The Animal That Therefore I Am.* Edited by Marie-Louise Mallet, translated by David Wills.

Jean-Luc Marion, *The Visible and the Revealed.* Translated by Christina M. Gschwandtner and others.

Michel Henry, *Material Phenomenology.* Translated by Scott Davidson.

Jean-Luc Nancy, *Corpus.* Translated by Richard A. Rand.

Joshua Kates, *Fielding Derrida.*

Michael Naas, *Derrida From Now On.*

Shannon Sullivan and Dennis J. Schmidt, eds., *Difficulties of Ethical Life.*

Catherine Malabou, *What Should We Do with Our Brain?* Translated by Sebastian Rand, Introduction by Marc Jeannerod.

Claude Romano, *Event and World.* Translated by Shane Mackinlay.

Vanessa Lemm, *Nietzsche's Animal Philosophy: Culture, Politics, and the Animality of the Human Being.*

B. Keith Putt, ed., *Gazing Through a Prism Darkly: Reflections on Merold Westphal's Hermeneutical Epistemology.*

Eric Boynton and Martin Kavka, eds., *Saintly Influence: Edith Wyschogrod and the Possibilities of Philosophy of Religion.*

Shane Mackinlay, *Interpreting Excess: Jean-Luc Marion, Saturated Phenomena, and Hermeneutics.*

Kevin Hart and Michael A. Signer, eds., *The Exorbitant: Emmanuel Levinas Between Jews and Christians.*

Bruce Ellis Benson and Norman Wirzba, eds., *Words of Life: New Theological Turns in French Phenomenology.*

William Robert, *Trials: Of Antigone and Jesus.*

Brian Treanor and Henry Isaac Venema, eds., *A Passion for the Possible: Thinking with Paul Ricoeur.*

Kas Saghafi, *Apparitions—Of Derrida's Other.*

Nick Mansfield, *The God Who Deconstructs Himself: Sovereignty and Subjectivity Between Freud, Bataille, and Derrida.*

Don Ihde, *Heidegger's Technologies: Postphenomenological Perspectives.*

Suzi Adams, *Castoriadis's Ontology: Being and Creation.*

Richard Kearney and Kascha Semonovitch, eds., *Phenomenologies of the Stranger: Between Hostility and Hospitality.*

Michael Naas, *Miracle and Machine: Jacques Derrida and the Two Sources of Religion, Science, and the Media.*

Alena Alexandrova, Ignaas Devisch, Laurens ten Kate, and Aukje van Rooden, *Re-treating Religion: Deconstructing Christianity with Jean-Luc Nancy.* Preamble by Jean-Luc Nancy.

Emmanuel Falque, *The Metamorphosis of Finitude: An Essay on Birth and Resurrection.* Translated by George Hughes.

Scott M. Campbell, *The Early Heidegger's Philosophy of Life: Facticity, Being, and Language.*

Françoise Dastur, *How Are We to Confront Death? An Introduction to Philosophy.* Translated by Robert Vallier. Foreword by David Farrell Krell.

Christina M. Gschwandtner, *Postmodern Apologetics? Arguments for God in Contemporary Philosophy.*

Ben Morgan, *On Becoming God: Late Medieval Mysticism and the Modern Western Self.*

Neal DeRoo, *Futurity in Phenomenology: Promise and Method in Husserl, Levinas, and Derrida.*

Sarah LaChance Adams and Caroline R. Lundquist, eds., *Coming to Life: Philosophies of Pregnancy, Childbirth, and Mothering.*

Thomas Claviez, ed., *The Conditions of Hospitality: Ethics, Politics, and Aesthetics on the Threshold of the Possible.*

Roland Faber and Jeremy Fackenthal, eds., *Theopoetic Folds: Philosophizing Multifariousness.*

Jean-Luc Marion, *The Essential Writings.* Edited by Kevin Hart.

Adam S. Miller, *Speculative Grace: Bruno Latour and Object-Oriented Theology.* Foreword by Levi R. Bryant.

Jean-Luc Nancy, *Corpus II: Writings on Sexuality.*

David Nowell Smith, *Sounding/Silence: Martin Heidegger at the Limits of Poetics.*

Gregory C. Stallings, Manuel Asensi, and Carl Good, eds., *Material Spirit: Religion and Literature Intranscendent.*

Claude Romano, *Event and Time.* Translated by Stephen E. Lewis.

Frank Chouraqui, *Ambiguity and the Absolute: Nietzsche and Merleau-Ponty on the Question of Truth.*

Noëlle Vahanian, *The Rebellious No: Variations on a Secular Theology of Language.*

Michael Naas, *The End of the World and Other Teachable Moments: Jacques Derrida's Final Seminar.*

Jean-Louis Chrétien, *Under the Gaze of the Bible.* Translated by John Marson Dunaway.

Edward Baring and Peter E. Gordon, eds., *The Trace of God: Derrida and Religion.*

Vanessa Lemm, ed., *Nietzsche and the Becoming of Life.*

Aaron T. Looney, *Vladimir Jankélévitch: The Time of Forgiveness.*

Robert Mugerauer, *Responding to Loss: Heideggerian Reflections on Literature, Architecture, and Film.*